Knowledge Management
in Organizations

Knowledge Management in Organizations

A CRITICAL INTRODUCTION

Second Edition

DONALD HISLOP

UNIVERSITY PRESS

Great Clarendon Street, Oxford OX2 6DP

Oxford University Press is a department of the University of Oxford.
It furthers the University's objective of excellence in research, scholarship,
and education by publishing worldwide in

Oxford   New York

Auckland Cape Town Dar es Salaam Hong Kong Karachi
Kuala Lumpur Madrid Melbourne Mexico City Nairobi
New Delhi Shanghai Taipei Toronto

With offices in

Argentina Austria Brazil Chile Czech Republic France Greece
Guatemala Hungary Italy Japan Poland Portugal Singapore
South Korea Switzerland Thailand Turkey Ukraine Vietnam

Oxford is a registered trade mark of Oxford University Press
in the UK and in certain other countries

Published in the United States
by Oxford University Press Inc., New York

British Library Cataloguing in Publication Data
Data available

Library of Congress Cataloging in Publication Data
Data available

Typeset by Macmillan Publishing Solutions
Printed in Italy by L.E.G.O S.p.A
ISBN 978–0–19–953497–5

1 3 5 7 9 10 8 6 4 2

For Catriona

PUBLISHER'S ACKNOWLEDGEMENTS

We are grateful to the following for permission to reproduce copyright material:

Academy of Management for the case studies in chapter 4: Siemens' sharenet initiative, drawn from Voelpel, Dous and Davenport, 'Five steps to creating a global knowledge-sharing system: Siemens' sharenet', *Academy of Management Executive* (2005) 19(2): 9–23; and in chapter 15: The relationship between empowering leadership, knowledge sharing and the performance of management teams, from Srivastava, Bartol and Locke, 'Empowering leadership in management teams: effects on knowledge sharing, efficacy and performance', *Academy of Management Journal* (2006) 49(6): 1239–1251.

Fairleigh Dickinson University for the case study in chapter 14: The impact of subcultures on organizational knowledge management activities, drawn from Alavi, Kayworth and Leidner, 'An empirical examination of the influence of organizational culture on knowledge management information systems', *Journal of Management Information Systems* (2006) 22(3): 191:224.

Strategic Planning Society for the case study in chapter 8: The inability to learn from failure, drawn from Baumard and Starbuck, 'Learning from failures: why it may never happen', *Long Range Planning* (2005) 38(3): 281–298.

Wiley-Blackwell for Figure 1.3: Schultze and Stabell's four discourses on knowledge management, from Schultze and Stabell, 'Four discourses on knowledge management', *Journal of Management Studies* (2004); Figure 4.1: Alvesson and Karreman's four knowledge management approaches', from Alvesson and Karreman, 'Knowledge Management Approaches', *Journal of Management Studies* (2001) 38(7): 995–1018; Figure 6.1: The modified Crossan *et al.* model, from Zietsma *et al*, 'The modified Crossan et al. model', *British Journal of Management* (2002) 13: S61–74; end-of-chapter case studies for chapter 2: The role played by the acquisition of tacit and explicit knowledge in improving task productivity, drawn from Haas and Hansen, 'Different knowledge, different benefits: towards a productivity perspective on knowledge sharing in organizations', *Strategic Management Journal* (2007) 28:1133–1153; and in chapter 5: Social capital and the acquisition and exploitation of knowledge in high technology organizations, drawn from Yli-Renko, Autio and Sapienza, 'Social capital, knowledge acquisition, and knowledge exploitation in young technology-based firms', *Strategic Management Journal* (2001) 22: 587–613; in chapter 7: Applying Nonaka's SECI framework to vehicle building, drawn from Dych, Starke, Mischke and Mauws, 'Learning to build a car: an empirical investigation of organizational learning', *Journal of Management Studies* (2005) 42(2): 387–416; in chapter 9: Knowledge hoarding within 'functional silos', drawn from Currie and Kerrin, 'Human resource management and knowledge management: enhancing knowledge sharing in a pharmaceutical company', *International Journal of Human resource*

Management (2003) 14(6): 1027–1045; in chapter 11: Cross community collaboration in the negotiation of safety on an Italian building site, drawn from Gherardi and Nicolini, 'Learning in a constellation of interconnected practices: canon or dissonance?', *Journal of Management Studies* (2005) 39(4): 419–436; and in chapter 12: The negotiation of meaning in a problem-solving context, drawn from Marshall and Rollinson, 'Maybe Bacon had a point: the politics of collective sensemaking', *British Journal of Management* (2004) 15: S71–86.

The institute for operations research and the management sciences for Table 3.6: Boundary spanning practices, from Orlikowski, 'Knowing in practice: enacting a collective capability in distributed organizing', *Organization Science* (2002) 13(3): 249–273; and Table 13.4: Trust facilitating behaviours and actions, from Jarvenpaa and Leidner, 'Trust facilitating behaviours and actions', *Organization Science* (1999) 10(6): 791–815; and for the case studies in chapter 3: A practice-based perspective on work activities in a global software development company, from Orlikowski, 'Knowing in practice: enacting a collective capability in distributed organizing', *Organization Science* (2002) 13(3): 249–273; and in chapter 10: The emergence and disintegration of a community of practice in a web design company, from Thompson, 'Structural and epistemic parameters in communities of practice', *Organization Science* (2005) 16(2): 151–164.

Cengage for Table 12.3, 'Power resources and modes of influence' from Hales, *Managing through organization: the management process, forms of organization and the work of managers* (1993).

Routledge for Figure 12.2: The structure of capitalist employment relations, from Tsoukas, 'What is management? An outline of a metatheory' in Ackroyd and Fleetwood (eds) (2000) *Realist perspectives on management and organizations*.

Emerald Journals for Table 14.2: Linking knowledge management initiatives to organizational culture, from McDermott and O'Dell, 'Overcoming cultural barriers to knowledge sharing', *Journal of Knowledge Management* (2001) 5(1): 76–85.

Sage for Figure 16.1: Suddaby and Greenwood's cycle of knowledge production and consumption, from Suddaby and Greenwood, 'Colonizing knowledge: commodification as a dynamic of jurisdictional expansion in professional science firms', *Human Relations Journal* (2001) 54 (7): 933–53; and the case studies in chapter 6: The difficulties and dynamics of project-based learning, from Scarborough, Bresnan, Edelman, Laurent, Newell and Swan, 'The process of project-based learning: an exploratory study', *Management Learning* (2004) 35(4): 491–506; and in chapter 13: How work practices shape the relevance and use of ICT-enabled knowledge management, from Hsiao, Tsai and Lee, 'The problem of embeddedness: knowledge transfer, coordination and reuse in information systems', *Organization Studies* (2006) 27(9): 1289–1317.

BRIEF CONTENTS

CONTENTS

PART 1   Epistemologies of Knowledge in the Knowledge Management Literature

LIST OF FIGURES

LIST OF TABLES

The Contemporary Importance of Knowledge and Knowledge Management

Introduction

'Some think the "knowledge turn" a matter of macro-historical change; citing Drucker, Bell, Arrow, Reich or Winter, they assert we have moved into an Information Age wherein knowledge has become the organization's principal asset.' (Spender & Scherer 2007, 6)

'The physical toil of manufacturing is being replaced by a world where we work more with our heads than our hands.' (Sewell 2005, 685–6)

'It is broadly accepted that systematic knowledge management is tightly linked with gaining and sustaining competitive advantage.' (Bogner & Bansal 2007, 165–6)

In a textbook on knowledge management it is important to put the subject in context, as this helps explain the growth of interest in it. Widespread interest in the topic of knowledge management among academics, public policy makers, consultants and business people occurred as recently as the mid-1990s.

The level of interest in knowledge management since then is visible in a number of ways. Firstly, the knowledge society rhetoric is used by and shapes the business and educational policy making of a number of governments including the UK, Scotland, Australia and the European Union (Fleming *et al.* 2004; Warhurst & Thompson 2006). While it is impossible to accurately quantify the number of business organizations which have attempted to develop and implement knowledge management systems, surveys such as those conducted by the consultants KPMG (2000, 2003) suggest large numbers of organizations have undertaken such initiatives. The beginning of the twenty-first century also witnessed a widespread interest in the topic amongst management consultancies such as McKinseys (see for example Kluge *et al.* 2001). Finally, a search on Amazon using the key term 'knowledge management' reveals the vast number of books and reports that have been written on the topic since 1995.

The late 1990s also witnessed an exponential increase in the number of academic articles and books published on the topic of knowledge management. Thus, surveys by both Scarbrough & Swan (2001) and Wilson (2002), revealed that prior to the mid-1990s interest in the topic was virtually non-existent, but from about 1996 onwards, the number of publications on knowledge management grew exponentially. Both these articles, however, suggested that there was a risk that knowledge management was a passing fad (Wilson is particularly scathing and talks of knowledge management as a bandwagon *'without wheels'*), and that there was likely to be an *'impending decline'* of interest in the topic (Scarbrough & Swan 2001, 56). However, contemporary analysis suggests such a decline has not occurred, and that the early years of the twenty-first century saw a sustained interest in the topic. Thus, as illustrated in Table 1.1, between 2000 and 2006, at least 110 articles per year were published on knowledge management, with the average number of articles per year being 129. This compares to the peak of just under 160 articles published on the topic in 1998 as reported by Scarbrough & Swan (2001).

The ongoing academic interest in knowledge management is also visible in a number of other ways, such as in the emergence of a number of conferences on the topic which have become regular annual events (see weblinks), as well as the topic of learning and knowledge now becoming regular themes at many long-standing management and organization conferences. Finally, in relation to academic journals, papers on learning and knowledge in organizations have consistently been published in top tier journals (such as *Journal of Management Studies, Organization Studies, Organization Science*) and there has also been the birth of a number of journals specifically concerned with issues of learning and knowledge management (such as the *Journal of Knowledge Management, Knowledge and Process Management* and *Knowledge Management: Research and Practice*). It thus appears that the current level of sustained interest in the topic of knowledge management is likely to continue in the academic arena for the foreseeable future.

Year	Number of publications
2000	111
2001	135
2002	152
2003	137
2004	110
2005	137
2006	121

Table 1.1 Number of articles on Proquest examining the topic of 'knowledge management'

Key assumptions in the knowledge management literature

The central idea uniting and underpinning the vast majority of the knowledge management literature, that it is important for organizations to manage their workforce's knowledge, flows from a number of key assumptions embodied in the three quotations which open the chapter. Firstly, Spender & Scherer's quotation illustrates the assumption that the end of the twentieth century witnessed an enormous social and economic transformation which resulted in knowledge becoming the key asset for organizations to manage. A second key assumption, flowing from the first one, and illustrated by Sewell's quotation, is that the nature of work has also changed significantly, with the importance of intellectual work increasing significantly. The third, related, key assumption, illustrated by Bogner & Bansal's quotation is that the effective management by an organization of its knowledge base is likely to provide a source of competitive advantage.

ILLUSTRATION

Knowledge Creation and the Link to Business Performance

Bogner & Bansal (2007) conducted research which tested the knowledge-based view of the firm (see Chapter 2 for a detailed exploration of the knowledge-based view of the firm). Specifically they examined whether an organization's ability to create and utilize new knowledge was linked to business performance. In their study they use patents as a measure of knowledge creation, and studied patent data in five patent-intensive industries (pharmaceuticals, semiconductors, forest products, oil & gas and automotive). Two of the hypotheses that their research data supported, which they argued provided support for the knowledge-based view of the firm, were that firstly, business performance was strongly linked to an organization's level of knowledge creation, and secondly, that business performance was also linked to an organization's ability to 'recycle' new knowledge and use it to improve future organizational knowledge creation activities.

While the growth of interest in knowledge management only took off during the mid-1990s the theoretical foundation for the assumptions it makes resonate with, and to some extent flow from Daniel Bell's post-industrial society concept (Bell 1973). Thus it is useful to examine his work in a little detail.

The knowledge society concept and its links to Bell's post-industrial society concept

The knowledge management literature is typically based on an analysis which suggests that since approximately the mid-1970s, economies, and society in general have become more information and knowledge intensive, with information/knowledge intensive industries replacing manufacturing industry as the key wealth generators (see DeFillippi *et al.* 2006; Neef 1999, for example). Arguably, the main source of inspiration for this vision was, and is, Daniel Bell's seminal book *The Coming of Post-Industrial Society*, which was first published in 1973. While earlier writers, notably von Hayek (1945) and one of his pupils, Machlup (1962), developed a similar analysis, Bell's work has provided the main inspiration for contemporary writers in the area of knowledge management. As a consequence, Bell's post-industrial society and contemporary conceptualizations of knowledge society bear more than a passing resemblance to each other. Burton-Jones (1999, 4), for example, explicitly links his knowledge capitalism model to Bell's thesis. Further, Bell himself has, over time, used the terms knowledge and information societies interchangeably with the post-industrial society concept (Webster 1996).

Bell's analysis is based on a typology of societies characterized by their predominant mode of employment (Webster 1996). Thus, industrial society is characterized by an emphasis on manufacturing and fabrication: the building of things. In post-industrial societies, however, which are argued to evolve out of industrial societies, the service sector has replaced the manufacturing sector as the biggest source of employment (see Figure 1.1). Another crucial characteristic of Bell's post-industrial society is that knowledge and information play a much more significant role in economic and social life than during industrial society, as work in the service sector is argued to be significantly more information and knowledge intensive than industrial work.

Finally, Bell suggests that not only has there been a quantitative increase in the role and importance of knowledge and information, but there has also been a qualitative change in the type of knowledge that is most important. In a post-industrial society, theoretical knowledge has become the most important type of knowledge. Theoretical knowledge represents abstract knowledge and principles, which can be codified, or at least embedded in systems of rules and frameworks for action. This is to a large extent because for Bell, in post-industrial societies professional service work is of central importance, and this type of work typically involves the development, use and application of

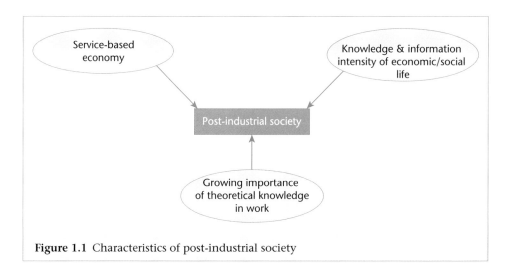

Figure 1.1 Characteristics of post-industrial society

abstract, theoretical knowledge more than manual work ever did. This relates not just to technical knowledge, such as may be used in R&D processes, but also encompasses a large and growing diversity of jobs which increasingly require the application and use of such knowledge—for example, formulation of government policy, architecture, medicine, software design, etc.

> **Definition** Post-industrial society
>
> A society where the service sector is dominant and knowledge based goods/services have replaced industrial, manufactured goods as the main wealth generators.

An important element of Bell's analysis is that post-industrial societies represent an advancement on industrial societies, as in general more wealth will be generated, and workers individually will have better, more fulfilling jobs. In fact, there is a tendency towards utopianism in aspects of Bell's vision, as he argues that: unpleasant, repetitive jobs will decline in number significantly; social inequality will reduce; (all) individuals will have increased amounts of disposable income to spend on personal services; society will be able to better plan for itself; and social relations will become less individualistic and provide greater scope for community development and collective support.

In order to empirically test and substantiate such claims, statistical evidence is typically mobilized to show the increasing importance of service work, and the simultaneous decline of manufacturing employment. Thus, statistics on the US economy in the mid-1970s were argued to show that 46% of its economic output was from the information sector, and 47% of the total workforce was employed in this sector (Kumar 1995). Castells (1998), in articulating his vision of a network/information society, mobilized an impressive amount of evidence from a wide range of economies which showed the long term, historical shift from industry to services, and from goods handling to information handling work (Figure 1.2).

Some empirical evidence on the growing skill intensity of much work also supports Bell's thesis. Zuboff (1988) suggested that advances in computer technology had the potential to make work more knowledge and skill intensive, through the potential for problem solving, and abstraction these technologies provide workers. This perspective is supported by research conducted by Gallie *et al.* (1998) in the UK in the mid-1990s, where almost 65% of workers surveyed reported experiencing an increase in the skill levels of their jobs. Further evidence also reinforces these conclusions (Felstead *et al.* 2000; NSTF 2000).

Overall therefore, aggregate statistical evidence appears to support the knowledge society/post-industrial society thesis. However, Bell's thesis has been the subject of a sustained, and not insignificant critique, much of which has relevance to the knowledge society vision developed by contemporary writers on knowledge management. The following section changes focus to consider these criticisms.

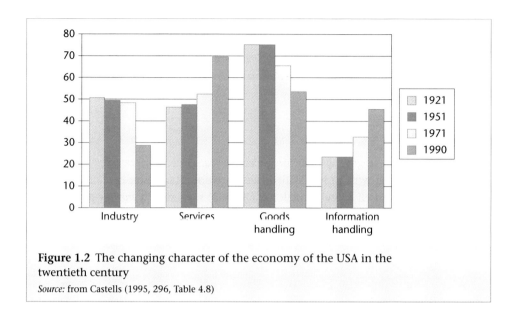

Figure 1.2 The changing character of the economy of the USA in the twentieth century

Source: from Castells (1995, 296, Table 4.8)

A critical evaluation of the knowledge society concept

One of the main criticisms of the arguments made by knowledge society, or post-industrial society theorists, is that they typically conflate knowledge work with service sector jobs. Thus, as outlined, aggregate statistics on the size of service sector employment is usually used to indicate the transition to a knowledge society (see Figure 1.2). However, not all service sector work can be classified as knowledge work, as the service sector is a residual employment category for all types of work which are not either manufacturing, or agricultural. Thus the service sector encompasses an enormously heterogeneous range of job types, including consultants and cleaners, marketing executives and milkmen (and women), as well as scientists and security guards. Thus, the service sector does not represent a coherent and uniform category of employment. While some service sector work such as consultancy, research etc. can be classified as being knowledge intensive, other types of service work, such as security, office cleaning and fast food restaurant work is low skilled, repetitive and routine (Thompson *et al.* 2001). Therefore to suggest that all service sector employment is knowledge intensive work does not acknowledge the reality of much service sector work.

TIME TO REFLECT CALL CENTRES AND KNOWLEDGE INTENSIVE WORK

While customer service work in call centres is typically highly controlled, routine and repetitive it also involves the use of computers and a significant amount of interaction with customers. To what extent can such work be regarded as more skilled and knowledge intensive than skilled or semi-skilled factory work?

The transition from an industrial to a post-industrial knowledge economy should produce an increase in the proportion of jobs which are knowledge intensive, and a more
general increase in the knowledge intensity of work. There is some evidence for this, as
statistical analyses typically show that managerial and professional work, work which
is typically regarded as knowledge intensive, has been one of the fastest growing occupational groups since the 1980s (Elias & Gregory 1994; Fleming *et al.* 2004). However,
focusing on this trajectory alone provides a partial and over-simplistic overview of the
way work has been changing.

Simultaneous to the growth in professional and managerial work there has been an
equally significant growth in low skilled, service work (Thompson *et al.* 2001). This is
leading to what Mansell & Steinmueller (2000, 403) suggest is *'a growing polarization of
the labour market between highly skilled, highly paid jobs, and low skilled, lower paid jobs . . .'*,
a conclusion reached by a growing number of writers (Fleming *et al.* 2004; Littler & Innes
2003; Warhurst & Thompson 2006). Thus, rather than there being a single trajectory in
the direction of upskilling and increasing knowledge intensity, there are two, simultaneous trends, moving in the opposite direction. Thus while such analyses provide some
support for the knowledge society thesis, they also suggest that the idea that there is a
universal increase in the knowledge intensity of work in general is simplistic and a little
misleading.

Another aspect of the knowledge society thesis that has been criticized is the privileging of theoretical knowledge over other types of knowledge (typically, tacit knowledge
and skills). An explicit example of this is Frenkel *et al.*'s analysis of knowledge work
(1995). In their analysis the knowledge intensity of any job can be measured on three
dimensions, one of which is the type of knowledge used. For Frenkel *et al.* theoretical
knowledge is used as a measure of knowledge intensity, while what they call 'contextual'
knowledge is not. However, this risks losing sight of the fact that, to some extent, all
work is knowledgeable work (Knights *et al.* 1993, 976), involving the use of significant
amounts of tacit knowledge (Manwaring & Wood 1985; Kusterer 1978). This therefore
leads to disputes and difficulties in defining what constitutes knowledge work, which
types of workers should be classified as knowledge workers, and leads to the knowledge
required in routine, manual work being underestimated (see Chapter 5 for this debate).

Questions have also been raised regarding the way knowledge was conceptualized by
Bell. His conception of theoretical knowledge as codifiable and objective draws on
classical images of scientific knowledge. However, much contemporary analysis views
knowledge as having substantially different characteristics, being partial, tacit, subjective
and context dependent (see Chapters 2 and 3 for these debates).

While aspects of the analytical frameworks developed by post-industrial society and
knowledge society theorists can be criticized and challenged, this does not mean that
society and economies have remained unchanged, or that every aspect of these analyses
is unfounded. Thus, it is undeniable that the last quarter of the twentieth century was a
period of profound change. For the advanced, industrial economies there was not only a
significant change in the type of products and services produced, and the nature of work
itself, but the role of information and knowledge, in many aspects of social and economic life, also increased substantially. However, it is arguably going too far to suggest

The changing character of work in Australia

Fleming *et al.* (2004) analysed employment statistics produced by the Australian government covering the years between 1986 and 2000 to evaluate the extent to which the Australian economy supports the knowledge economy rhetoric. This was done through looking at both highly aggregated data related to changes in broad occupational categories and more disaggregated data at the level of particular types of jobs. At the aggregate level their data doesn't support the knowledge society rhetoric as it, 'calls into question the claim that there is a generalized trajectory towards the growth of high-skilled jobs and the decline of low-skilled jobs' (p. 733). Instead their aggregate level data reinforces the polarization thesis with growth occurring not only in highly skilled professional occupations (the occupational category which increased the most between 1986 and 2002), but also in lower skilled occupations such as intermediate and elementary level clerical, sales and service occupations. At the most disaggregated level a further degree of complexity emerged. At this level only the three occupational groups with the highest levels of growth were examined. Fleming *et al.* found that for each of the occupational groups examined, rather than finding a homogeneous picture of relatively equal levels of growth among all the jobs in each occupational category, there was significant diversity. For example, with regard to jobs in the professional occupational category, some jobs (such as accountants and computer professionals) had experienced high levels of growth while others had remained static and some even declined in employment terms (such as dental practitioners, and librarians). Overall therefore, Fleming *et al.* found that the changes that had occurred in Australian employment patterns did not provide unequivocal support for the knowledge society thesis.

that these changes represent a fundamental rupture, witnessing the birth of a new type of society. This is because while much change has occurred, there have also been significant elements of continuity—organizations remain driven by the same imperatives of accumulation, and the general social relations of capitalism remain unchanged. Thus, Kumar (1995, 31) suggests,

> 'capitalist industrialism has not been transcended, but simply extended, deepened and perfected.'

Such a conclusion is reinforced by McKinlay (2005, 242), who suggests that one of the key drivers for knowledge intensive firms, such as those in the pharmaceutical industry, to develop knowledge management systems is '*new competitive pressures within capitalism for perpetual innovation in products, services and organization by leveraging the tacit knowledge of their employees.*'

Thus to challenge Bell's conceptualization of a post-industrial society as representing a fundamental rupture with existing social and economic structures is not to suggest that there has been no change. Equally, such critiques cannot be used to conclude that knowledge is not important to contemporary business organizations.

Aims, philosophy and structure

The final objective of this chapter is to articulate the general aims and philosophy of this book, as well as outlining the themes and issues examined in each chapter. A useful way to articulate the aims and philosophy of this textbook is to sketch out an overview of the various perspectives on knowledge and knowledge management that exist in the academic literature and locate the perspective adopted here within this framework. As will be seen, one of the features of this academic literature is the diversity of quite different perspectives that exist. However, despite the heterogeneity of the literature on knowledge management, a number of broad perspectives can be identified.

One of the key distinctions in the knowledge management literature relates to epistemology. As outlined in the introduction to Part 1 on epistemology and while different writers use a number of different labels (see Table 2 in the introduction to Part 1), there is a general consensus that two identifiable perspectives on epistemology dominate. These perspectives are here labelled the objectivist and practice-based perspectives on knowledge. The objectivist perspective assumes that knowledge is an entity that can be codified and separated from the people who possess and use it. In contrast, the practice-based perspective challenges the entitative conceptualization of knowledge and instead assumes that knowledge is embedded in, developed through and is inseparable from people's workplace, practices and the contexts in which they occur. In Part 1 which follows, Chapters 2 and 3 are devoted to fully articulating each of these two epistemologies.

Another useful framework that helps to characterize the knowledge management literature, and simultaneously highlight issues which are typically neglected in it, was developed by Schultze & Stabell (2004), which is itself based on Burrell & Morgan's (1979) sociological paradigms framework. As with Burrell & Morgan's (1979) work on sociological paradigms, they articulate a two dimensional framework which produces four distinctive knowledge management discourses. Due to the different perspectives on epistemology, outlined above, this is one of the dimensions in their framework. What is here labelled the objectivist perspective, Schultze & Stabell label the epistemology of dualism, and what is here referred to as the practice-based perspective, Schultze & Stabell label them the epistemology dualism.

What is distinctive about Schultze & Stabell's framework is that they add a second dimension to the epistemology one. The second dimension in their framework relates to social order, with differences existing on the extent to which existing social relations are regarded as consensual and unproblematic. In relation to the social order dimensions Schulze & Stabell suggest two distinct perspectives dominate. The consensus perspective is where existing social relations are regarded as unproblematic and where challenging them is not considered. The dissensus perspective, by contrast assumes that existing social relations are problematic, that conflict is rife, that they typically reinforce power differentials which result in exploitation. The four discourses on knowledge management which emerge when these dimensions are put together are illustrated in Figure 1.3.

What this analysis reveals, and one of the key insights flowing from Schultze & Stabell's framework, is the extent to which the consensus-based perspective on social order predominates in the knowledge management literature. Thus most literature on the topic regards the management of organizational knowledge as being positive and progressive, and unquestioningly benefiting all organizational members, which consequently results in issues of conflict, power and disagreement being marginalized, if not ignored.

Further, of the four discourses outlined by Schultze & Stabell the neo-functionalist one is by far the most dominant in the knowledge management literature (a conclusion also made by Goles & Hirscheim 2000). This literature not only assumes that the management of knowledge is positive and has potential benefits for all organizational members, but also that the object like status of knowledge in organizations makes it a resource amenable to managerial control.

This book, while describing the neo-functionalist discourse on knowledge management (see Chapter 2) is concerned with giving voice to and drawing on work from the other three knowledge management discourses. Thus, its primary purpose is to provide readers with a rich understanding of the debates and diversity of perspectives that exist through drilling down below the surface assumptions that typically go unquestioned in the mainstream knowledge management literature (regarding both the manageability of knowledge and the extent to which knowledge management involves conflict,

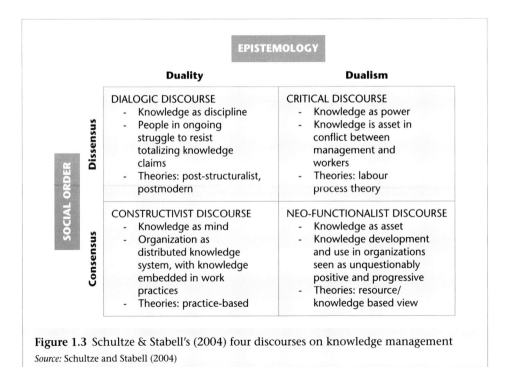

Figure 1.3 Schultze & Stabell's (2004) four discourses on knowledge management
Source: Schultze and Stabell (2004)

power and politics). This necessarily means utilizing perspectives other than that which Schultze and Stabell label the neo-functionalist discourse. This will allow an in-depth exploration of the issues underlying the theme of knowledge management and provide students with an insight into the debates and disagreements that continue to characterize the knowledge management literature, which would remain invisible if the focus was narrowly on the neo-functionalist perspective.

Thus, the book provides a critical introduction to knowledge management through examining ideas and assumptions that typically are not questioned in the mainstream knowledge management literature. Undertaking such an analysis reveals fundamental and important questions, which are likely to be of perennial interest, such as what is knowledge? Can it be controlled? Can it be codified? What are the difficulties involved in sharing or codifying it? Why might people be unwilling to participate in knowledge management initiatives? How these issues are structured in the book is described below.

The book is organized into four distinctive parts, each of which are focused around particular themes. Part 1 addresses one of the fundamental questions in the knowledge management literature, how knowledge is conceptualized. This issue is explored in detail in Chapters 2 and 3. These chapters separately examine the two dominant perspectives on epistemology that predominate in the knowledge management literature. Chapter 2 focuses on elaborating the objectivist perspective on knowledge, which Schultze & Stabell label the epistemology of dualism. While Schultze & Stabell's (2004) analysis links two discourses with this perspective on knowledge (the neo-functionalist and the critical), the central focus here is largely on the neo-functionalist discourse alone. This is primarily because, as outlined it represents the mainstream perspective on the knowledge management literature, and few analysts utilize the critical discourse. Further, issues raised by writers who adopt what Schultze & Stabell (2004) label the critical discourse are examined later, in Chapter 12, on power, politics and conflict.

Chapter 3 then elaborates the practice-based perspective on knowledge, which Schultze & Stabell label the epistemology of duality. As with Chapter 2, while Schultze & Stabell (2004) identify two knowledge management discourses as being associated with this epistemology (the dialogic and constructivist discourses), the focus in Chapter 3 is narrowly on what they label the constructivist discourse. This is largely because substantially more writing on knowledge management has utilized the constructivist discourse. Of Schultze & Stabell's (2004) four discourses the dialogic discourse is the least utilized, with only one piece of work explicitly adopting such a perspective (Sewell 2005). The issues raised by Sewell (2005) are examined in Chapter 12.

Part 2 is concerned with examining and elaborating key concepts and is organized into three chapters. Chapter 4 engages with the questions of what knowledge management is and shows that providing a simple definition is problematic. This is due to the wide range of strategies that have been advocated and adopted for managing knowledge in organizations. A number of different typologies and frameworks are then utilized to categorize and structure them. Chapter 5 focuses on the key and related concepts of knowledge work, knowledge workers and knowledge-intensive firms. The chapter examines and explores the debates that have developed around all these concepts, which, as with the idea of knowledge management itself, makes providing a straightforward definition for them difficult. Chapter 6, the final chapter in Part 2 engages with the topic of learning and the learning organization, exploring how the concepts and practices of learning and knowledge management in organizations are closely related. The chapter also examines the contrasting viewpoints on the learning organization that have emerged, specifically engaging with the debate on whether the learning organization increases opportunities for self development or simply represents a new method of control and exploitation for workers.

The two chapters in Part 3 focus on processes of organizational innovation, but each examines quite different aspects of it. Chapter 7 examines innovation through the creation and use of new knowledge. The central focus of this chapter is on Nonaka and his various collaborators, whose work on knowledge creation is arguably the most well known and used of all writing on knowledge management. The chapter will provide a critical evaluation of his work highlighting a number of ways in which it has been criticized.

Chapter 8 examines an equally important aspect of organizational innovation processes, though one which is often neglected in the knowledge management literature, the process of forgetting, unlearning or giving up knowledge which may be perceived as not having contemporary relevance. This chapter is put beside the chapter on knowledge creation as to some extent unlearning and forgetting represent the opposite of knowledge creation, but can equally be regarded as being innovative.

Part 4, the last, but largest section of the book examines a diverse range of human and social issues related to managing knowledge in organizations, all of which have emerged as being important to organizational attempts at knowledge management. Part 4 begins with Chapter 9 which examines the question of how knowledge processes in organizations are intimately linked to the topic of motivation. The chapter challenges the assumption that people are likely to be willing to share their knowledge, and explores why this is the case. This chapter utilizes the now copious literature that argues for a greater sensitivity to human and social factors.

Chapters 10 and 11 look at the dynamics of knowledge sharing, and knowledge generation in two distinctive types of group situation. These chapters both illustrate different aspects of the collective and shared nature of much organizational knowledge. Chapter 10 uses the community of practice concept to consider the dynamics of knowledge sharing and knowledge production in a homogenous group context, where the people working together have well established social relations, a significant degree of common knowledge, and a sense of collective identity. It closes by examining the potential dark side of communities of practice, which has been relatively unexplored in the communities of practice literature. Chapter 11 considers knowledge processes in group contexts where there are limited social relations, a limited degree of common knowledge, and a limited sense of collective identity (for example in international project teams). This chapter shows how the dynamics of knowledge sharing and production in such a context are significantly different from those that are typical within communities of practice.

Chapter 12 builds from some of the issues touched on in Chapter 9—how knowledge processes are shaped by the conflict and politics that are an inherent part of organizational life. In general, the chapter considers how and why knowledge and power are inextricably linked, and specifically examines how conflicts in the development and use of knowledge can also be linked to the fundamental character of the employment relationship. The chapter examines the contrasting perspectives on knowledge and power developed within what Schultze & Stabell label the critical and discursive discourses on knowledge management.

Chapter 13 examines one of the most heated debates in the knowledge management literature—the role that information technology can play in knowledge management processes. Perspectives range from those that suggest that IT can play a crucial role, to diametrically opposed perspectives that argue that the nature of knowledge makes it impossible to share knowledge electronically. In examining this debate the chapter links back to issues of epistemology, and the definitions of knowledge that are discussed in Chapters 2 and 3.

Chapter 14 examines the way that organizations have, and can attempt to shape the knowledge behaviours of their staff through developing specific HRM policies and practices, or culture management exercises. Chapter 15, the final chapter in Part 4 examines the topic of leadership considering the role that senior management in organizations can play in facilitating and inhibiting knowledge management processes.

The book then concludes in Chapter 16 by considering the extent to which knowledge management is likely to continue being a topic of great importance to business organizations, evaluating how the role of the various groups such as business organizations, academics, government policy makers and consultants have evolved with regard to knowledge management over time.

Review and discussion questions

1   What is your position on the knowledge society debate? Do you believe that the economy and society in the country you live have the characteristics of a knowledge society? What evidence supports and undermines your argument?

2   The critical and dialogical discourses raise the idea that knowledge management initiatives may not always be in the best interests of everyone working in an organization. To what extent do knowledge management initiatives create conflicts of interest between senior managers and workers in business organizations?

3   To what extent is the dissensus based perspective on knowledge management (the critical and dialogical discourses) neglected in the knowledge management literature. Can you think of any examples of work which utilizes either of these perspectives?

4   One of the dominant assumptions in much of the knowledge management literature is that knowledge can be objective and universal. To what extent do you agree with the postmodern criticism of such ideas which suggests that there is no such thing as objective knowledge as all knowledge is subjective and socially constructed?

Suggestions for further reading

1   R. DeFillippi *et al.* (2006). *Knowledge at Work: Creative Collaboration in the Global Economy*. Oxford: Blackwell.

This represents a good example of a text clearly embracing the knowledge society thesis and examining the implications of it for organizations and managers.

2   H. Scarbrough & J. Swan (2001). 'Explaining the Diffusion of Knowledge Management', *British Journal of Management*, 12: 3–12.

Examines the growth of interest in knowledge management from the point of view of the fads and fashions literature.

3   U. Schultze & C. Stabell (2004). 'Knowing What you Don't Know? Discourses and Contradictions in Knowledge Management Research', *Journal of Management Studies*, 41: 549–573.

A useful analysis which provides a way to categorize the diverse range of work published on knowledge management.

4   F. Webster (1996). *Theories of the Information Society* (particularly chapter 3). London: Routledge.

Provides a comprehensive description and critique of Bell's post-industrial society thesis.

Take your learning further: Online Resource Centre

Visit the supporting Online Resource Centre for resources which will extend your understanding of knowledge management in organizations. As well as web links to sites of interest, the author has provided case studies looking at knowledge management in virtual and knowledge intensive firms, and in global multinationals. These will help you with your research, essays and assignments; or you may find these additional resources helpful when revising for exams.

 www.oxfordtextbooks.co.uk/orc/hislop2e/

PART 1

Epistemologies of Knowledge in the Knowledge Management Literature

Chapter 1 has introduced the idea that increasingly knowledge is seen as representing the most important asset organizations possess, and that society has witnessed a significant increase in both the number of knowledge workers, and knowledge intensive organizations. This begs a number of questions, not least of which is, what is knowledge? This represents one of the most fundamental questions that humanity has grappled with, and has occupied the minds of philosophers for centuries. Furthermore, even in contemporary times, interest in the topic of knowledge stems from more than the growth of interest in knowledge management. For example, postmodern philosophy has raised questions about the assumed objectivity of knowledge, and in the process has sparked an enormous debate. Therefore, in engaging with the question of the fundamental character of knowledge it is tempting to look beyond the knowledge management literature and engage with the wider historical and philosophical literature on the topic. However, this temptation is resisted here, for two primary reasons.

Firstly, it is way beyond the scope of this book to attempt to provide any kind of adequate review, however brief, of the debates regarding the nature of knowledge (such as what distinguishes knowledge from belief, opinion etc), or to describe, compare and contrast the different perspectives on knowledge that have been developed by different writers (from Plato and Aristotle to nineteenth century philosophers such as Hume, Kant and Nietzsche to twentieth century writers such as Ryle or Polanyi[1]). The second reason for not engaging with such issues and writers here is that few writers on knowledge management do so. This is largely because, as Styre (2003) argues, writers on knowledge management appear both less interested in knowledge per se, having a narrow focus on knowledge in workplaces that has practical utility and can contribute to an organization's competitive advantage, and also because they appear unwilling to embrace the idea that knowledge is not ultimately amenable to management control. However, where knowledge management writers do engage directly with such issues and philosophers, such as the use of Polanyi's work in discussions of tacit knowledge, reference will be made to relevant philosophers.

Thus, this section of the book deliberately chooses to focus narrowly on how knowledge is conceptualized in the knowledge management literature. Even with this restricted focus, addressing the question of the nature of knowledge is by no means simple. This is to a large extent because in the contemporary literature on knowledge management there are an enormous diversity of definitions, and from the way knowledge is described by different writers it is obvious that it is conceptualized in hugely divergent ways. Thus, rather than suggest that there is one single 'true' definition of what knowledge is, the book reflects the fragmented nature of the contemporary debate on this topic and presents the differing definitions and descriptions. As will be seen, the competing conceptualizations examined are based on fundamentally different epistemologies.

Definition   Epistemology

Philosophy addressing the nature of knowledge. Concerned with questions such as: is knowledge objective and measurable? Can knowledge be acquired or is it experienced? What is regarded as valid knowledge, and why?

As outlined in Chapter 1, Schultze & Stabell (2004), drawing on Burrell & Morgan's (1979) analysis of sociological paradigms, suggested that two distinctive epistemologies exist in the knowledge management literature, the epistemologies of dualism and duality. This is a similar conclusion to that reached by a number of other writers (see Table 2), who label their epistemologies differently from Schultze & Stabell. This part of the book is structured to reflect these findings, with a separate chapter being devoted to each epistemology, with Chapter 2 examining what is here labelled the objectivist perspective, and Chapter 3 examining what is here labelled the practice-based perspective (see Table 2).

These chapters examine not only how knowledge is conceptualized within each perspective, but also how the management and sharing of knowledge is characterized, based on their different assumptions about knowledge. Therefore, to best understand these competing perspectives, and to allow an effective comparison of their differences, it is useful to read these chapters in parallel, and consider them as being two halves of a debate.

---

1. Anyone interested in developing an understanding of such issues should find and read one/some of the many books which provide an introduction to and overview of the philosophy and theory of knowledge.

Author	Objectivist perspective	Practice-based perspective
Schultze & Stabell (2004)	Epistemology of duality	Epistemology of dualism
Werr & Stjernberg (2003)	Knowledge as theory	Knowledge as practice
Empson (2001a)	Knowledge as an asset	Knowing as a process
Cook & Brown (1999)	Epistemology of possession	Epistemology of practice
McAdam & McCreedy (2000)	Knowledge as truth	Knowledge as socially constructed
Scarbrough (1998)	'Content' theory of knowledge	'Relational' view of knowledge

Table 2 Competing epistemologies

While the practice-based perspective, as will be seen, is founded on a critique of the objectivist perspective, the objectivist perspective, largely via what Schultze and Stabell (2004) label the neo-functionalist discourse, remains by far the dominant, mainstream perspective on knowledge in the knowledge management literature. Thus having an understanding of both perspectives is useful. These represent probably the most difficult chapters to read, as they are dealing with relatively abstract ideas. However, they provide a useful foundation to the issues addressed in the remainder of the book. Therefore a thorough grasp of these issues should facilitate a deeper understanding of what follows.

2

The Objectivist
Perspective on Knowledge

Introduction

The purpose of this chapter is to fully articulate the objectivist perspective on knowledge. In this book the term 'objectivist' perspective is used instead of the various terms adopted by other writers (see Table 2 in the introduction to Part 1 of the book). This is because this label embodies and highlights what are here regarded as two of this perspective's foundational assumptions: not only that much organizational knowledge is typically considered as being objective in character, but also that such knowledge can be separated from people via codification into the form of an object, or entity (explicit knowledge).

This chapter is structured as follows. Firstly, it begins by outlining the key assumptions and characteristics of the objectivist perspective on knowledge. The characteristics of this perspective are further elaborated in the second section which examines and gives examples of work utilizing the knowledge-based theory of the firm, which, as outlined, is one of the most important and well known theories associated with the neo-functionalist variant of the objectivist perspective. The third section of the chapter examines one of the key consequences of the either/or logic that dominates within this perspective on knowledge, the development of knowledge typologies that highlight and differentiate between distinctive categories of knowledge (the most well known being tacit and explicit knowledge). The final section of the chapter concludes by considering how those adopting an objectivist perspective on knowledge typically conceptualize the sharing and management of organizational knowledge.

Objectivist perspectives on knowledge

The primary aim of this section is to describe the principles and characteristics of the objectivist epistemology of knowledge (see Table 2.1), outlining both the way it characterizes knowledge and how those adopting this perspective conceptualize knowledge management processes. Cook and Brown (1999) refer to this perspective as the

Character of knowledge from an objectivist epistemology
Knowledge is an entity/object
Based on a positivistic philosophy: knowledge regarded as objective 'facts'
Explicit knowledge (objective) privileged over tacit knowledge (subjective)
Knowledge is derived from an intellectual process

Table 2.1 The objectivist character of knowledge

'epistemology of possession' as knowledge is regarded as an entity that people or groups possess.

Within the objectivist perspective the entitative character of knowledge represents its primary characteristic. Knowledge is regarded as an entity/commodity that people possess, but which can exist independently of people in a codifiable form. Such knowledge can exist in a number of forms including documents, diagrams, computer systems or be embedded in physical artefacts such as machinery or tools. Thus, for example, a text-based manual of computer operating procedures, whether in the form of a document, CD or web page, represents a form of explicit knowledge. From the objectivist perspective, the idea that explicit knowledge can exist in a textual form stems from a number of assumptions about the nature of language, including that language has fixed and objective meanings, and that there is a direct equivalence between words, and that which they denote.

A further assumption about the nature of knowledge is that it is regarded as objective. The assumption is that it is possible to develop a type of knowledge and understanding that is free from individual subjectivity. This represents what McAdam & McCreedy (2000) described as the *'knowledge is truth'* perspective, where explicit knowledge is seen as equivalent to a canonical body of scientific facts and laws which are consistent across cultures and time. These ideas are deeply rooted in the philosophy of positivism, the idea that the social world can be studied scientifically, i.e. that social phenomena can be quantified and measured, that general laws and principles be established, and that objective knowledge is produced as a result.

Definition Positivism

While Comte, a nineteenth century French philosopher founded what is now called Positivism, Durkheim was arguably the first to translate these ideas into the realm of sociology. Durkheim was concerned to make sociology into a science, and advocated the use of positivistic philosophy. This philosophy assumes that cause and effect can be established between social phenomena through the use of observation and testing, and that general laws and principles can be established. These general laws and principles constitute objective knowledge.

ILLUSTRATION

The prioritization of explicit over tacit knowledge in a bakery

Yanow (2004) suggests that the privileging and prioritizing of what she calls expert or theoretical knowledge can result in local, contextual tacit knowledge becoming so marginalized that it can often be neglected if not ignored. One of the most vivid organizational examples she gives to illustrate her argument concerns the knowledge of some delivery drivers employed by a bakery. The owners of the bakery decided that they wanted to better understand the changing nature of the tastes and demands of the final customers who bought their goods (which they bought from the shops that were the bakery's direct customers). Despite the fact that some of the bakery's own employees (the delivery drivers who took their goods to the shops) arguably possessed such knowledge, through the ongoing conversations they had with the shops' owners that happened when deliveries were made, this source of knowledge wasn't used. Instead, the bakery's owners spent a significant amount of money employing external consultants to conduct some market research. For Yanow, the reason that the delivery drivers' knowledge was overlooked and not used was due to its character. Fundamentally, this knowledge was tacit, subjective, experience based and context specific and was possessed by workers low down in the organizational hierarchy. For the owners of the bakery this was regarded as a less legitimate and less objective form of knowledge to that which the market research consultants could provide (which was regarded as objective, abstract, generalizable and 'scientific').

Yanow suggests that this is far from an isolated example and that the privileging of theoretical knowledge over local contextual, tacit knowledge is an attitude which is prevalent in many, if not the majority of organizations.

1. Do you agree with this conclusion regarding the dominance of this perspective?
2. From any organizational experiences you have can you think of other, similar examples where potentially important and useful knowledge is overlooked and neglected due to its tacit, contextual and experiential character?

The third key element of the objectivist epistemology is that it privileges explicit knowledge over tacit knowledge. Primarily, explicit knowledge is regarded as equivalent to objective knowledge. Tacit knowledge on the other hand, knowledge which is difficult to articulate in an explicit form, is regarded as more informal, less rigorous and highly subjective, being embedded within the cultural values and assumptions of those who possess and use it. Nonaka *et al.* (2000), for example, make this explicit by suggesting that,

> 'explicit knowledge can be expressed in formal and systematic language and shared in the form of data, scientific formulae . . . In contrast, tacit knowledge is highly personal . . . Subjective insights, intuitions and hunches fall into this category of knowledge.'

A key element of Nonaka's perspective on epistemology, as will be seen in Chapter 7, is that he challenges the privileging and prioritization of explicit knowledge, which he regards as being characteristic of the way knowledge is conceptualized in 'western' societies, and suggests that greater attention requires to be paid to the role of tacit knowledge.

The final major assumption is that knowledge is regarded as primarily a cognitive, intellectual entity (but which is ultimately codifiable). As Cook & Brown (1999, 384) suggest, knowledge '*is something that is held in the head*'. From this perspective, the development and production of knowledge comes from a process of intellectual reflection (individual or collective), and is primarily a cognitive process.

The knowledge-based theory of the firm

The knowledge-based theory of the firm represents the dominant theory which adopts the objectivist perspective on knowledge. Effectively, it represents the mainstream perspective on knowledge. For example, Nonaka & Peltokorpi's (2006) analysis of the twenty most cited knowledge management articles found that articles using or developing the knowledge (and/or resource) based theory of the firm were prominent in this list. Hence it is worth spending time examining it in a little detail.

The knowledge-based theory of the firm, which represents a specific development from the resource-based view of the firm, has been articulated and developed by a number of writers including Spender (1996), Kogut & Zander (1996), and Grant (1996). Over time the theory has been developed and refined partly through theoretical development, and partly through empirical testing (Berman *et al.* 2002; Bogner & Bansal 2007; Haas & Hansen 2007; Nahapiet & Ghoshal 1998; Voelpel *et al.* 2005).

The compatibility of the knowledge-based view of the firm with Schultze and Stabell's (2004) neo-functionalist discourse is visible in the fundamental, unquestioned assumptions made by those adopting this perspective (such as those listed at the end of the previous paragraph) that organizational knowledge is an increasingly important source of competitive advantage for firms and further that the interests of workers and organizational managers and owners in attempting to do this are compatible and not contradictory.

The compatibility of the knowledge-based view of the firm with the characteristics of the objectivist perspective on knowledge just outlined is also typically quite apparent. For example, such work typically adopts an entitative view of knowledge (see for example Szulanski 1996), with Glazer (1998) explicitly talking about '*knowledge as a commodity*' (p. 176). Second, as is apparent with the two examples of the knowledge-based theory of the firm outlined in this chapter, (see Berman *et al.* (2002, 25) and Haas & Hansen (2007, 30) for examples), this perspective is also founded on the idea that there are separate and distinctive types of knowledge, such as tacit and explicit, and group and individual knowledge. Finally, assumptions in this perspective regarding the objective character of knowledge are apparent in the view that the quality and character of organizational knowledge can be quantified and measured. For example, one of the key objectives of Glazer's article is to facilitate efforts to 'develop reliable and valid measures of knowledge', (1998, 176). Further, Haas and Hansen (2007), in examining how the acquisition of tacit and explicit knowledge can improve task performance assume unproblematically that it is possible to measure the quality of both types of knowledge (defined as '*rigour, soundness and insight*' (p. 1137)) through asking relevant questions in a survey.

Finally, the compatibility of those utilizing and developing the knowledge-based theory of the firm with the objectivist perspective on knowledge is evident in the use of positivistic methods to investigate and analyse organizational knowledge and knowledge management processes. This is apparent in the assumptions that the variables under investigation can be objectively measured (typically via quantitative methods involving the collection of large bodies of statistical data), and that objective causal relationships between these variables can be revealed via the development and testing (via statistical analysis) of specific hypotheses. Such characteristics are visible in both the illustrated examples provided in this chapter.

One of the most widely cited articles utilizing and developing the knowledge-based view of the firm is Nahapiet and Ghoshal's (1998). They begin from the assumption that intellectual capital ('*the knowledge and knowing capability of a social collective, such as an organization, intellectual community or professional practice*' (p. 245)) is an increasingly important source of competitive advantage for firms. Further they suggest that firms provide better institutional conditions for the development of intellectual capital than markets do. Their theoretical contribution to the development of the knowledge-based view of the firm is to conceptualize the relationship between social and intellectual capital within firms. Their analysis builds from the assumptions in social capital theory that the networks of social relations people have can provide useful resources for social action. They build from this by suggesting that business organizations provide institutional conditions conducive to the development of dense networks of social capital, and that this social capital facilitates the development and creation of intellectual capital.

Typologies of knowledge

As has been outlined, one of the primary features of the objectivist perspective on knowledge is the privileging of explicit/objective knowledge over tacit/subjective knowledge. This distinction between tacit and explicit knowledge, which are regarded as quite separate and distinct types of knowledge, flows from the either/or logic of binary oppositions which is a fundamental character of this perspective (see Figure 1.3, and also Nonaka & Peltokorpi 2006). Thus, one feature of the writing of those adopting an objectivist perspective on knowledge is to make and develop typologies that identify and distinguish between fundamentally different types of knowledge. Two of the most common distinctions made, which are examined here are between tacit and explicit knowledge, and individual and collective or group knowledge.

Tacit and explicit knowledge

The tacit–explicit dichotomy is largely ubiquitous in analyses into the characteristics of organizational knowledge. Explicit knowledge, from an objectivist perspective is synonymous with objective knowledge, as outlined above (see Table 2.2). Therefore, it is unnecessary to restate in detail its characteristics. Suffice to say that explicit knowledge is regarded as objective, standing above and separate from both individual and social value systems and secondly that it can be codified into a tangible form.

Tacit knowledge on the other hand represents knowledge that people possess, but which is inexpressible. It incorporates both physical/cognitive skills (such as the ability to juggle, to do mental arithmetic, to weld, or to create a successful advertising slogan), and cognitive frameworks (such as the value systems that people possess). The main characteristics of tacit knowledge are therefore that it is personal, and is difficult, if not impossible to disembody and codify. This is because tacit knowledge may not only be difficult to articulate, it may even be subconscious (see Table 2.2).

This distinction between tacit and explicit knowledge is by no means unique to the objectivist epistemology of knowledge, but the specific way that the distinction is theorized within this perspective is quite particular. Importantly, as will be seen later in the chapter, some major implications flow from this depiction of the dichotomy in terms of the way knowledge sharing processes are conceptualized. Within the objectivist epistemological framework the either/or logic that predominates results in tacit and explicit knowledge being regarded as separate and distinctive types of knowledge. This characterization of the dichotomy is explicit in the following quotation, '[t]here are *two types of knowledge: explicit knowledge and tacit knowledge*' (Nonaka *et al.* 2000). Thus

Tacit knowledge	Explicit knowledge
Inexpressible in a codifiable form	Codifiable
Subjective	Objective
Personal	Impersonal
Context specific	Context independent
Difficult to share	Easy to share

Table 2.2 The characteristics of tacit and explicit knowledge

	Individual	Social
Explicit	Conscious	Objectified
Tacit	Automatic	Collective

Table 2.3 Generic knowledge types
Source: adapted from Spender (1996)

from this perspective tacit and explicit knowledge do not represent the extremes of a spectrum, but instead represent two pure and separate forms of knowledge.

Typically, this polarized dichotomy is argued to be based on the work of Michael Polanyi (1958, 1983). Nonaka for example makes this reference explicit. However, as will be shown in Chapter 3, there is another, distinctly different interpretation of Polanyi's work, which questions this conceptualization of the tacit–explicit dichotomy.

Individual–group knowledge

While Nonaka argues that knowledge can only ever exist at the level of the individual, this idea is disputed by a range of other writers. These writers argue that while much knowledge does reside within individuals, there is a sense in which knowledge can reside in social groups in the form of shared work practices and routines, and shared assumptions or perspectives. This insight is used as the basis for a further dichotomy of knowledge types: into individual and group/social level knowledge. One of the most well known advocates of such a perspective is Spender (1996), who combined the tacit–explicit dichotomy, with the individual–group dichotomy to produce a two by two matrix with four generic types of knowledge (Table 2.3).

Objectified knowledge represents explicit group knowledge, for example a documented system of rules, operating procedures or formalized organizational routines. *Collective* knowledge on the other hand represents tacit group knowledge, knowledge possessed by a group that is not codified. Examples of this include informal organizational routines and ways of working, stories and shared systems of understanding. For example, the value systems that people possess have a collective element, as they are related to values and ideas that circulate within the particular social milieu that people work within. The massive expansion of the culture management industry that has occurred since the mid-1980s, which attempts to inculcate specific value systems within organizations, suggests that there is an optimism amongst organizational management that such shared systems of values can be developed. As the following example suggests, coordination among team mates on sports teams can involve the use of collective, group tacit knowledge.

However, the organizational context is by no means the only level at which group knowledge can exist. One specific, more micro-level type of collective knowledge that is increasingly being referred to is that possessed and held within communities of practice (see Chapter 10). At a more macro level, Lam (1997) also found that the national cultural context could play an important role in shaping the nature of organizational knowledge (see Chapter 3 for details of her study, its findings and conclusions).

ILLUSTRATION

Linking group tacit knowledge to team performance in the National Basketball Association (NBA)

Berman *et al.* (2002) utilize the empirical context of National Basketball Association (NBA) in the USA to examine the role that group tacit knowledge plays in team performance. One of the key tenets of the knowledge-based view of the firm is that tacit knowledge can be an important source of competitive advantage. For Berman *et al.* group tacit knowledge is a form of 'collective mind', where a team of people individually possess related and overlapping knowledge. This knowledge is tacit in form when people use it to coordinate their actions with others without the aid of any verbal communication and even where eye contact does not exist. The most explicit example of this would be when someone successfully executes a 'blind pass' to a team mate, whereby they anticipate the movement of a team mate by passing the ball to where they believe they will be while not looking either at their colleague, or in the direction they are throwing the ball. Such knowledge is argued to be developed experientially, through collective practice, where team mates work together over time.

In testing their hypothesis, they used shared team experience as a proxy for group tacit knowledge, with this being measured via the amount of time that players played for the same team continuously. They found that, as they had predicted, there was an inverse 'u' shaped relationship between the level of group tacit knowledge and team performance. Thus, group tacit knowledge was positively related to team performance, but that due to the law of diminishing returns, the extent of performance increased eventually declined. Further, beyond a certain level of group tacit knowledge, team performance started to decline. This decline in performance with high levels of group tacit knowledge was due to what they termed 'knowledge ossification', whereby high levels of group tacit knowledge resulted in group/team behaviours, values and mindsets becoming rigid and difficult to change, which could create an unwillingness to learn and adapt.

1. What are the implications of this study for business organizations? Are these findings relevant to business organizations, or is the context quite different?
2. Should organizations attempt to foster and develop group tacit knowledge?
3. What, if anything could management do in a business organization to avoid the risk of group performance declining when levels of group tacit knowledge reach a certain level?

An objectivist perspective on the sharing and management of knowledge

Having examined both the fundamental character of knowledge, and the way knowledge can be categorized into different types, the final section of this chapter examines the implications of these ideas for the sharing and management of knowledge. This section begins by making explicit the general model of knowledge sharing which flows from objectivist assumptions regarding knowledge, before concluding by outlining the way knowledge management processes are characterized.

Conduit model of knowledge sharing

The assumptions in the objectivist perspective outlined earlier that knowledge can be externalized from people into a separate and discrete object or entity, and that knowledge can also be objective has profound implication for how knowledge sharing processes are conceptualized.

Building from such assumptions the sharing of knowledge from an objectivist perspective represents what has been referred to as the conduit or transmitter/receiver model (see Figure 2.1). This model suggests that knowledge is shared by the transferral of explicit, codified knowledge (in the form of text, a diagram or an electronic document, etc.) from an isolated sender, to a separate receiver. The metaphor of knowledge sharing as being similar to the posting of a letter is thus appropriate. The idea behind this model is that the sender, in isolation from the receiver, can produce some wholly explicit knowledge, and then transfer it remotely to the receiver. The receiver then takes this knowledge and is able to understand it and use it without any other form of interaction with the sender. Further, it is assumed that no important aspects of this explicit knowledge are lost in the transfer process, and that both sender and receiver derive the same meaning from the knowledge.

Such assumptions are often made explicit. For example, Szulanski (1996), while acknowledged that most organizational knowledge has tacit components, and can be embedded in organizational routines suggests that knowledge sharing involves *'the exchange of organizational knowledge between a source and a recipient'* (1996, 28). Voelpel *et al.*'s (2005) case study of Siemens' ShareNet knowledge management initiative (which is examined at the end of Chapter 4) also reveals similar assumptions, as utilizing the resource-based theory of the firm, they use terms such as *'source unit's knowledge'*, *'transmission channels'* and *'receiving unit'* (p. 10) to conceptualize knowledge transfer processes.

Figure 2.1 The conduit model of knowledge sharing

Knowledge management processes

Building from these assumptions regarding the sharing of knowledge, we can now examine the nature of knowledge management processes from an objectivist perspective (Table 2.4).

Based on the strict dichotomy on which the objectivist perspective is founded, where tacit and explicit knowledge are regarded as distinctive and separate types of knowledge with quite specific characteristics, the sharing of tacit and explicit knowledge are also regarded as being fundamentally different (the case study by Haas & Hansen at the end of this chapter is a good illustration of this). From this perspective, while the sharing of tacit knowledge is acknowledged to be difficult, complex and time consuming, the sharing of explicit knowledge, by contrast is regarded as much more straightforward. In fact, from the objectivist perspective, the easy transferability of explicit knowledge represents one of its defining characteristics. For example, Grant (1996, 111) suggests that *'explicit knowledge is revealed by its communication. This ease of communication is its fundamental property.'*

The typical starting point in objectivist conceptualizations of knowledge management is the processes of codifying relevant knowledge, converting tacit to explicit knowledge (a process which Nonaka and his collaborators refer to as *'externalization'*—see Chapter 7). From this perspective there is an acknowledgement that much organizational knowledge may be tacit. But this is accompanied by an optimism that it is possible to convert much of this knowledge to an explicit form. For example, while all the assembly instructions for putting together a car, or all the stages in a telesales customer interaction may not be totally explicit, with effort and work it is assumed to be possible to make all this knowledge explicit, and codify it into a complete set of instructions/body of knowledge. This can be achieved by getting relevant workers to articulate all their knowledge about such processes, making explicit all the assumptions, behaviours and actions they utilize in accomplishing the task being examined.

Thus, the first stage in any knowledge management initiative, from this perspective, is to identify what knowledge is important and then make it explicit. The typical optimism that exist with regard to the extent to which tacit knowledge can be made at least partially explicit means that the difficulties involved in sharing tacit knowledge, and the nature of such processes are not typically central to objectivist models of knowledge management. These issues are therefore not examined here. Instead, they are considered in Chapter 3, as the sharing of tacit knowledge is a more fundamental element of the practice-based perspective on knowledge.

Knowledge management: objectivist perspective
Convert tacit to explicit knowledge (codification)
Collect knowledge in central repository
Structure/systematize knowledge (into discrete categories)
Technology plays a key role

Table 2.4 An objectivist perspective on knowledge management

TIME TO REFLECT 'EXTERNALIZING' TACIT KNOWLEDGE

Think about an example of tacit knowledge that you possess. To what extent could this knowledge be converted into an explicit form? Could it be codified such that someone else could utilize it? Further, how easy, and how time consuming is this process likely to be?

The next stage in the knowledge management process involves collecting all the codified knowledge together into a central repository, and then structuring it in a systematic way to make it easily accessible to others. Thus for example, the knowledge may be collected in a central database, where it is not only stored, but also categorized, indexed and cross-referenced. The importance of doing this effectively is related to the final part of the knowledge management process: making this knowledge accessible to all people who may want to use it. One of the primary rationales for organizations managing their knowledge, is to allow knowledge to be more widely and effectively shared within organizations (so that 'best practices' can be shared, etc.). This makes organizing knowledge, and making it accessible, equally as important as the codification process.

Finally, technology typically plays a key role in knowledge management processes utilizing the objectivist perspective. For example technology can play an important role in almost every element of the knowledge management process. Firstly, it can provide a repository (for example databases). Secondly it can play a role in the organizing of knowledge (for example with electronic cross referencing systems). Finally it can provide conduits and mechanisms through which knowledge can be transferred into, or extracted from a central repository (for example through an intranet system or search engine). The role of technology in knowledge management processes is examined more fully in Chapter 13.

These characteristics are visible in the majority of the earliest knowledge management initiatives. For example, Ruggles (1998) reports the findings of a survey of 431 US and European companies. The emphasis of these initiatives was heavily technological (the top four reported priorities of these projects all had a significant technological element): conceptualize knowledge as a codifiable asset, and focus on the codification, storage, and making accessible, of this codified knowledge (see Table 2.5). *Management Review*

Knowledge management project priorities	% of respondents
Create an intranet	47
Data warehousing/create knowledge repositories	33
Implementing decision support tools	33
Implementing groupware	33

Table 2.5 Priorities of ongoing knowledge management projects
Source: adapted from Ruggles (1998, 83, Chart 2)

(Management Review & AMA 1999) reports on a survey of 1600 US managers conducted in 1998/99, and reached similar conclusions. In this survey the top priorities were: (1) identify useful information; (2) establish repositories and retrieval systems; (3) gather knowledge from customers; and (4) create and maintain employee talent.

ILLUSTRATION

An objectivist approach to knowledge management in Globalbank

Globalbank is a Dutch based, globally dispersed bank. From the mid-1990s onwards it invested significantly in intranet technologies, as this was perceived as facilitating the sharing of knowledge across divisions. One specific intranet based knowledge management system which was ultimately successful, was developed by the IT support function.

Globalbank's IT function was enormous, employing 1500 staff in Amsterdam, where it was centred, and approximately 5000 staff worldwide. There was felt to be a significant need for a knowledge management system, to support IT staff, as staff were typically widely dispersed, both geographically and divisionally, and were involved in doing similar tasks for different divisions. The objectivist assumptions regarding knowledge were apparent in a number of ways. Firstly, in terms of knowledge, the project team had an entitative conception of knowledge, which was apparent from the assumption that relevant knowledge could be codified. Secondly, there was a large technological emphasis to the project, with it being assumed that the knowledge which had been codified could be stored in databases linked to an intranet system. A significant part of the intranet project team's work was also concerned with categorizing this knowledge using an indexing system which made it easy for staff to find and access what they were looking for. Finally, with regards to knowledge sharing, the project exemplified the transmitter–receiver logic of the objectivist perspective: knowledge sharing happened through staff firstly codifying their knowledge, putting it in the database, where other staff would then be able to access and utilize it without a need to personally interact together.

Once the system had been developed and implemented it was deemed relatively successful, as staff in the IT support function made frequent use of the system, and found it to be helpful in their work.

1. With such systems what is likely to happen to any knowledge which cannot be codified?

2. The success of such intranet based knowledge management systems is dependent upon people being willing to codify and store their knowledge. Are workers typically likely to be willing to do this? Secondly, what factors are likely to affect workers willingness to do so?

Conclusion

This chapter has outlined the defining characteristics of the objectivist perspective on knowledge, which represents the mainstream perspective in the knowledge management literature on how to conceptualize knowledge. The most fundamental features of this perspective on knowledge are that it assumes that knowledge can take the form of a discrete entity, separate from people who may understand or use it. While within this perspective there is an acknowledgement that knowledge can take different forms, most importantly between tacit and explicit knowledge, and there is an assumption and optimism that much of the organizational knowledge possessed by workers can be codified into an explicit form. Some subsidiary features of this perspective on knowledge are that tacit and explicit knowledge are regarded as quite separate and distinctive types of knowledge, with explicit knowledge typically being privileged and prioritized over tacit knowledge. This is largely because explicit, or codified knowledge is typically characterized as being objective, while tacit knowledge is, in contrast, assumed to be more personal, subjective and context specific.

These assumptions about the nature of knowledge have significant implications for how the management and sharing of knowledge is conceptualized. The privileging of explicit knowledge within this perspective means that there is a bias towards and focus upon the management and sharing of explicit, codified knowledge. The emphasis on codified knowledge is also due to assumptions that it is much easier to manage and share codified knowledge, than it is to manage and share tacit knowledge. The optimist regarding the codifiability of knowledge means that those adopting an objectivist perspective on knowledge typically emphasize processes of codification. Thus, from this perspective, an initial step in the management and sharing of knowledge is to codify as much knowledge as possible. The sharing of such knowledge between people has the characteristics of a 'transmitter–receiver' model, where it is assumed codified, explicit knowledge can be passed from one person to another unmodified. This perspective on knowledge typically also suggests that computer and communication technologies can play a key role in knowledge management processes, through providing one important medium, or conduit, via which codified knowledge can be shared.

Case study

The role played by the acquisition of tacit and
explicit knowledge in improving task productivity

Haas & Hansen (2007) explicitly concern themselves with both conceptually developing and empirically testing the knowledge-based view of the firm. The basic propositions they develop and test relate to the impact that the acquisition by work groups of tacit and explicit knowledge from beyond their group/team have on what they call task productivity. This was done within the empirical context of sales teams in a large management consultancy firm in the USA, examining how the external knowledge the teams utilized impacted on the effectiveness of their work efforts. Their paper is based upon most of the typical assumptions made by those utilizing the knowledge-based theory of the firm and adopting an objectivist view of knowledge. For example they argue that tacit and explicit knowledge are distinctive knowledge types (shared via different mechanisms), that the effective use and sharing of knowledge is an increasingly important source of competitive advantage for firms, and they adopt the 'conduit' model of knowledge sharing (talking about the 'providers' and 'receivers' of knowledge).

Their paper also conceptually develops the knowledge-based view of the firm in a number of ways. Firstly, while much research has examined the barriers to knowledge sharing that exist, and the impact of knowledge sharing on organizational performance, little has been done on the impact of knowledge sharing on task performance/productivity. Secondly, this study goes beyond the common assumption that the greater level of knowledge sharing that exists the better it is for organizations, by examining at a more micro level the different consequences that the sharing and acquisition of different types of knowledge has on particular organizational tasks.

The management consultancy firm examined by Haas & Hansen provided tax and audit advice to clients in a wide range of industries including energy, communications, healthcare, automotive and financial services. The firm was both large, and highly dispersed, employing over 10,000 consultants in over 100 offices spread across the USA. The study focused narrowly on particular work tasks, examining the acquisition and use of knowledge in the work done by sales teams in pitching for business with prospective clients. These sales teams were typically *ad hoc* and temporary, bringing together groups of consultants deemed to have relevant knowledge and expertise to prepare particular bids. One of the key elements involved in preparing such bids, which was the knowledge sharing/acquisition process examined by Hass and Hansen, was the work done by consultants to draw on and utilize knowledge or experience from previous bids that they felt was relevant.

The data on the knowledge and work processes they examined was acquired from surveys that were distributed to the team leaders of a random selection of sales bids carried out during a particular time period. Of the 259 team leaders who were emailed, 191 responded, giving a response rate of 74%. Three dimensions of task productivity were examined. These included time saved, task quality, and the extent to which the bid team were considered to be competent by external stakeholders such as clients. In terms of knowledge sharing, two mechanisms were examined, with one being related to each type of knowledge that was examined. Fundamentally it was assumed that explicit knowledge was shared through the acquisition and use of documentation, whereas tacit knowledge was acquired through person-to-person interaction. Finally, for both tacit and explicit knowledge they examined the impact that both process and content factors had on task productivity, with process factors relating to the extent to which the knowledge acquired had to be adapted and customized, and content factors relating to the inherent quality of the knowledge acquired.

The most fundamental and general finding of their study was that, as their hypotheses predicted, tacit and explicit knowledge did both impact on task productivity, but in quite different ways. For example, in relation to the task productivity measure of time saved, the use of explicit/codified knowledge did have positive time saving benefits, but the acquisition of tacit knowledge did not. Further, the higher the quality of the explicit/codified knowledge that was used, the greater the time saving. By contrast, the sharing of tacit knowledge had different benefits and impacts on task productivity, improving both task quality and client's perception of competence, with both being positively related to the quality of the tacit knowledge that was shared.

This study doesn't privilege tacit over explicit knowledge and shows that both tacit and explicit knowledge have their own distinctive benefits for task productivity.

1. Does this empirical evidence undermine assumptions regarding the superiority of explicit over tacit knowledge?

Source: Haas, M., & Hansen, M. (2007). 'Different Knowledge, Different Benefits: Towards a Productivity Perspective on Knowledge Sharing in Organizations', *Strategic Management Journal*, 28: 1133–1153.

 For further information about this journal article visit our Online Resource Centre at
www.oxfordtextbooks.co.uk/orc/hislop2e/

Review and discussion questions

1 Think about your experience of social/group knowledge in the workplace. Is it largely tacit or explicit? Did it exist in the form of systems of rules, routines, stories, etc.?

2   National culture and communities of practice have been discussed as two types of social context/setting where collective knowledge can be seen to exist. What other social contexts, in your own experience, have you witnessed collective knowledge to exist— organization, family, geographic region, peer group, friendship network, profession?

3   Does the use of IT as part of a knowledge management system always indicate an objectivist perspective on knowledge? Have any of the organizations you have worked in developed IT centred knowledge management systems? Did they embody objectivist assumptions regarding knowledge? How successful were these initiatives?

4   Do you agree with the idea that the objectivist perspective on knowledge represents the most dominant perspective in the knowledge management literature? Think about what you regard as being the most well known and important works on the topic of knowledge management. Do they represent examples of the objectivist perspective on knowledge or the knowledge-based view of the firm? What features of their assumptions and analysis reveal their perspective on knowledge?

Suggestions for further reading

1   **R. Grant (1996). 'Towards a Knowledge Based Theory of the Firm',** *Strategic Management Journal*, **17, Winter Special Issue: 109–122.**

One of the earliest papers explicitly concerning itself with articulating and theoretically developing the knowledge-based view of the firm.

2   **J.-C. Spender (1996). 'Organizational Knowledge, Learning and Memory: Three Concepts in Search of a Theory',** *Journal of Organizational Change Management*, **9(1), 63–78.**

Articulates characteristics of and relations between four generic knowledge types.

3   **Berman** *et al.* **(2002). 'Tacit Knowledge as a Source of Competitive Advantage in the National Basketball Association',** *Academy of Management Journal*, **45(1), 13–31.**

An interesting article which is founded on the idea that group tacit knowledge exists and can be developed, and which examines its role in shaping performance of basketball teams.

4   **D. Yanow (2004). 'Translating Local Knowledge at Organizational Peripheries',** *British Journal of Management*, **15, Special Issue: s71–86.**

A description (and critique) of the idea that the privileging of explicit over tacit knowledge that is typical in organizations can lead to the role and importance of tacit knowledge becoming neglected and ignored.

Take your learning further: Online Resource Centre

Visit the supporting Online Resource Centre for resources which will extend your understanding of knowledge management in organizations. As well as web links to sites of interest, the author has provided case studies looking at knowledge management in virtual and knowledge intensive firms, and in global multinationals. These will help you with your research, essays and assignments; or you may find these additional resources helpful when revising for exams.

 www.oxfordtextbooks.co.uk/orc/hislop2e/

3

The Practice-Based Perspective on Knowledge

Introduction

Chapter 2 provided one specific answer to the question 'what is knowledge?' However, the objectivist perspective has been widely challenged, and for a number of different reasons. Arguably the most fundamental challenge and critique of it is that it is based on flawed epistemological assumptions. Chapter 3 therefore presents an alternative answer to the question 'what is knowledge?' This chapter is based on fundamentally different epistemological assumptions, and as will be seen, characterizes knowledge and knowledge management practices quite differently from the objectivist perspective.

The practice-based perspective conceptualizes knowledge not as a codifiable object/entity, but instead emphasizes the extent to which it is embedded within and inseparable from work activities or practices. Cook & Brown (1999) labelled this perspective an '*epistemology of practice*' due to the centrality of human activity to its conception of knowledge. Further, Gherardi (2000, 218) argues that '*practice connects "knowing" with "doing"*'. Thus, the embeddedness of knowledge in human activity (practice) represents one of the central characteristics of this epistemological perspective. This is therefore why the label practice-based epistemology is here preferred to Schultze & Stabell's (2004) terminology, the epistemology of duality.

Definition   Practice

Practice refers to purposeful human activity. It is based on the assumption that activity includes both physical and cognitive elements, and that these elements are inseparable. Knowledge use and development is therefore regarded as a fundamental aspect of activity.

While the objectivist perspective was closely aligned with a positivistic philosophy, the practice-based perspective is compatible with a number of different philosophical perspectives (Table 3.1). However, constraints of space prevent an examination of these perspectives and their similarities and differences.

Writer	Theoretical perspective
Empsom (2001a)	Interpretive
Blackler (1995)	Activity theory
Tsoukas (1996)	Ethnomethodology/interpretive philosophy
Cook & Brown (1999)	American pragmatists
Lave & Wenger (1991)	Situated learning theory
Suchman (2003)	Actor network theory

Table 3.1 Theoretical perspectives related to the practice-based perspective

The chapter follows a similar structure to Chapter 2, and begins by firstly outlining the way knowledge is characterized within the practice-based perspective. Following this, the chapter then examines how knowledge management processes are conceptualized. As the chapter proceeds, the vast differences that exist between practice-based, and the objectivist perspective on knowledge will become more apparent.

Features of a practice-based perspective on knowledge

The practice-based epistemology can be understood in terms of six specific, but inter-related factors, each of which are now examined in turn (Table 3.2).

The embeddedness of knowledge in practice

Perhaps the most important difference between the objectivist and practice-based epistemologies of knowledge is that the practice-based perspective challenges the entitative conception of knowledge. From this perspective, knowledge isn't regarded as a discrete entity/object that can be codified and separated from people. Instead, knowledge, or as some of the writers from this perspective prefer, knowing, is inseparable from human activity (Orlikowski 2002). Thus all activity is, to some extent knowledgeable, involving the use and/or development of knowledge. Conversely, all knowledge work, whether

Characteristics of knowledge from practice-based epistemology
1. Knowledge is embedded in practice
2. Tacit and explicit knowledge are inseparable
3. Knowledge is embodied in people
4. Knowledge is socially constructed
5. Knowledge is culturally embedded
6. Knowledge is contestable

Table 3.2 Practice-based characteristics of knowledge

using it, sharing it, developing it or creating it, will involve an element of activity. Blackler (1995, 1023) summed this up as follows,

> 'rather than regarding knowledge as something that people have, it is suggested that knowing is better regarded as something they do.'

As well as challenging the knowing–doing dichotomy, this perspective also challenges the mind–body dichotomy that is inherent to the objectivist perspective. As outlined, the objectivist perspective, drawing on the classical images of science, conceptualizes knowledge as being primarily derived from cognitive processes, something involving the brain but not the body. The practice-based perspective instead views knowing and the development of knowledge as occurring on an ongoing basis through the routine activities that people undertake. Knowing thus can be seen as less of a purely cognitive process, and more of a holistic process involving the whole body (Gherardi 2000). Thus, from this perspective, thinking and doing are fused in knowledgeable activity, the development and use of embodied knowledge in undertaking specific activities/tasks. The involvement of the body in processes of knowing is illustrated in the following example. However it is important to say that the involvement of the body in processes of knowing is as much a part of managerial, professional, white collar work as it is in manual work.

These ideas can be illustrated through considering a number of examples. Firstly, Orr's (1990) widely referenced study of photocopier engineers emphasizes how their knowledge

ILLUSTRATION

Sensible knowledge and work practices

Strati (2007) contributes to the development of the practice-based perspective on knowledge through the development of the term sensible knowledge. Central to Strati's conceptualization of knowledge is the idea that knowing is not an activity conducted purely within the brain, with knowing involving the whole body. For Strati (p. 67), work practices and processes of knowing in organizations are, 'not only mental and logical-analytical but also corporeal and multi-sensorial'. The concept of sensible knowledge relates to knowing that involves workers using the human senses of touch, sight, taste, hearing and smell, with a number of empirical examples being given to illustrate the arguments being made. One of these examples concerned sawmill workers from the north east of Italy (Strati 2007, 67–69). In this example, the workers in the mill (who did not wear gloves), were able to identify the thickness of the planks they were moving without formally measuring them, simply through the process of lifting and feeling them. Their sense of touch was such that they were able to differentiate between planks whose thicknesses varied by half a centimetre. For Strati this represented an example of sensible knowing, where the sawmill workers hands, through their sense of touch was intimately involved in knowing how thick the planks they handled were.

developed through a process of dialogue and improvization, which involved the adaptation of existing knowledge to new and novel situations. Similarly, Patriotta (2003), in a study of a Fiat Auto plant in Italy, showed the embeddedness of knowledge in the narratives possessed by workers, and how these narratives evolved in the resolution of 'disruptive occurrences' (p. 349). Thirdly, DeFillippi & Arthur (1998) in a study of film (i.e. movie) production, showed that for apprentice technicians processes of learning by watching were crucial. Knowledge in this context tended to develop through processes of socialization, observation and practice.

Tacit and explicit knowledge are inseparable

One key difference between the objectivist and practice-based perspectives on knowledge, as highlighted by Schultze & Stabell (2004) is their attitudes towards binary oppositions. Within the objectivist perspective an either/or logic dominates, which results, as outlined in Chapter 2, in the development of taxonomies of distinctive categories of knowledge. However, such a logic is rejected by those advocating and utilizing a practice-based perspective on knowledge who suggest that while such an approach may have analytical benefits, it misrepresents the complexity of organizational knowledge. Tsoukas (1996), for example suggests that dichotomies such as tacit–explicit and individual–group are unhelpful as they disguise the extent to which these elements are inseparable, and mutually defined. Blackler (1995, 1032) makes a similar point by suggesting that,

> '. . . knowledge is multi-faceted and complex, being both situated and abstract, implicit and explicit, distributed and individual, physical and mental, developing and static, verbal and encoded.'

Thus the practice-based perspective rejects the taxonomy based approach to categorizing knowledge into distinctive types which are independent of each other. Instead of the objectivist perspective's either/or logic, a both/and logic predominates. This perspective is most obvious in how those utilizing a practice-based perspective conceptualize the relationship between tacit and explicit knowledge. The practice-based perspective suggests that rather than tacit and explicit knowledge representing separate and distinctive types of knowledge, they represent two aspects of knowledge and in fact are inseparable, and are mutually constituted (Tsoukas 1996; Werr & Stjernberg 2003). One consequence of this is that there is no such thing as fully explicit knowledge, as all knowledge will have tacit dimensions. Clark (2000) uses the term '*explacit knowledge*' to linguistically symbolizes their inseparability (Table 3.3). For example text, which is often referred to as a form of codified knowledge, has tacit components, without which no reader could make sense of it. Examples of these tacit elements include an understanding of the language in which they are written, or the grammar and syntax used to structure them. Polanyi (1969, 195) suggests that,

> 'The idea of a strictly explicit knowledge is indeed self-contradictory; deprived of their tacit co-efficients, all spoken words, all formulae, all maps and graphs, are strictly meaningless.'

ILLUSTRATION

This book as partially explicit knowledge

This book represents a piece of partially explicit knowledge for two reasons. Firstly, as an author I have not been able to make fully explicit all the ideas, assumptions, theoretical frameworks and values which underpin what I have written. From the point of view of the reader it can also be considered partially explicit, as to read it you require to have a good grasp of the English language, and have some knowledge of other relevant academic topics.

While, as outlined in Chapter 2, Polanyi's work is often used to justify the idea that tacit and explicit knowledge are two separate and distinctive types of knowledge, a number of writers suggest that this misunderstands his analysis (Brown & Duguid 2001; Prichard 2000; Tsoukas 2003). These writers challenge this and suggest that his analysis is grounded more in the practice-based perspective which builds from the assumption that there are tacit and explicit dimensions to all knowledge, and that they are inseparable. Thus, from this perspective, there is no such thing as pure tacit, or pure explicit knowledge, as all knowledge contains elements of both.

The both/and logic of the practice-based perspective shapes not only how tacit and explicit knowledge are inter-related, but, as suggested by the Blackler (1995) quotations described earlier and the previous illustration of the mind–body dualism and Strati's (2007) sawmill workers, it extends to understanding how other variables are related. Three dichotomies, which are challenged by those adopting the practice-based epistemology are outlined in Table 3.3. For example, those adopting a practice-based perspective (such as Strati and his example of sawmill workers) reject the Cartesian distinction between mind and body, which assumes that knowing is primarily an intellectual and cognitive process related to the brain and instead assumes that knowing and doing are inseparable, with all knowing involving some element of doing or action and vice versa.

Knowledge is embodied

The objectivist perspective on knowledge assumes that knowledge can exist in a fully explicit and codified form and can exist independently of human beings. This position is fundamentally challenged by the practice-based perspective on knowledge, which

Challenging objectivist dichotomies
Explicit knowledge (tacit and explicit knowledge)
Knowledgeable activity (knowing and doing)
Sensual cognition (brain & body)

Table 3.3 Challenging dichotomies

TIME TO REFLECT THE MULTIDIMENSIONALITY OF KNOWLEDGE

Think of some specific organizational knowledge that you possess. Can it be classified into a neat category, such as tacit–collective, or does it have multiple dimensions
simultaneously?

assumes all knowledge, or knowing is personal. The practice-based perspective therefore
assumes that it is impossible to totally disembody knowledge from people into a fully
explicit form. This assumption is therefore closely related to, and flows from the previous two issues examined, that all knowledge has tacit dimensions, and that knowledge is
embedded in, and inseparable from practice. Thus, knowledge that is embedded in work
practices is simultaneously embodied by the workers who carry out these practices.

The practice-based nature of knowing/knowledge assumes that knowledge develops
through practice: people's knowledge develops as they conduct activities and gain experience. Further, the inseparable and mutually constituted nature of tacit and explicit
knowledge means that it is not possible to make such knowledge fully explicit. There will
always be an element to which knowledge resides in the head/body of those who developed and possess it. Thus while it may be possible to partially convert tacit knowledge
into an explicit form, in contradiction with the objectivist perspective, the practice-based
perspective assumes that such processes can never be complete. For example, in terms of a
situation most readers are likely to be familiar with from one context or another, consider
the nature of knowledge sharing in 'master–apprentice' type relations, where someone
experienced attempts to share their knowledge with a more inexperienced colleague. The
practice-based perspective assumes that the practice-based nature of the knowledge and
expertise the 'master' possesses means that this knowledge will be to some extent embodied, and cannot be fully articulated and made explicit. Further, the practice-based perspective assumes that for the apprentice to learn the knowledge of the master requires that they
communicate, interact and work together, typically over an extended period of time.

A further sense in which knowledge is embodied (and simultaneously embedded in practice) relates to what Tsoukas (1996) referred to as the *'indeterminacy of practice'*, where the
essential distinctiveness of all situations that people act in requires them to continually make
personal judgements. No matter how explicit and well defined the rules are that may guide
action, there will always be some element of ambiguity or uncertainty that creates a need for
actors to make inferences and judgements. For example, applying this insight to the perspective of the 'apprentice' just discussed, no matter how formalized, structured and explicit the
knowledge they have acquired, there will always be circumstances that emerge where an element of judgement will be required. Thus, knowledge/knowing involves the active agency of
people making decisions in light of the specific circumstances they find themselves.

The socially constructed and culturally embedded nature of knowledge

Two factors that are closely interwoven are that knowledge is socially constructed and
culturally embedded. It is therefore necessary to examine them simultaneously. In
stark contrast to the 'knowledge is truth' assumption of the objectivist perspective on

The embodiment of knowledge in pre-operative anaesthetics

Hindmarsh & Pilnick's (2007) study of medical teams conducting operations in a UK teaching hospital provides an interesting example of the embodied nature of knowledge. Hindmarsh & Pilnick's research is primarily concerned with the role of the human body in teamworking and inter-personal interaction, which was studied via analysing videos they took of how surgical staff spoke, moved and interacted during the preparation for and execution of various surgical procedures. While surgery was a team based process, Hindmarsh & Pilnick refer to the teams they studied as 'ephemeral' as they involved temporary and relatively short term collaboration between people who often hardly knew each other and hadn't previously worked together. One of the key examples they describe concerns the way pre-operative anaesthetic procedures were carried out, and the specific process of tracheal intubation (inserting a plastic tube into the trachea of a patient to allow them to breathe effectively while anaesthetized). This procedure typically involved the coordinated efforts of two people, the anaesthetist and their assistant. The procedure required the patient's head to be moved into an appropriate position (typically done by the anaesthetist) before a laryngoscope (a metal instrument) is used to open the patient's trachea. This procedure requires to be done very quickly, as during it the patient is unable to breathe properly, and requires smooth coordination between the anaesthetist and their assistant as the assistant typically is responsible for passing the laryngoscope to the anaesthetist at the appropriate time and in the appropriate way. From the observations of Hindmarsh and Pilnick this procedure was typically done with little verbal communication or eye contact occurring between the anaesthetist and their assistant. It appeared that despite the lack of such communication the assistant was able, through reading the body language of the consultant, to anticipate when, and in what way to pass them the laryngoscope. This represents an example of the embodiment of knowledge in two senses, as the assistant has to develop a knowledge of the anaesthetist's physical movements and how they relate to particular stages in a surgical procedure as well as requiring the assistant to learn how to coordinate the movements of their own body in attempting to seamlessly co-ordinate their bodily actions with the anaesthetist's.

1. Can you think of other examples of teamworking in a work context which requires co-ordination and interaction between people with only limited verbal and visual communication occurring?

knowledge, where it is suggested that codified knowledge can exist in an objective form independent of social and cultural values, the epistemology of practice perspective argues that all knowledge is socially constructed in nature, which makes it somewhat subjective and open to interpretation. Thus, knowledge is never totally neutral and unbiased, and is, to some extent, inseparable from the values of those who produce it.

As with the objectivist perspective, this viewpoint is based on a particular understanding about the nature of language. The objectivist perspective assumes that language has fixed and objective meanings, and that there is a direct equivalence between words and that which they denote. Instead, the practice-based perspective suggests that language has no such fixed meanings, and that in fact the meaning of language is inherently ambiguous. This subjectivity or interpretive flexibility in language thus undermines any claims about the objective status of any knowledge, whether it is highly tacit and personal, or whether it is partially explicit and codified. However, the socially negotiated nature of language limits the scope individuals have to modify and interpret the meaning and use of language (Sayer 1992; Tsoukas 1996).

The socially constructed nature of knowledge applies to both its production, and its interpretation. Polanyi (1969) referred to these two processes as sense giving and sense reading, while Boland & Tenkasi (1995) used the terms perspective making and perspective taking. Thus both the production of knowledge, and the reading/interpretation required to develop an understanding of it, involves an active process of meaning construction/inference. For example, a written report is a piece of partially explicit knowledge, whose meaning is constructed by its author/s. However, different readers may infer a different meaning and analysis. This aspect of the practice-based perspective therefore has profound implications for the way knowledge is shared and managed, as the attractive simplicity of the transmitter–receiver model is questioned.

Further, this process of meaning construction/inference is typically culturally embedded. As Weir & Hutchins argue (2005, 89) *'knowledge cannot be understood outside of the cultural parameters that condition its emergence and modes of reproduction'*. For example, the meanings people attach to language/events are shaped by the values and assumptions of the social and cultural context in which they live and work. One way in which pre-existing values and assumptions influence these processes of knowledge construction/ knowledge interpretation is through the filtering of data-information in deciding what is considered 'relevant'. A dramatic and tragic example of such a filtering process was one of the contributory factors to the Challenger Space Shuttle accident (Baumard 1999; Starbuck & Milliken 1988). In this case NASA engineers neglected what turned out to be important information regarding O-ring erosion, as based on the assumptions they had, such a situation was regarded as presenting a minute risk.

The socially constructed and culturally embedded nature of organizational knowledge is perhaps best illustrated through considering how national cultural factors impact on

TIME TO REFLECT PERSPECTIVE MAKING & TAKING

Can you think of an example from any organizational experience you may have of where a range of people inferred different meanings from a report? Could these differences partly be explained by the fluidity of meaning in language?

both the nature of organizational knowledge and the character of knowledge management processes. For example, Lam (1997), in examining the knowledge involved in a joint technology development project involving extended collaboration between a Japanese and a UK company, found the knowledge of all relevant staff to be deeply embedded in the social context the engineers were socialized into and worked within, and that further, the knowledge base and organizational context of both organizations were significantly different. While in the UK company there was an emphasis on formalized knowledge, developed through education, in the Japanese company tacit knowledge accumulated through experience was more important. Secondly, in the UK company there was a clear demarcation of job boundaries, limited use of job rotation, and a tendency for people to develop narrowly specialized knowledge bases. In the Japanese company, by contrast, due to the emphasis on team working the demarcation between jobs was blurred, and due to the use of job rotation, people's knowledge bases were typically broad. Finally, there were also significant differences in the way knowledge was shared and developed throughout the product cycle. In the UK division, product design and the development of detailed specifications was principally the domain of design staff. In the Japanese company, by contrast, production and design staff both had an important role in the development of product specifications. These differences made the process of knowledge sharing and joint technology development extremely complicated. Overall Lam concluded that the socially embedded character of all knowledge means that sharing knowledge between any different social and cultural contexts is likely to be both complex and time consuming.

Further, a number of writers have suggested that Nonaka & Takeuchi's (1995) SECI model of knowledge creation isn't universally applicable as it is based upon social and organizational characteristics that are specific to Japan (Glisby & Holden 2003; Weir & Hutchins 2005). This is an issue that is returned to in Chapter 7, when the work of Nonaka & Takeuchi is considered in detail.

TIME TO REFLECT THE COMPLEXITY OF CROSS CULTURAL KNOWLEDGE SHARING

These ideas suggest that the sharing of knowledge between people from different cultures is likely to be difficult. Such situations are likely to be common in multinational corporations. From a management point of view, what, if anything can management in multinationals do to address such problems?

The contestable nature of knowledge

The final key aspect of the practice-based perspective is the acknowledgement that the subjective, socially constructed and culturally embedded nature of knowledge means that what constitutes knowledge is open to dispute. This therefore challenges and undermines the idea central to the objectivist perspective that it is possible to produce truly objective knowledge. Thus, competing conceptions of what constitute 'legitimate' knowledge can occur where different groups/individuals develop incompatible and contradictory analyses of the same events, which may lead to conflict due to attempts by these groups to have their knowledge legitimated.

One of the main consequences which flow from this, therefore, is that issues of power, politics and conflict become more important than are acknowledged by the objectivist perspective. Most fundamentally, Foucault's conception of power/knowledge suggests that these concepts are inseparable (Foucault 1980; McKinlay 2000). Relatedly, Storey & Barnett (2000)

ILLUSTRATION

Competing truth claims and the politics of introducing change

Pharma-co is a UK pharmaceutical company. Until the early 1980s it had been a government owned research laboratory, and by the mid-1990s there was still evidence of the technically focused culture which had historically predominated. During the mid-1990s a decision was made to implement a new information management system. The dominant rhetoric used by the project team to justify the need for change was that the changing nature of their markets required significant changes to be made to improve the competitiveness of their production facilities. An important figure to Pharma-co's project was the World Manufacturing Director, who strongly championed it. When the project started he had been a relatively recent recruit to the organization. As part of Pharma-co's long term strategy of adopting more commercial and cost sensitive operating practices a need had been identified to introduce such attitudes to its senior management. The recruitment of the World Manufacturing Director represented one of the key ways in which this was done. Thus his 'commercial' knowledge from working outside of the company was highly regarded by senior management. However, resistance to the proposed changes emerged from middle managers within the production function. They suggested the proposed changes were fundamentally unnecessary, and that Pharma-co could remain competitive through staying focused on the development and production of technically innovative products. The traditional culture which had been historically predominant within Pharma-co was focused around production. One of the main factors strengthening the argument of production management was their detailed knowledge of the company's internal manufacturing practices. Thus at the start of Pharma-co's change project there was a highly political conflict between those for and against change which centred on the validity of their knowledge and the way they used it to legitimate their different analyses of the extent to which change was needed.

1. In such situations, to what extent is it possible to objectively evaluate the competing arguments and decide on the appropriate course of action?

2. What does the different perspectives of these interest groups say about the cultural embeddedness of knowledge? To what extent are the viewpoints of those in conflict derived from the values and ideas of the organizational communities they have worked in?

suggest that all knowledge management initiatives require to be seen as highly political, and are likely to be accompanied by what they describe as '*turf wars*' by different organizational interest groups attempting to gain some control over these projects. The importance of acknowledging and taking account of the contested and political nature of knowledge is magnified by the fact that this aspect of knowledge and knowledge management initiatives is typically either neglected or ignored by the majority of the knowledge management literature. These issues are examined more fully in Chapter 12. However, the following example illustrates these issues through considering a case where distinctively different and competing knowledge claims existing regarding the need for organizational change.

Implications for the nature of the organizational knowledge base

The above outlined characteristics of knowledge have profound implications with regard to the nature of organizational knowledge bases, as a growing number of writers recognize. The practice-based perspective on knowledge suggests that rather than being unitary and coherent, organizational knowledge bases are in fact fragmented and dispersed, being made up of specialized and specific knowledge communities, which have some degree of overlapping '*common knowledge*' (Kogut & Zanger 1992). This led Brown & Duguid (1991, 53) to suggesting that organizations require to be conceptualized as a '*community-of-communities*', and Blackler *et al.* (2000) as decentred and distributed knowledge systems. Finally, as will be seen in the following section, these insights have enormous implications for the sharing and management of knowledge in organizations.

The fragmentation of the organizational knowledge base relates closely to the idea that knowledge is embedded in practice. Typically, the practices undertaken by organizational staff, and hence the knowledge they possess, are localized and specific, being shaped by the particular demands of their context (local customers, market conditions, character of national/regional regulation and legislation, etc.). The degree of fragmentation and specialization will also be related to the culture of the organization, and the extent to which it encourages and supports autonomous or standardized working practices.

Becker (2001) suggests that while the dispersed nature of organizational knowledge is a neglected topic in the knowledge management literature, this feature of organizational knowledge poses particular managerial challenges and problems. Becker suggests that there are three particular problems, each of which produces their own distinct management challenges (see Table 3.4). Firstly is the problem of 'large numbers', which broadly increases with the number of people employed by an organization. This problem creates two managerial challenges. There is the issue of opaqueness, which refers to the difficulties of developing an overview when knowledge is fragmented and dispersed, which is a problem that increases as the level of dispersal, or number of fragments, increases. There is also the issue of resource requirements involved in bringing together the fragments of a dispersed knowledge base, which is a problem that again increases proportionally with organizational size.

Secondly is the problem of knowledge and learning asymmetries which means that knowledge and learning isn't evenly dispersed throughout an organization, with the

Problems of dispersed knowledge	Implications
Large numbers	• Limited overview (opaqueness) • Higher resource requirements
Asymmetries	• Differentiated knowledge and learning • Different cognitive frameworks
Uncertainty	• Decision problems

Table 3.4 Management problems caused by dispersed knowledge
Source: from Becker (2000, 1041, Figure 1)

knowledge of individuals being related to the nature of the tasks and social contexts they work in. Such asymmetries create two challenges for management. Firstly they require and create the need for collaboration between people with differential knowledge resources. Secondly, not only is people's knowledge different (i.e. specialized and specific), but it may also be based on qualitatively different assumptions, values, and interpretative frameworks. Brown & Duguid (2001) referred to these as '*epistemic differences*'. For example, the communication and interaction difficulties between staff from different functions of an organization (such as production and R&D, or finance and R&D), or between staff from different disciplinary backgrounds (such as in a multidisciplinary project team) can be, to some extent, explained by such differences. As will be seen in Chapter 11, where this issue is explored in detail, this significantly affects the dynamics of knowledge sharing processes.

The third and final problem of dispersed knowledge relates to the uncertainty it can create which poses challenges to management in the area of decision making, where the high and unavoidable levels of uncertainty created by the dispersed nature of organizational knowledge makes it impossible for individual organizational actors to make decisions with full and relevant knowledge.

A practice-based perspective on the management and sharing of knowledge

Having considered in detail how the practice-based epistemology conceptualizes knowledge it is now time to examine the implications of these ideas for understanding the character of organizational knowledge sharing and knowledge management processes (see Table 3.5).

One of the central components of the practice-based perspective on knowledge management is that it eschews the idea that it is possible for organizations to collect knowledge together into a central repository, or for middle and senior managers to fully understand the knowledge of those who work for them (Goodall & Roberts 2003). Tsoukas (1996, 15), quoting Hayek suggests that a belief in the ability to achieve such a state represents the '*synoptic delusion . . . that knowledge can be surveyed by a single mind*'. Thus managerial understanding of organizational knowledge will always be fragmented and incomplete, and attempts to collect knowledge in a central location likely to be limited. The following

Knowledge management from a practice-based epistemology

1. Knowledge sharing/acquisition requires 'perspective making' and perspective taking'—developing an understanding of tacit assumptions

2. Knowledge sharing/acquisition through
   * 'rich' social interaction
   * immersion in practice—watching and/or doing

3. Management role to facilitate social interaction

Table 3.5 A practice-based perspective on knowledge management

quotation from Tsoukas (1996, 22) sums this up, and points towards the practice-based perspective's conceptualization of knowledge sharing processes:

'the key to achieving coordinated action does not so much depend on those "higher up" collecting more and more knowledge, as on those "lower down" finding more and more ways to get connected and interrelating the knowledge each one has.'

The practice-based perspective further suggests that the transmitter–receiver model of knowledge sharing is questionable because the sharing of knowledge does not involve the simple transferral of a fixed entity between two people. Instead, the sharing of knowledge involves two people actively inferring and constructing meaning. This perspective suggests that to be effective the sharing of knowledge requires individuals to develop an appreciation of (some of) the tacit assumptions and values on which the knowledge of others is based—the processes of 'perspective making' and 'perspective taking' outlined earlier (Boland & Tenkasi 1995). This challenges the assumption embedded in the transmitter–receiver model that the knowledge exchanged in such processes is unchanged. Bolisani & Scarso (2000) suggest the practice-based perspective on knowledge sharing represents a 'language game', due to the importance of dialogue and language to such processes. Boland & Tenkasi (1995, 358) argue that effective knowledge sharing involves,

'a process of mutual perspective taking where distinctive individual knowledge is exchanged, evaluated and integrated with that of others in the organization.'

Definition Perspective making and taking

Perspective making is the process through which a community develops, strengthens and sustains its knowledge and values. Perspective taking is the process through which people develop an understanding of the knowledge, values and 'worldview' of others.

The logic of the 'language game' model complicates the nature of knowledge sharing processes, as the inherent ambiguity of language, combined with the fact that those involved in the knowledge sharing process have different cognitive frameworks means that there is always scope for differing interpretations. Thus, as you read this book, a piece of partially explicit knowledge, the meaning you take from it may vary from the meaning I intend to convey.

These perspective making and perspective taking processes typically require an extensive amount of social interaction and face-to-face communication, which is a conclusion reached by a number of empirical studies (see for example Lam 1997, 2000; Leonard-Barton 1995; Swan *et al.* 1999). The acquisition and sharing of knowledge typically occur through two distinct, but closely inter-related processes:

1. Immersion in practice—for example learning by doing, or learning by watching.
2. 'Rich' social interaction—for example, an interaction which allows people to develop some level of trust with each other, as well as develop some insights into the tacit knowledge, values and assumptions of each other.

These processes are inter-related because learning by doing is likely to simultaneously involve an element of social interaction, and vice versa, the sort of *'discursive practice'* referred to by Gherardi (2000, 221).

From a practice-based perspective, the managerial role in facilitating the management and sharing of knowledge is therefore to encourage and facilitate the type of communication and social interaction processes that will allow effective perspective making and taking to occur. This can be done through an enormously diverse range of ways including (to highlight just a few examples):

- developing a knowledge sharing culture (through rewarding people for sharing);
- facilitating the development of organizational communities of practice;
- providing forums (electronic or face-to-face) which encourage and support knowledge sharing;
- implementing a formalized 'mentoring' system to pair experienced and inexperienced workers

These issues are examined in more detail in subsequent chapters, with Chapter 9 looking at general issues of motivation to share knowledge, Chapters 10 and 11 looking at the specific dynamics of knowledge sharing within and between communities, Chapter 12 looking at the political nature of knowledge sharing, while Chapter 13 considers the role that information systems may be able to play in facilitating perspective making and taking processes. Finally, Chapter 14 considers the role that organizations can play through their human resource management policies and culture management practices.

Conclusion

In conclusion, Chapters 2 and 3 have outlined two distinctive epistemological perspectives, which characterize knowledge in extremely different ways. These perspectives also conceptualized knowledge sharing and knowledge management processes differently. They therefore have very different managerial implications with regard to how knowledge management efforts should be organized and structured:

- *Objectivist perspective:* focus on the codification and collection of knowledge, create mechanisms to allow this knowledge base to be searched and accessed, such as setting

ILLU

**Kn
m**

While
this is
attemp
to fail
knowl
sharin
knowl
feel 'c
manag
proces
knowl
lizing
ability

To wl

The mo
that kno
ers sugg
tional k
Firstly
ageabili
*managei
interests
resents*
ally unn
the kno
McCree
ambigu
it a resc
do have
A rela
is that t
tems. F
perspec
and tha
puter si

up a searchable database and encouraging staff to codify their knowledge and store it there.

• *Practice-based perspective:* facilitate inter-personal knowledge sharing and processes of perspective making and taking through diverse forms of interaction and communication.

Case study

A practice-based perspective on work activities in a global
software development company

Orlikowski (2002) used a practice-based perspective on knowledge in developing an analysis of the work that was conducted in a globally distributed software development company. In saying that 'knowledge is not primarily a factual commodity or compendium of facts', (p. 252), she explicitly rejects an objectivist perspective on knowledge. Instead, Orlikowski (2002) makes explicit her adoption of a practice-based perspective on knowledge by arguing that 'knowledge and practice are reciprocally constitutive', (p. 250) and that knowing is, 'an ongoing social accomplishment, constituted and reconstituted as actors engage the world in practice', (p. 252). Thus people sustain, develop, transform and demonstrate their knowledgeability in their everyday work activity. As will be seen below, Orlikowski found that the knowing of Kappa's staff was sustained through the particular 'repertoire' of work practices they utilized.

Kappa is the pseudonym Orlikowski gave to the global software company she studied. Research data was collected via a range of qualitative methods including interviews, observation and the analysis of company documentation. While based in the Netherlands, Kappa is a globally dispersed organization employing over 2000 engineers spread across 15 development units spread over five continents, each of which has design responsibilities on different projects. The work of the engineers was project based, with each project typically lasting about 18–24 months. Kappa deliberately splintered development responsibilities between sites, and created project teams involving members from different development units. Thus Kappa's project teams always required extensive virtual/dispersed collaboration between staff who had limited opportunities to meet and work face to face.

Orlikowski's analysis suggested that the knowing of the engineers in Kappa was developed through and sustained via a 'repertoire' of five mutually constitutive practices, activities and forms of knowing (see Table 3.6).

The relationship between the practices, activities and knowing identified by Orlikowski can be illustrated by examining one of these five practices, that of sharing identity. In globally dispersed organizations such as Kappa developing strong and coherent organizational values and getting workers to identify with them can be challenging. Kappa was relatively successful at achieving this, with all the engineers who were interviewed talking about the distinctive 'Kappa way' of working which was common across all their sites, and which they identified with and valued. These organizational values were initially articulated to the engineers through the organization's induction training and socialization, but were sustained over time through the engineers using the values, mind-set and practices of the 'Kappa way' to organize their work. Thus, while these values were initially communicated in organizational training sessions, they were sustained by the day-to-day basis actions of the engineers. Thus the practice of sharing identity was related to knowing the organization (the Kappa way), both of which were sustained and developed through the ongoing activities of the engineers.

TIME TO REFLECT THE NATURE OF ORGANIZATIONAL STRATEGY MAKING PROCESSES

To what extent do stage model conceptualizations of organizational strategy making reflect the reality of what happens inside organizations? Do sequential stage models of strategy making processes provide an unrealistic and over-simplified picture of how such processes occur?

management literature (Zack 1999), and that as a consequence strategy models are thus relatively basic and unsophisticated. Empirical support for the *ad hoc* and emergent model of strategy making is provided by Moreño-Cerdan *et al.* (2007). They report on a study looking into the knowledge management strategies adopted by a selection of Spanish and Austrian small and medium sized enterprises (SMEs). One of the main conclusions from their study was few of the SMEs examined had clear, deliberate and consistent approaches to the management of knowledge.

Thus far, the discussion of strategy has been relatively abstract and general. However, it is useful to be a little more specific and identify some of the market and/or organizational factors that are likely to have a significant effect on the role knowledge in organizations and thus impact on the type of knowledge management strategies relevant to particular organizations.

Firstly there is the type of knowledge processes that organizations require to undertake which can include knowledge creation (where innovation is an important and intrinsic part of an organization's work), knowledge searching, knowledge sharing/reuse, knowledge classification and codification. Secondly, due to the embodied and tacit nature of much knowledge, the nature of the labour markets that organizations recruit from can have significant implications for their knowledge management strategies. For example, research on knowledge-intensive work suggests that labour market shortages in particular sectors can make it easy for knowledge workers to move between firms, making the retention of such workers difficult (see Chapter 14). In such circumstances, methods developed to retain such workers can be conceived of as being an important element of an organization's knowledge management strategy. Thirdly, the nature of an organization's markets and the character of competition in them are also likely to be important factors. Thus whether markets are highly competitive or not and whether competition is on the basis of cost, product quality or product/service innovation are factors likely to affect the strategic role of knowledge processes within firms. Fourthly, as has been discussed above, the particular strategy that an organization adopts will also influence the type of knowledge resources and processes that are key to organizational performance. Fifthly, and finally, the character of an organization's product/service, for example whether they are standardized and generic or individually customized to the particular requirements of individual customers, will influence the type of knowledge processes that are important.

This is not intended to be a comprehensive list, outlining all the strategic factors firms need to account for in developing their knowledge management strategies. Instead it is an indicative list that highlights some of the most important factors affecting such processes. Overall however it can be concluded that the particular type of knowledge management strategy that particular companies adopt should take account of the type of strategic factors just discussed, and as a consequence, the type of knowledge management strategies and initiatives that organizations adopt are likely to be highly varied.

To conclude this section, one further level of complexity can be added. In considering the relationship between an organization's general business strategy and its knowledge management strategy this raises the question of how its IT and HRM strategies link in to the development of both business strategy and knowledge management strategy. Of primary relevance here is the relationship between knowledge management strategy and IT & HRM strategy. Put another way, the focus here is on the choices organizations make regarding the prominence and roles they give to IT systems and HRM practices in their knowledge management initiatives. These issues have been examined in a number of papers, with Hendriks (2001) examining the relationship between IT and knowledge management strategy in detail and Haesli & Boxall (2005) examining the relationship between knowledge management and HRM strategy via using Hansen *et al.*'s (1999) typology of knowledge management strategies. These issues are examined both in the following, final section of this chapter, which outlines various knowledge management typologies, and also in Chapter 13 on technology and knowledge management and Chapter 14 on the role of HRM policies and culture management practices on knowledge management initiatives.

Conceptualizing the diversity of knowledge management strategies

It should now be obvious that there is not one single way for an organization to manage knowledge. Arguably there are virtually an infinite number of ways organizations can attempt to manage the knowledge of their workforce. To take account of this diversity, the following, generic and broad brush definition of knowledge management is developed.

Definition   Knowledge management

Knowledge management is an umbrella term which refers to any deliberate efforts to manage the knowledge of an organization's workforce, which can be achieved via a wide range of methods including directly, through the use of particular types of ICT, or more indirectly through the management of social processes, the structuring of organizations in particular ways or via the use of particular culture and people management practices.

While the focus thus far in the chapter has generally been on the general and strategic factors which can shape the type of KM strategies organizations adopt, the focus shifts here to provide some specific details on some of the diversity of knowledge management methods that organizations can utilize and a number of frameworks and typologies that have been developed to characterize them.

Hansen *et al.*'s (1999) codification versus personalization framework

Hansen *et al.* (1999), in what is arguably the most well known knowledge management framework differentiate between two broad knowledge strategies: codification and personalization (see Table 4.3). The codification strategy is argued to be most relevant for companies whose competitive advantage is derived from the reuse of codified knowledge and is centrally concerned with creating searchable repositories for the storage and retrieval of codified knowledge. The personalization strategy, by contrast, is most relevant for companies whose competitive advantage is derived from processes of knowledge creation and the provision of innovative, customized products/services. The personalization knowledge strategy assumes that much of the key knowledge of its workers is tacit and can't be codified, and thus focuses on ways to improve the face-to-face sharing of this tacit knowledge between workers.

In terms of the link between knowledge management and HRM, Hansen *et al.* (1999) make clear that the HRM implications of the codification and personalization knowledge strategies are different, and argue that it is thus important for organizations to ensure that their knowledge and HRM strategies are aligned (see Table 4.3). For example, with the codification strategy, the main motivation issue is persuading workers to codify their knowledge, whereas with the personalization strategy it is related to persuading people to share their knowledge with others. HRM policies and practices thus need to be directed toward the achievement of these quite different objectives. Thus for example, in terms of recruitment and selection, it will be important to identify and recruit people with suitable personalities to these different knowledge activities (knowledge reuse versus knowledge creation). Equally, training and development implications also require to

Knowledge strategy	Codification	Personalization
Business–knowledge link	Competitive advantage through knowledge reuse	Competitive advantage through knowledge creation
Relevant knowledge process	Transferring knowledge from people to documents	Improving social processes to facilitate sharing of tacit knowledge between people
HRM implications	• Motivate people to codify their knowledge • Training should emphasize the development of IT skills • Reward people for codifying their knowledge	• Motivate people to share their knowledge with others • Training should emphasize the development of inter-personal skills • Reward people for sharing knowledge with others

Table 4.3 Codification and personalization knowledge strategies
Source: from Hansen *et al.* (1999)

Linking HRM and KM strategies in two high technology manufacturing companies

Haesli & Boxall (2005) present a case study based analysis of the link between knowledge management and human resource management in two New Zealand high technology design and manufacturing companies. Their focus on high technology manufacturing companies was based on the assumption in the knowledge-based view of the firm that the knowledge of organizational employees was a key source of competitive advantage. In such contexts, the recruitment and retention of employees with relevant knowledge is likely to be a vital part of an organization's knowledge management strategy. Thus their analysis of the linkage between knowledge management and human resource management compared the type of knowledge management strategies utilized to the types of recruitment and retention policies utilized by the two case study companies. Due to concerns about anonymity, few details of the companies examined were given. AlphaCo produced electrical goods for New Zealand and export markets, adopted a 'first mover' strategy and operated in niche markets. BetaCo was also a high technology manufacturing company which operated in niche markets, was considered a market leader with an internationally recognized brand, but was less concerned than AlphaCo with being a first mover in new markets.

AlphaCo's predominant knowledge management strategy was classified as being close to Hansen *et al.*'s personalization approach as knowledge sharing occurred more through the face-to-face interaction of engineers than through the codification of knowledge in documentation. Part of the reason for this approach was that avoiding the development of excessive levels of documentation was regarded as helping to ensure fast product development cycles, which was important to their first mover strategy. In terms of HRM policies the focus was on retention rather than recruitment. AlphaCo was successful at retaining staff, employing a significant proportion of engineers with long tenure levels and had both low turnover levels and high levels of employee satisfaction. The risk with this approach to knowledge sharing was that when key engineers did leave the company this did lead to the loss of valuable knowledge from the organization, as little effort had been made to codify their knowledge or expertise. Thus, AlphaCo's use of a personalization based knowledge management strategy was wedded to a retention-based HRM strategy.

BetaCo by contrast placed a much greater emphasis on a codification based approach to knowledge management through the use of extensive amounts of documentation in their product development process. In BetaCo engineers were required to keep up to date logbooks of their work, with these being shared with others through project debriefing meetings. In contrast to AlphaCo, employee

(continued)

satisfaction levels were lower, and employee turnover levels were higher. As a consequence, in terms of HRM policies, BetaCo's focus was on recruitment rather than retention and were involved in recruiting staff on an almost constant basis. Thus BetaCo's codification based strategy was wedded to a recruitment focussed approach to HRM.

In conclusion, the analysis found that the KM–HRM configuration adopted by both companies was different, but that it was difficult to judge which was superior. The risk with AlphaCo's personalization-retention configuration was that when key engineers left AlphaCo this did lead to a loss of knowledge, thus having effective retention strategies are key to this configuration working. On the other hand, BetaCo's codification-recruitment configuration had the disadvantage of both slowing down development times, and inhibiting the autonomy of the engineers in doing their work.

They also propose the opposite configurations could be possible, with personalization being linked to recruitment and codification with retention.

1. To what extent are these configurations likely to succeed?

be different, with companies pursuing codification strategies requiring to emphasize the development of IT skills, whereas those organizations pursuing a personalization strategy require to place a substantially greater emphasis on developing the social networking and inter-personal skills of their workers. Finally, payment and appraisal systems should reward behaviours appropriate to the organization's knowledge strategy. The IT implications of these two strategies are also obviously different, with codification strategy being much more IT based, and the personalization strategy being much more HRM based.

Earl's (2001) seven schools of knowledge management

The second taxonomy of knowledge management approaches was developed by Michael Earl, a professor of Information Management (Earl 2001). This is a more complicated taxonomy than Hansen *et al.*'s as it identifies seven specific schools which are organized into three broad approaches (see Table 4.4). This taxonomy takes account of the choices organizations face with regard to the role they allocate in knowledge management initiatives to IT systems and HRM practices through the varying extent and character of the role they play in each of the seven schools.

Earl to some extent acknowledges the complexity of the choices organizations require to make about the role of IT systems in their knowledge management initiatives by identifying three different and distinctive schools of knowledge management all of which give a prominent (but different) role to IT systems, which are classified together as making up the technocratic approach to knowledge management.

The first of the technocratic approaches to knowledge management is the *Systems School*. With the systems school the main concern is with the codification of knowledge into databases with this knowledge then being available for use as an organizational resource.

	Technocratic			Economic		Behavioural		
	Systems	Cartographic	Engineering	Commercial	Organizational	Spatial	Strategic
Focus	Technology	Maps	Processes	Income	Networks	Space	Mindset
Aim	Knowledge bases	Knowledge directories	Knowledge flows	Knowledge assets	Knowledge pooling	Knowledge exchange	Knowledge capabilities
Unit	Domain	Enterprise	Activity	Know-how	Communities	Place	Business
IT role	Knowledge based systems	Internet directories	Shared databases	Intellectual asset register	Groupware and intranets	Access tools	Eclectic
Philosophy	Codification	Connectivity	Capability	Commercialization	Collaboration	Contactivity	Consciousness

Table 4.4 Earl's seven schools of knowledge management

Source: adapted from Earl (2001, Table 1)

Knowledge sharing thus occurs not in a direct face-to-face exchange between people, but indirectly via people codifying knowledge which others then subsequently utilize.

Earl's second IT based approach to knowledge management is the *Cartographic School*. With this approach IT systems are used to facilitate the creation of inter-personal connections between people who possess relevant expertise through the creation of searchable directories of expertise which effectively provides a map of an organization's knowledge base. With such systems, anyone seeking a source of particular expert knowledge can use such directories to find and develop links with relevant people. Thus, while IT systems play a key role in this school, ultimately knowledge sharing typically occurs directly between people, once relevant sources of knowledge and expertise have been identified.

The third and final IT based approach to knowledge management identified by Earl is the *Engineering School*. With this school IT systems are used to provide people with task and process oriented knowledge on operational processes and procedures through the codification of knowledge in databases that are available to relevant people. The difference between this approach and the Systems School of knowledge management is the focussing of knowledge around operational tasks and processes.

The second broad approach to knowledge management identified by Earl is the economic approach, which has only one specific school of knowledge management, the *Commercial School*. With this approach to knowledge management the main aim of knowledge management activities is to effectively commercialize an organization's knowledge such that an organization can achieve measurable economic benefits from such efforts. With this approach knowledge activities are focussed on producing products and services that produce value, and attempting to protect such knowledge assets via patents, trademarks etc.

The final broad approach to knowledge management identified by Earl, within which he identified three distinctive schools is the behavioural approach to knowledge management. This approach contrasts with the technocratic approach as its emphasis is much more on people management practices and processes than on managing knowledge via the use of IT systems. Fundamentally, this approach is focussed on creating processes, spaces and mechanisms which facilitate the inter-personal sharing of knowledge between people.

The first of the behavioural approaches is the *Organisational School*. This school of knowledge management is concerned with facilitating the creation of inter-personal networks, or communities of people who have common interests and who can benefit from sharing their knowledge and experience with each other. The success of such efforts depends upon people participating in such communities developing a strong sense of identity with them, and also that there are adequate levels of trust between people within them to facilitate knowledge sharing. While such communities can interact on a face-to-face basis, there is also scope for IT systems to play a role in such communities through the role they can play in supporting the remote, IT mediated interaction of community members.

The second of the behavioural approaches to knowledge management is the *Spatial School*. This method of knowledge management is focussed on the creation of spaces, both physical and virtual, which can provide opportunities to bring people together, and allow them to share knowledge and experiences when they do so. Examples of physical spaces that can be developed for such purposes are formal meeting and training rooms, or more informal meeting spaces such as water-coolers and kitchens. McKinlay (2002) provided an example of a virtual space that was created for such purposes in his research on a global pharmaceutical company which developed an online, virtual café which workers could enter and share knowledge relatively informally via discussion boards and chartrooms.

The final of the behavioural approaches to knowledge management identified by Earl is the *Strategic School*. This approach to knowledge management is concerned with shaping

ILLUSTRATION

The spatial approach to knowledge management at the BBC

Chaundy (2005) describes a knowledge management activity utilized by the BBC's Nations & Regions division to facilitate inter-personal knowledge sharing. The Nations & Regions division is both large (employing nearly 7000 staff) and highly dispersed, being spread over more than 50 separate sites in the UK. Most sites were focussed on the provision of local and regional television and radio news. However, the physical separation of staff across such a large number of sites made it difficult to share knowledge and experience between offices. One solution developed and supported by the BBCs knowledge management team to deal with this problem was the creation of a training site which would allow staff from different regional offices to come together and share their experiences. This site, name SON&R (Sharing Opportunities across Nations and Regions) was developed in Bristol in an existing BBC building.

The idea of SON&R was to facilitate knowledge sharing through bringing together people from different sites who performed similar functions for 2–5 day workshops during which they would have the opportunity to developing social relations and share experiences. Overall, the idea was to create an, 'exciting and safe atmosphere where participants would feel happy to share their experiences and be inspired to enhance working practices' (p. 25). The centre opened in September 2002 and by the time Chaundy wrote her article over 3500 Nations & Regions staff had attended an event at the SON&R facility. Role based sessions have brought together people performing a range of different jobs including sports journalists, weekend producers, assistant editors, football commentators, religious producers, weather presenters and 'front of house staff'. For example in 2003, 30 'front of house staff' such as receptionists and security guards had a workshop. Prior to its start, 10 of the staff participated in a job swap, while 10 others visited front of house functions in other organizations. Participants in these events gave feedback on their experiences during the workshops. All participants in the workshop felt they had had a positive experience, had learned something new and had developed a sense of being part of a wider community.

attitudes and values which facilitate effective knowledge management behaviours rather than directly shaping knowledge processes. It can be labelled the culture management based approach to knowledge management as it uses a wide range of mechanisms such as vision statements, business plans, communication programmes and training activities to develop a consciousness within employees that knowledge management processes matter. The expectation with this approach is that if such interventions are successful, people will voluntarily choose to undertake and participate in relevant knowledge management processes.

Alvesson & Kärreman's (2001) four knowledge management approaches

Alvesson & Kärreman (2001) used the framework of four management philosophies outlined earlier as the basis for developing four specific approaches to knowledge management (see Figure 4.1). Alvesson & Kärreman, as with Earl, make clear that the distinction they make between the four different approaches to knowledge management they make are analytical rather than empirical. Thus, they suggest that organizations are unlikely to exclusively use one approach to knowledge management and that management in any particular organization are likely to simultaneously use a combination of their four approaches. The four approaches to knowledge management they identify are structured around two dimensions: the mode of managerial intervention, and the medium of interaction (see Figure 4.1). The mode of managerial intervention dimension relates to the strength of managerial control dimension outlined earlier, with the 'co-ordination' mode relating to a relative weak philosophy of management, and the 'control' mode referring to a stronger form of management control. The medium of interaction dimension relates to the distinction, outlined earlier, between, management systems focussed on controlling behaviour and those focussed on workers' attitudes with the 'social' dimension relating to attitudinal focussed control, and the 'technostructural' dimension relating to behavioural focussed controls. The four approaches that result from the combination of these dimensions are described below.

Starting at the bottom left of Figure 4.1 is the *Extended Library* approach to knowledge management, which combines technostructural focussed controls with a relatively weak form of co-ordinated management. This approach to knowledge management is relatively bureaucratic, centrally controlled and top down in character. IT systems play an important role with this approach, with senior management creating central databases and archives where employees are encouraged to codify their knowledge and experiences. Such databases are searchable and can be accessed by staff looking for sources of particular types of knowledge.

The *Community* approach to knowledge management combines the co-ordinated form of weak and limited managerial interventions with socially focussed managerial controls. This approach to knowledge management gives a very limited role to IT systems, due to the acknowledgement that much organizational knowledge is highly tacit, with it being focussed around encouraging the direct sharing of knowledge

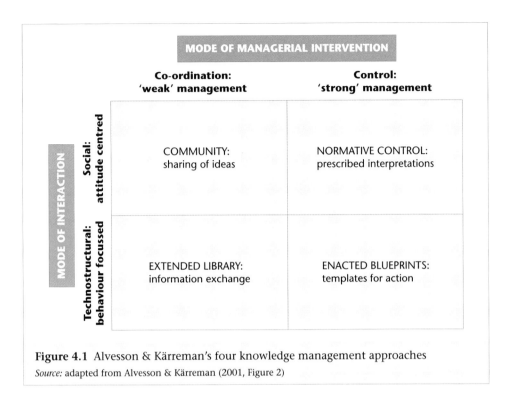

Figure 4.1 Alvesson & Kärreman's four knowledge management approaches

Source: adapted from Alvesson & Kärreman (2001, Figure 2)

between people. Management efforts with this approach are focussed on creating a positive environment, context or culture which is likely to encourage staff to share knowledge with each other, for example through facilitating the development of communities of practice.

The *Normative Control* approach to knowledge management combines the same focus on socially focussed control as the community approach, but allies it with a stronger form of managerial intervention. This is knowledge management via culture management, whereby management invest significant efforts at creating a culture which encourages, values and rewards employee participation in organizational knowledge processes, and encourages employees to 'buy into' the culture.

Alvesson & Kärreman's final approach to knowledge management is the *Enacted Blueprints* method which combines a strong form of managerial intervention with technostructural type managerial controls. As with the normative control approach to knowledge management the enacted blueprints model involves significant managerial efforts. These efforts are focussed on creating codified databases of knowledge focussed around particular roles and tasks that provide employees which provide templates which guide their action. This means of knowledge management is intended to facilitate the codification and dissemination of 'best practice' ways of work. However, the way in which this method limits the scope of workers to use their autonomy leads Alvesson & Kärreman to label it a form of Taylorism.

An extended library approach to knowledge management in AXA

AXA UK's updating of its intranet systems, described by Kirby (2006) represents an example of Alvesson & Kärreman's extended library approach to knowledge management. The need for the restructuring of its intranet systems was the results of an acquisition based growth strategy. All the different organizations that made up the newly formed AXA UK group were meant to operate as one integrated division. However, following the acquisitions, there were four separate intranet systems in different divisions which made it virtually impossible to share information and knowledge across divisions. To address this problem these intranets were integrated together with the objective of 'facilitating knowledge management and collaborative working through document sharing and online collaboration tools' (p. 11). This was done via a single, top down project called 'One UK intranet'. The architecture of the new intranet system was initially developed by a centralized project team. However, to get user input on it the second phase of the project involved users from a range of business areas and job types using the intranet and providing feedback on their experiences.

Conclusion

Following on from Chapters 2 and 3, where the different perspectives on the character of knowledge in the knowledge management literature were examined, this chapter moved on to grapple with the question of what is knowledge management. The general conclusion of the chapter, which was illustrated through examining three separate knowledge management typologies (those of Earl, Hansen *et al.*, and Alvesson & Kärreman) was that there are a large diversity of ways in which to manage knowledge in organizations. For some organizations knowledge management may simply be a broad philosophy, for others it may be centred around managing people and organizational culture in certain ways, while another alternative again is to give a prominent role to information and communication technologies in knowledge management efforts. Thus, talking of 'knowledge management' as a coherent management practice is problematic.

The chapter also considered the factors that influence the approach to knowledge management that organizations adopt. In this respect it was found that a large diversity of heterogeneous factors came into play including how organizations conceptualize knowledge, their objectives for attempting to manage knowledge, the nature of the products/services they develop and provide, and the type of business strategy they pursue. Another important factor examined, which also influences the approach to knowledge management organization's adopt, but which is typically neglected in the knowledge management literature, is the approach to management adopted by an organization. Using Alvesson & Kärreman's (2001) analysis the concept of management was examined and unpacked, with it being concluded that 'management' itself doesn't represent a unified and coherent set of objectives or practices and that there are a diversity of ways for organizations to manage.

Case study

Siemens' ShareNet initiative

Voelpel *et al.* (2005) provide a description and analysis of how Siemens implemented a global knowledge sharing system called ShareNet. ShareNet is argued to be one of the few examples of a successful global knowledge management system which spanned international borders. Siemens is a Munich based global corporation, employing over 400,000 staff spread across 190 countries. Its business is focussed on the electronics industry with it being involved in a wide range of different product and service markets including semiconductors, health case products, household appliances and lighting products. It has a decentralized corporate structure with every business unit operating autonomously.

The ShareNet initiative was implemented within Siemens' Information and Communication Networks (ICN) Division, which employed 33,000 staff across the globe. The system was to be used by the divisions 17,000 sales and marketing staff. This division was formed in 1998 following a corporate restructuring exercise which was driven by competitive and regulatory changes in some of Siemens' key markets. The ICN group brought together what had previously been a number of separate business units. The ShareNet initiative was one of the key mechanisms utilized by senior management in the ICN division to facilitate knowledge sharing between sales and marketing staff. The idea of the system was to allow the experiences of sales and marketing staff in particular regions to be shared with sales and marketing staff across the globe. Voelpel *et al.* classify the ShareNet initiative using Hansen *et al.*'s framework as a codification type initiative as it was primarily concerned with sharing explicit knowledge, and encouraging staff to try and codify and share important tacit knowledge they possessed.

ShareNet was designed to include a number of separate and distinct elements including a knowledge library, a forum for dealing with urgent requests and platforms that would allow the sharing of 'rich' amounts of knowledge. The library represented the most important element of ShareNet and consisted of a database of project team experiences gained from working on particular sales bids. Information on project experiences was logged via a web-based questionnaire style form with the questions being designed to try and encourage reflection so as to capture some of the tacit knowledge people possessed. The urgent request platform was the second most important element of ShareNet. It was a platform where people could post and respond to urgent questions and requests for information. One example of such a post was where a sales team working in South America posted a question about laying cables in a jungle situation which was responded to by someone in Senegal who had had relevant experience. The third element of ShareNet, the platform for sharing 'rich' knowledge consisted of news bulletins, bulletin boards, discussion groups focussed around particular topics and live chat rooms.

Voelpel *et al.* classify the ShareNet initiative as a codification based knowledge management strategy.

1. How would you classify it using Earl's and Alvesson & Kärreman's knowledge management typologies?

Source: Voelpel, S., Dous, M., & Davenport, T. (2005). 'Five Steps to Creating a Global Knowledge-Sharing System: Siemens' ShareNet', *Academy of Management Executive,* 19/2: 9–23.

 For further information about this journal article visit our Online Resource Centre at www.oxfordtextbooks.co.uk/orc/hislop2e/

Review and discussion questions

1 McKinlay (2002) suggested that one of the limits that exist to managerial efforts to control and manage knowledge relate to the difficulty of managing informal, unregulated

encounters, such as when groups of colleagues socialize together. What, if anything, can organizations do to manage knowledge in such contexts?

2   Think about the link between the three taxonomies of knowledge management examined. What similarities and overlaps exist between the different approaches to knowledge management identified. For example, to what extent is Earl's systems approach similar to Hansen *et al.*'s codification based strategy?

3   Earl suggests that organizations can adopt more than one school of knowledge management simultaneously. For example, an organization could simultaneously utilize a strategic and commercial approach to knowledge management. Can you identify any of Earl's schools of knowledge management which are unlikely to be compatible with each other?

Suggestions for further reading

1   **M. Alvesson & D. Kärreman (2001). 'Odd Couple: Making Sense of the Curious Concept of Knowledge Management',** *Journal of Management Studies*, **38/7: 995–1018.**

An interesting and wide ranging article which contains a useful discussion on the importance of conceptualizing 'management' and a useful typology of distinctive knowledge management approaches.

2   **A. Haesli & P. Boxall (2005). 'When Knowledge Management Meets HR Strategy: An Exploration of Personalization-Retention and Codification-Recruitment Configurations',** *International Journal of Human Resource Management*, **16/11: 1955–1975.**

Makes use of Hansen *et al.*'s knowledge management typology to analyse how two organizations link their knowledge management (and human resource management) strategies to their different business strategies.

3   **M. Earl (2001). 'Knowledge Management Strategies: Towards a Taxonomy',** *Journal of Management Information Systems*, **18/1: 215–233.**

Develops a useful taxomomy of seven different knowledge management strategies which highlights the different role that IT systems and people management practices can play in knowledge management initiatives.

4   **A. McKinlay (2002). 'The Limits of Knowledge Management',** *New Technology, Work and Employment*, **17/2: 76–88.**

A case study of one global pharmaceutical company's knowledge management initiative which discusses the limits that can exist on managerial efforts to manage and control knowledge.

Take your learning further: Online Resource Centre

Visit the supporting Online Resource Centre for resources which will extend your understanding of knowledge management in organizations. As well as web links to sites of interest, the author has provided case studies looking at knowledge management in virtual and knowledge intensive firms, and in global multinationals. These will help you with your research, essays and assignments; or you may find these additional resources helpful when revising for exams.

 www.oxfordtextbooks.co.uk/orc/hislop2e/

Knowledge Intensive Firms and Knowledge Workers

Introduction

As was discussed in Chapter 1, many commentators and writers characterize contemporary society as being a knowledge society, with the importance of knowledge to work and economic activity having grown enormously in the last quarter of the twentieth century. The growing importance of knowledge to the world of work is also argued to have transformed both the character of the work activities people undertake, as well as the nature of organizations. Key to these transformations has been the growing importance of knowledge workers and knowledge intensive firms. In fact, if contemporary society is a knowledge society, then almost by definition knowledge intensive firms and knowledge workers represent constituent elements of it (Neef 1999).

This chapter has two primary purposes. Firstly it provides a detailed definition of the terms knowledge intensive firms and knowledge workers and secondly it examines the character of the knowledge and the dynamics of the knowledge processes within knowledge intensive firms. However, as the chapter progresses it will be shown that a number of debates exist on these topics, most fundamentally with the definition of knowledge workers and the extent to which they are distinctive from other types of worker being topics on which there is much disagreement (Hislop 2008).

The chapter begins by looking at how writing on knowledge workers and knowledge intensive firms is typically embedded in the knowledge society rhetoric. Following this, sections two and three present different perspectives on the definition of knowledge work, starting in section two with the mainstream 'professional knowledge work' perspective, and then in section three moving onto the alternative 'all work is knowledge work' perspective. Section four then examines the extent to which ambiguity represents a distinguishing feature of, and inherent element in, knowledge work. The fifth section then considers the character of knowledge and knowledge processes within knowledge intensive firms, which links back to the topic of social capital outlined in Chapter 2. The sixth and final section of the chapter examines the debate regarding the extent to which knowledge workers represent the ideal employee, being always willing to participate in relevant knowledge processes, and work long hours for their employers. Finally, a topic not examined here, as it is dealt with in Chapter 14, is what organizations can do to manage knowledge workers.

The rise of the knowledge worker

In the last quarter of the twentieth century, as discussed in Chapter 1, the character of work changed enormously. These changes are argued to have produced an enormous expansion in the number of knowledge workers, and knowledge intensive firms. More specifically, such analyses typically utilize the post-industrial/knowledge society rhetoric and argue that not only have the number of knowledge workers increased, and the knowledge intensity of work gone up, but that knowledge is now the most significant source of competitive advantage, and that abstract and theoretical knowledge has taken on a heightened level of importance. However, such analyses have not gone unchallenged.

One writer who was among the first to popularize such analyses was Robert Reich (Blackler 1995; Rifkin 2000). Reich's analysis was focused largely on the USA, but his argument was relevant to all of the most industrialized economies (Reich 1991). He argued that the shift towards high value added, knowledge intensive products and services in these economies gave rise to what he termed 'symbolic analysts'. These are workers who, firstly '*solve, identify and broker problems by manipulating symbols*' (p. 178), and secondly need to make frequent use of established bodies of codified knowledge (p. 182). Thus, typical of symbolic analytical occupations are research and product design (problem solving), marketing and consultancy (problem identification) and finance/banking (problem brokering). According to Reich's analysis, by the late 1980s this category of work had grown to account for 20% of employment in the USA, and was one of the USA's three key occupational categories. Statistical analysis from the UK suggests that the proportion of professional/knowledge intensive workers in Britain was also 20% in the early 1990s (Elias & Gregory 1994).

Chapter 1 presented a critique of the knowledge society rhetoric. However it is useful to briefly revisit two elements of it here as they question the way the rise of the knowledge worker has been conceptualized. Firstly, while there has been a growth in knowledge intensive occupations, there has simultaneously been a growth in relatively low-skilled and routine work (Elias & Gregory 1994; NSTF 2000; Thompson *et al.* 2001). Thus, suggestions that the expansion of knowledge intensive work is the only, or main aspect in the contemporary restructuring of occupations are over-simplistic.

TIME TO REFLECT HOW IMPORTANT ARE KNOWLEDGE WORKERS?

If knowledge workers constitute approximately 20% of the workers in the most industrialized nations, does this suggest that their importance to these economies has been exaggerated, or is their contribution to knowledge creation and wealth generation disproportional to their numbers?

Another critique of the knowledge work/er rhetoric, drawing on Foucault's concept of power/knowledge (see Chapter 12), suggests that this rhetoric requires to be understood as less of an objective/scientific statement, and more of a truth claim which attempts to legitimate contemporary social change as positive and emancipatory (Knights *et al*. 1993).

Defining knowledge workers and knowledge intensive firms: the professional knowledge work perspective

While the growing importance of knowledge workers and knowledge intensive firms has been widely articulated, and has to a large extent become a taken for granted truth, providing a precise definition of a knowledge worker and describing their general characteristics has proved much more difficult. This section begins by presenting the mainstream definition of these terms, before introducing the critique of this perspective in the following section, which leads to another definition of the term knowledge worker.

It is useful to begin by outlining the definition and characteristics of knowledge intensive firms, as there is more of a consensus on this than there is on the definition of knowledge work. While a number of papers present their own particular definitions of a knowledge intensive firm, one of the most widely used is that provided by Alvesson (2000, 1101) as, '*companies where most work can be said to be of an intellectual nature and where well qualified employees form the major part of the workforce.*' Swart *et al*. (2003) expand

ILLUSTRATION

A software development company as a knowledge intensive firm

The small software development company from the south west of England, SoftWareCo, examined by Swart & Kinnie's (2003) represents an example of a knowledge intensive firm as it has all the above listed characteristics. Firstly, while it is unclear what academic qualifications SoftWareCo's engineers typically possessed, they are described as being highly qualified and in possession of specialist software skills. Secondly, the work was non routine and required significant levels of creativity to design bespoke software systems to the particular needs of individual clients. Further, it operated in what was regarded as a very competitive market, and the particular knowledge and skills of its software engineers were regarded as its key asset and source of competitive advantage. Finally, it had a very flat and fluid organizational structure with only three layers in the organization, with work typically being organized around project teams, with engineers being allocated to projects on the relevance of their knowledge and on the extent of their prior experience.

client knowledge is as important as technical knowledge. Thus, without a detailed knowledge of the client, a knowledge intensive firm would not be able to provide an effectively customized product/service. It is only through the acquisition of such knowledge that the ambiguity in client needs that often exists at the start of projects (see previous section) can be reduced.

Empson (2001b) further suggests that both types of knowledge used by knowledge workers can be divided into three subcategories. In the case of technical knowledge this can be illustrated by an example: engineering consultants working in the aerospace industry. Industry level technical knowledge could be knowledge of wing vibration dynamics, which are well understood, and shared across most companies operating in the industry. Organizational level knowledge in this context could be an understanding of an organizational specific system/process for testing wing vibration dynamics. Finally, in the same context, individual technical knowledge would be the expertise that individual consultants had built up over time, for example of conducting wing vibration tests and analyses.

The three types of client knowledge identified by Empson can also be illustrated through the use of an example, that of the film industry in the USA. In this context industry level client knowledge would be knowledge of the factors at industry level that affect the chances of having a film funded, such as the characteristics of a typical Hollywood blockbuster. Organizational level knowledge in this context would be an understanding of the specific tastes and preferences of particular film companies, such as Disney or United Artists. Finally, individual client knowledge would be having an acquaintance with, and understanding of important, key individuals within particular companies who are able to influence decisions on the commissioning of films.

In understanding the character of work processes within knowledge intensive firms it is not enough to know the types of knowledge that knowledge workers possess and use, it is equally important to have an insight into the types of knowledge processes that occur. It is to this topic that the chapter now turns.

Knowledge processes

The key knowledge processes within knowledge intensive firms can be divided into three broad categories: knowledge creation/application, knowledge codification, and knowledge acquisition and sharing, each of which are briefly described.

Knowledge creation/application

One of the key aspects of the work in knowledge intensive firms is that it is typically not routine, repetitive work. Instead knowledge intensive firms provide customized, specifically designed products/services, rather than off the shelf ones. For example, Robertson & Swan (2003, 833) suggest one of the key characteristics of knowledge intensive firms is '*their capacity to solve complex problems through the development of creative and innovative solutions*'. The production/creation of such client-specific, customized solutions requires and involves both the application of existing bodies of knowledge, and the creation of new knowledge (Morris 2001). Thus, the ongoing creation and development of knowledge represents an important and intrinsic feature of a knowledge worker's work.

Knowledge codification

Typically, the knowledge created and developed within knowledge intensive firms is held either by individual workers, or by all the staff working on a particular project. Morris (2001) and Swart & Kinnie (2003) argue that because of this there is an incentive in knowledge intensive firms to try and share project specific knowledge and learning across the organization. One way this can be done is through codification (Quinn *et al.* 1996). Werr & Stjernberg (2003) also argue that the codification of some knowledge helps with the communication and sharing of tacit knowledge. However, the difficulties of doing so are significant. Firstly, much of this knowledge is highly tacit, and is not amenable to codification. Secondly, much project knowledge is specialized and context-specific in nature, and has only limited general relevance. Finally, in an issue examined more fully later, knowledge workers may not be willing to facilitate the codification of the specialist knowledge they possess.

Knowledge acquisition/sharing

The development of client-specific, customized solutions involves more than the application and creation of knowledge, it also involves the sharing and integration of different bodies of knowledge, both between workers in knowledge intensive firms, and between the workers in knowledge intensive firms and staff from client organizations (Fosstenlokken *et al.* 2003). Due to this need to acquire and share knowledge, and the limits to codification that exist, other ways are typically utilized by people, projects and organizations to acquire and share relevant knowledge. Most typically this is done through inter-personal interaction. To understand the character and dynamics of such knowledge acquisition and sharing processes it is useful to utilize the concept of social capital that was touched on very briefly in Chapter 2, which is a concept increasingly used by analysts examining knowledge intensive firms (Swart & Kinnie 2003; Yli-Renko *et al.* 2001).

Social capital relates to the networks of personal relationships that people possess and are embedded within, and the resources people can draw on and utilize through such networks. Social capital theory is typically predicated on the assumption that the resources available to people through such networks can aid action. However, the close and inseparable relationship that exists between the networks of relations that people possess and the resources they have access to through them, means that there is a lack of consensus within the social capital literature about the precise definition of social capital. For some, social capital refers purely to the networks of relations people possess, while to others it encompasses not only these networks, but also includes the resources people have access to through them (Nahapiet & Ghoshal 1998). Here it is used in the narrow sense, to refer purely to the networks of social relationships that people have. Further, Nahapiet & Ghoshal (1998) suggest that social capital has three key dimensions or facets: the structural, the relational and the cognitive (see Table 5.6).

In the context of knowledge intensive firms, the importance of social capital to knowledge workers is that it is only through having it that they are able to access the different

Dimension	Character
Structural	The overall pattern of social relations a person possesses. For example, the number of contacts, and the type of people in the network
Relational	The strength of the relationship between people. Can vary from weak relations, to strong relationships involving high levels of trust. This dimension of social capital typically built up over time, through repeated interactions
Cognitive	The extent to which people have shared cognitive resources such as shared knowledge, common assumptions, interpretations and beliefs

Table 5.6 The three dimensions of social capital

types of knowledge (outlined previously) that they require in order to be able to do their work effectively (Swart & Kinnie 2003). This is because for people to be willing to share knowledge with others some degree of inter-personal trust is required (a topic that is discussed more extensively in Chapters 9 and 11), and the existence of social capital implies that an element of trust exists between people (the relational dimension of social capital).

The types of knowledge that knowledge workers use in their work (both technical and client knowledge) requires their networks of social capital to include both staff from their own organization (but who may be working on different projects), and staff in client firms (Swart *et al.* 2003; Yli-Renko *et al.* 2001). As outlined, the project based nature of work in knowledge intensive firms means that their knowledge bases are typically fragmented. Having a network of social relations (social capital) that spans such project boundaries thus provides knowledge workers with a way of accessing potentially relevant knowledge possessed by colleagues working on other projects. The importance for knowledge workers of possessing social capital with representatives of their client firms is that such networks can provide access to relevant client knowledge which is necessary for their work. However, as outlined, the need by knowledge workers to continually interact with representatives of their client firms over the course of a project typically means that the development of social capital and good relations with specific client staff is not difficult to develop (Alvesson 2000; Fosstenlokken *et al.* 2003). The role of client related social capital in the work of knowledge intensive firms will be examined again at the end of this chapter, as this topic is the focus of this chapter's extended illustrative example.

The willingness of knowledge workers to participate in knowledge processes: contrasting perspectives

One of the key themes developed and examined in Part 4 of this book is that the willingness of any worker to participate in organizational knowledge management processes should *not* be taken for granted. In fact, dealing with such motivational issues, and creating a socio-cultural environment where workers are prepared to participate in knowledge management initiatives represents one of the key challenges and difficulties of knowledge management. However, another area of divergence in the literature on knowledge workers and knowledge intensive firms relates to the extent to which knowledge workers are always willing to participate in knowledge management processes and initiatives, with two contrasting perspectives existing, both of which are outlined below.

Knowledge workers: the ideal employee?

A reasonable amount of (largely case study) evidence exists to suggest that in many ways knowledge workers represent the ideal employees. Primarily, this evidence suggests that such workers are prepared to invest significant amounts of time and effort into their work, and that motivating them to do so is typically not difficult (Alvesson 1995; Deetz 1998; Kunda 1992; Robertson & Swan 2003). As these workers are prepared to make such efforts with minimal levels of supervision, and without regarding such effort as being problematic, Alvesson suggests such workers represent the ideal subordinates (2000, 1104). Alvesson (2000) suggests four reasons why knowledge workers are prepared to make such efforts:

1. They find their work intrinsically interesting and fulfilling.
2. Such working patterns represent the norms within the communities they are a part of.
3. A sense of reciprocity, whereby they provide the organization with their efforts in return for good pay and working conditions.
4. Such behaviour reinforces and confirms their sense of identity as a knowledge worker, where hard work is regarded as a fundamental component.

Robertson & Swan (2003) provide a further explanation: the structure of the employment relationship is less clear than for other workers, and the potential for conflict on the basis of it thus becomes dissipated. Primarily they suggest that the employer/employee, manager/managed relationship is not as clear cut in knowledge intensive firms, as in other, more hierarchically based organizations. In knowledge intensive firms such boundaries are fuzzy, and evolve over time, and therefore the interests of employers and employees are more likely to be in common.

Factors inhibiting knowledge workers' work efforts and knowledge management activities

As will be discussed in more detail in Chapters 9 and 12, two general factors which may inhibit workers from participating in organizational knowledge management efforts is the unavoidable potential for conflict between worker and employer embedded in the employment relationship, and the potential for intra-organizational conflict (between people and groups/teams) that arguably exists in all organizations. In contrast to the perspective of writers adopted in the previous section, some analysts suggest that these two potential sources of conflict are as likely in knowledge intensive firms as in any other type of organization, and that the willingness of knowledge workers to participate in knowledge management initiatives should not be taken from granted. Thus Starbuck (1993) described the knowledge intensive company he examined as being, '*internally inconsistent, in conflict with itself. . . . An intricate house of cards.*' Further, Empson (2001b) presented an example of a knowledge intensive firm in a post-merger situation, where workers from the two pre-merger companies were unwilling to share their knowledge with each other.

A number of writers highlight the issue of the conflicting sense of identities that knowledge workers may experience, and how this may shape and inhibit their willingness to participate in organizational knowledge management processes (Alvesson 2000). Due to the amount of time that many knowledge workers can spend working with individual client organizations and particular staff within them (see previous section), one source of identity based conflict knowledge workers can experience is feeling a sense of belonging to both their employer and to their client's firm (Swart *et al.* 2003). Ravishankar and Pan (2008) present a case of where such client based identity by the knowledge workers they studied (an Indian IT outsourcing vendor) resulted in some staff being unwilling to participate in their employer's knowledge management initiatives.

Other evidence which suggests that knowledge workers may have divergent interests from their employers relates to the problem many knowledge intensive firms experience in trying to retain their employees for extended periods. Fundamentally many knowledge intensive firms have quite high turnover rates, which suggests that knowledge workers have only a limited amount of loyalty to their employing organization. This is

ILLUSTRATION

Conflict over commercial considerations in an art gallery

Beaumont & Hunter (2002) examined the management of a collection of art galleries, and found that, following the implementation of more commercially orientated working practices and funding procedures, conflict emerged between these new commercial values and the more public sector ethos maintained by a number of the galleries' key knowledge workers. The publicly managed organization examined was responsible for four different art galleries, which employed a total of over 800 staff. While one third of this staff was low paid warders and gallery assistants, most of the staff, consisting of collections and restoration staff, could be described as being knowledge workers. The introduction of commercially oriented management values and systems resulted in government funding for the galleries being reduced from 100% to 50–60%, with the rest to be raised through fundraising. Simultaneously, galleries were set performance targets regarding the number of visitors they should have. Traditionally, under the historical system of full public funding, while pay levels had not been high, and promotion potential was limited, the collections and restoration staff had had a significant amount of professional autonomy. While many of the younger collection and restoration staff were happy to embrace the new, more commercially focussed culture, most of the older staff were against it. This was for two main reasons. Firstly, they perceived that the performance targets and requirement to find commercial funding had diminished their autonomy. Secondly, they also felt that these values not only devalued their expertise, but also dumbed down art. Thus, the move towards a commercially focused culture challenged the professional values of the older collections and restoration staff.

1. Could this conflict have been avoided through better or different management?
2. What could gallery management have done to minimize or avoid this conflict?

partly due to labour market conditions, where the skills and knowledge of knowledge workers are typically relatively scarce, creating conditions for knowledge workers which are favourable to labour market mobility (Flood *et al.* 2001; Scarbrough 1999).

Having a high turnover rate is a potentially significant problem for knowledge intensive firms (Alvesson 2000; Beaumont & Hunter 2002; Flood *et al.* 2000; Lee & Maurer 1997). As Table 5.3 suggests, two important types of knowledge important to, and used within, knowledge intensive firms is the individual technical knowledge and client knowledge of their workforce. For example, client knowledge or social capital, the knowledge of and relationships with key individuals within their client organizations, can be a key source of knowledge for knowledge intensive firms. Individual knowledge workers develop such knowledge and social capital through working closely with clients. Such knowledge is typically tacit and highly personal, therefore, when a knowledge worker leaves their job, they take such knowledge with them. Not only that but through the social capital they possess with individuals in client firms there is also a risk for their employer that when a knowledge worker leaves they may take some clients with them. The question of how to develop the loyalty and commitment of such workers is one of the key issues addressed in Chapter 14.

Conclusion

The importance of knowledge workers and knowledge intensive firms is closely tied to the rhetoric regarding the contemporary rise and emergence of the knowledge society, which has not gone unquestioned. In the debate over defining knowledge workers and knowledge intensive firms, two perspectives were shown to exist. While the mainstream perspective suggests that knowledge workers are a distinctive and elite element in the contemporary workforce, others argue that this neglects to account for the extent to which all work is knowledge work, and thus how all workers can be defined as knowledge workers.

In relation to the work in knowledge intensive firms it was shown that the possession and use of client related knowledge was as important as technical knowledge. Further the acquisition of such knowledge requires knowledge workers to possess and utilize any networks of social capital they have and that such knowledge is acquired from both their colleagues (who may work on different projects) and staff from the clients they work with.

Finally, while some case study evidence suggests that knowledge workers arguably represent the ideal employee, due to their willingness to work autonomously, others suggest that for a number of reasons, such as tensions that may exist between a knowledge worker and their employer over how their knowledge is utilized, knowledge workers cannot always be assumed to be willing to participate in the knowledge management processes their employers may desire.

Case study

Social capital and the acquisition and exploitation of knowledge in high technology organizations

Yli-Renko *et al.* (2001) report their findings on a study into the role that client related social capital had on some of the knowledge processes within some relatively new knowledge intensive firms in the UK. Specifically they were looking at how the relationships these organizations had with their major clients affected firstly their ability to acquire external knowledge and secondly the relationship between these knowledge acquisition processes and the firm's knowledge exploration and utilization processes, and competitive advantage. The assumptions being tested were that, firstly, the greater the amount of social capital possessed the better would be the firm's ability to acquire knowledge, and secondly, the greater the firm's ability to acquire such external sources of knowledge, the more it would improve their knowledge exploration/utilization processes.

In taking account of the three dimensions of social capital (see Table 5.6) the first assumption about the relationship between levels of social capital and the firms ability to acquire knowledge was developed into three specific hypotheses. To test the cognitive dimension of social capital they hypothesized that the greater the amount of social interaction that occurred with staff from the client firm (which provides opportunities for the development and sharing of common knowledge) the greater would be the firm's ability to acquire external knowledge from the client firm. To test the relational dimension of social capital they hypothesized that the greater the extent to which levels of trust and goodwill existed with staff from the client firm the greater would be the firm's ability to acquire external knowledge. Finally, to test the structural dimension of social capital they hypothesized that the more client contacts provided access to other people and firms, the greater would be the firm's ability to acquire external knowledge.

These relations were tested via the statistical analysis of a survey of 180 young technology based firms from the UK (firms had to operate in one of five sectors: pharmaceuticals, medical equipment, communications technology, electronics or energy/environmental technologies, and be between 1–10 years old).

Of the three hypotheses discussed here, the first and third hypotheses, which concerned the relationship between the level of social interaction and amount of network ties and the firm's ability to acquire external knowledge were both strongly supported. However, in relation to their second knowledge acquisition hypothesis, on how relationship quality affected levels of knowledge acquisition, they found the opposite to what was hypothesized. Thus their findings suggested that relationship quality was *negatively* related to levels of external knowledge acquisition, suggesting that the stronger the relationship quality, the poorer would be a firm's ability to acquire external knowledge. A suggested explanation for this related to the idea of 'over-embeddedness'. It was suggested that if firms become too closely linked to particular client firms this could inhibit the acquisition of external knowledge from sources other than this close client. Effectively they become insulated and blinkered from other new and potentially useful sources of knowledge possessed by other external people.

Finally the three hypotheses on how the firms' ability to acquire knowledge was related to their ability to be both competitive and to also utilize and exploit this knowledge was also supported, suggesting that the ability of knowledge intensive firms to acquire external knowledge can have a positive impact on their competitiveness. Overall therefore, the possession and use of client facing social capital was found to positively affect not only a firm's ability to acquire external knowledge but also their ability to utilize such knowledge and develop and sustain their competitiveness.

This case study focussed narrowly on client related social capital. Produce a list of other types of social capital that are important for the type of new, knowledge intensive firms examined by Yli-Renko *et al.* Is client related social capital the most important? Further, are these other forms of social capital likely to be developed and sustained in a similar way to client related social capital?

Source: Yli-Renko, H., Autio, E., & Sapienza, H. (2001). 'Social Capital, Knowledge Acquisition, and Knowledge Exploitation in Young Technology-Based Firms', *Strategic Management Journal,* 22: 587–613.

 For further information about this journal article visit our Online Resource Centre at www.oxfordtextbooks.co.uk/orc/hislop2e/

Review and discussion questions

1   What do you think of the 'all work is knowledge work' perspective? Can all forms of work be defined as knowledge work even if they don't require the use of abstract/conceptual knowledge? Think about a range of jobs and the types of knowledge, skills and level of creativity involved in them. Can you identify any that you don't feel should be labelled 'knowledge work'?

2   One of the factors that was found to be a potential source of conflict and tension for knowledge workers, and that could affect their attitude to participating in organizational knowledge management initiatives, was their identification with both their employer and the client firms they work for. Given the nature of the work undertaken by knowledge workers and the typical need that exists to work extensively with their clients, is it likely to be inevitable that knowledge workers will typically always have some level of identification with and loyalty to client firms?

Suggestions for further reading

1   M. Alvesson (2001). 'Knowledge Work: Ambiguity, Image and Identity', *Human Relations*, 54/7: 863–886.

Good discussion, analysis and critique of the mainstream literature on knowledge workers and knowledge intensive firms.

2   M. Robertson & J. Swan (2003). '"Control—What Control?"' Culture and Ambiguity Within a Knowledge Intensive Firm', *Journal of Management Studies*, 40/4: 831–858.

Contains a detailed examination of the role of culture in knowledge intensive firms, based on an analysis of a case study company.

3   D. Hislop (2008). 'Conceptualizing Knowledge Work Utilizing Skill and Knowledge-Based Concepts: The Case of Some Consultants and Service Engineers', *Management Learning*, 39/5: 579–597.

Elaborates the debate on how knowledge work is defined and illustrates argument via use of two contrasting examples.

4   H. Yli-Renko, E. Autio, & H. Sapienza (2001). 'Social Capital, Knowledge Acquisition, and Knowledge Exploitation in Young Technology-Based Firms', *Strategic Management Journal*, 22: 587–613.

Interesting analysis which highlights the importance of social capital to the performance of knowledge intensive firms.

Take your learning further: Online Resource Centre

Visit the supporting Online Resource Centre for resources which will extend your understanding of knowledge management in organizations. As well as web links to sites of interest, the author has provided case studies looking at knowledge management in virtual and knowledge intensive firms, and in global multinationals. These will help you with your research, essays and assignments; or you may find these additional resources helpful when revising for exams.

 www.oxfordtextbooks.co.uk/orc/hislop2e/

Frameworks	Concepts/levels	Description
Learning modes	Cognitive	Learning as a change in intellectual concepts and frameworks (at individual or group level)
	Cultural	Change in inter-subjective, group based values, concepts or frameworks
	Behavioural/action based	Learning occurs primarily through action followed by a process of critical reflection
Learning types	Single-loop	Incremental changes within a coherent framework of theory
	Double-loop	Learning where existing theories/ assumptions are questioned and reflected on
	Deutero	The highest level of learning which involves the process of learning and reflection itself being questioned
Learning levels	Individual	Changes in the behaviour or theories and concepts of an individual
	Group	Changes in group level, shared understandings or practices
	Organizational	Institutionalization at organizational level of changes in behaviour/theory
	Inter-organizational	Learning at supra-organizational level— for example within a network or sector

Table 6.1 Typologies of learning

different mechanisms and processes. These can be characterized into three distinctive types: learning via formal training and education, learning via the use of interventions in work processes, and learning that is embedded in and emerges from day-to-day work activities (and people's reflections on them).

Before learning became a fashionable idea it was a relatively neglected backwater of a subject and was regarded as being most closely linked to the topics of training and education. Thus, from this perspective, learning occurred and was facilitated via workers attending and participating in formal processes of training and education. The growing interest in the topic of learning led to an acknowledgement that learning could also occur in and be facilitated by a range of practices, values and activities embedded in work processes. From this perspective learning can be facilitated via the creation of 'learning cultures', where learning, reflection, debate and discussion are encouraged (López *et al*. 2004; Raz & Fadlon 2006), the embedding of learning opportunities in organizational decision making processes (Carroll *et al*. 2006), and where project based work is common, via processes such as post-project reviews (Ron *et al.* 2006; von Zedtwitz 2002). Finally, writers who adopt a practice-based perspective on knowledge see learning as occurring via and embedded in day-to-day work practices (see for example Contu & Willmott 2003; Styhre *et al.* 2006).

In conclusion, there is significant diversity and disagreement in the literature on learning on both the topics of what learning is, and how it occurs in organizations. The chapter now changes focus to consider the dynamic inter-relationship between individual, group and organizational levels of learning.

The dynamics of organizational learning

While the central concern of the chapter is on learning within organizations, this does not mean that there is an exclusive focus on organizational level learning. As will be seen, learning in organizations can be characterized as involving a dynamic reciprocity between learning processes at the individual, group and organizational level (Antonocopoulou 2006). Before presenting a conceptual model that outlines the inter-relationship between these processes it is useful to define and discuss the term organizational learning. Organizations can be understood to learn, not because they 'think' and 'behave' independently of the people who work within them (they cannot), but through the embedding of individual and group learning in organizational processes, routines, structures, databases, systems of rules etc. (Hedberg 1981; Shipton 2006; Shrivastava 1983). For example, organizational learning would be where insights developed by an individual or group result in a systematic transformation of the organizations work practices/values. However, it is wrong to equate organizational learning as being simply the sum of individual and group learning processes (Vince 2001). Organizational learning only occurs when learning at the individual or group level impacts on organizational level processes and structures. But such a transition is by no means automatic. For this to be achievable organizations need to be able to sustain critical reflection on their established norms and practices. It is thus possible, as will be seen in the illustration of Hyder presented later in the chapter that learning can occur at individual and group levels, but *not* produce learning at the organizational level. The literature on project based working also shows how project based learning is often not transferred to an organizational level (Scarbrough *et al.* 2004a & b—see end of section example for an illustration of the dynamics of project based learning and the relationship between project and organizational level learning).

Definition   Organizational learning

The embedding of individual and group level learning in organizational structures and processes, achieved through reflecting on and modifying the norms and values embodied in established organizational processes and structures.

Resisting and embracing learning in MacMillan Bloedel

Zietsma *et al.* (2002) present an interesting case study of an organization which for long periods actively resisted change, but which eventually undertook a radical transformation. MacMillan Bloedel (MB) is a Canadian forestry company, which for a long time was in the vanguard of defending the use of 'clear cutting' forestry management in the face of extensive and widespread opposition from a range of environmental protesters who felt that this means of forestry management was environmentally damaging.

In terms of the Crossan framework this was because MB was focused on exploitation/feedback learning processes, which involved the utilization and refinement of existing practices and values. In MB, these institutionalized norms were extremely powerful and dominant, which actively inhibited if not prevented feed forward, or exploration based learning which challenged the existing values in any way. In MB this meant the logic of clear cutting forestry management was never seriously questioned. This occurred because MB developed a specific form of competency trap, which Zietsma *et al.* labelled a 'legitimacy trap', which significantly inhibited learning.

A legitimacy trap occurs where the arguments of an individual/group are ignored or regarded as worthless as the legitimacy of the group/individual to make relevant arguments are questioned. In the case of MB, the arguments of the protesters were disregarded as senior management believed that they did not understand the detailed technical and economic factors affecting forestry business practices. Resistance to the arguments of the protesters was also related to individual level emotional issues. Thus, many of MB's senior managers were reluctant to listen to the arguments of the protesters as they felt this challenged and undermined the morality of their traditional values and business practices. However over time, change and learning did begin to occur, with various isolated individuals in MB (including public relations staff and field managers) adapting their thinking. This occurred not simply through a process of intuition, but also through an active process Zietsma *et al.* label as 'attending' (see Table 6.2), where these individuals actively engaged in a dialogue with the protesters to develop a better understanding of their perspective and arguments. These isolated, individual learning processes then developed into isolated group level learning through processes of group level interpretation and experimenting. This involved groups of individuals coming together not only to share their views, but actively experiment with alternative forestry management practices. Finally, after a new CEO was appointed this learning became institutionalized, with the viewpoints of the protesters becoming accepted and discussed at board level. This institutionalization of learning became highly visible when MB eventually gave up clear cutting practices altogether and shifted to a different style of forestry management.

This case suggests that the competency traps which inhibited MB from learning for a long time were shaped by the attitudes and values of senior management in the company.

1. In general terms, are the attitudes and behaviour of management always likely to play a crucial role in the extent to which organizations can learn?

The learning organization: emancipation or exploitation?

As outlined in the introduction, the literature on organizational learning is characterized by a diversity of theoretical perspectives. One specific topic that has produced an enormous amount of debate, and heated argument is the learning organization. It is worthwhile examining the contours of this debate, as doing so sheds light on some key issues.

Crudely, those engaged in this debate can be classified into two broad camps: the visionaries, or utopian propagandists, and the sceptics, or gloomy pessimists (Friedman *et al.* 2001). The visionary/propagandists camp, whose most well-known and prolific writers include Peter Senge (1990) and Mike Pedler (Pedler *et al.* 1997), is largely dominated by consultants and industrial practitioners (Driver 2002) and is very prescriptive in nature (Shipton 2006). This camp portrays the learning organization as an achievable ideal with significant benefits for both organizations and their workers. The sceptic/pessimistic campwhich is largely populated by academics challenges this perspective and pours scorn on the claims of the learning organization propagandists (Levitt & March 1988; Weick & Westley 1996). Primarily these writers, with Coopey (1995, 1998) being one of the most incisive, argue that despite the emancipatory rhetoric of the learning organization discourse, in reality it is likely to provide a way to buttress the power of management and is thus likely to lead to increased exploitation of and control over workers, rather than in their emancipation and self-development.

This section examines the two dominant perspectives in this debate, uncovering and examining issues such as power, the nature of the employment relationship and trust, which as will be shown later in Chapters 9 and 12 connect the topics of learning and knowledge management as they are factors which can also play a crucial role in shaping organizational knowledge management processes.

The learning organization: the advocates vision

Constraints of space make it impossible to elaborate all the different learning organization frameworks developed by its different advocates (Pedler, Senge, Garvin, among others—see Shipton 2006). This section focuses centrally on the way Pedler *et al.* conceptualize it. However, there is much commonality to these frameworks, therefore there is a general resonance between the broad characteristics of these different models. Pedler *et al.* (1997, 3) define the learning organization as an *'organization which facilitates the learning of all its members and consciously transforms itself and its context'*. Their learning organization framework is also elaborated into eleven specific characteristics (see Table 6.3). A key element of

Focus	Core characteristics	Description
Strategy	1. Learning approach to strategy	Strategy making/implementation/ evaluation structured as learning processes—for example with experiments and feedback loops
	2. Participative policy making	Allow all organizational members opportunity to contribute to making of major policy decisions
Looking in	3. Informating	Use of IT to empower staff through widespread information dissemination and having tolerance to how it is interpreted and used
	4. Formative accounting and control	Use of accounting practices which contribute to learning combined with a sense of self-responsibility, where individuals/groups encouraged to regard themselves as responsible for cost management
	5. Internal exchange	Constant, open dialogue between individuals and group within an organization, and encouraging collaboration not competition
	6. Reward flexibility	New ways of rewarding people for learning contribution which may not be solely financial, and where principles of reward system are explicit
Structures	7. Enabling structures	Use of loose and adaptable structures which provide opportunities for organizational and individual development
Looking out	8. Boundary workers as environmental scanners	The bringing in to an organization of ideas and working practices developed and used externally—an openness and receptivity to learning from others
	9. Inter-company learning	Use of mutually advantageous learning activities with customers, suppliers etc.
Learning opportunities	10. Learning climate	Facilitate the willingness of staff to take risks and experiment, which can be encouraged by senior management taking the lead. People not punished for criticizing orthodox views
	11. Self development opportunities for all	Have opportunities for all staff to be able to develop themselves as they see appropriate

Table 6.3 The learning company framework of Pedler *et al.* (1997)

this definition is that there is a mutual, positive synergy between the organizational context and the learning of its members. Thus in a learning organization, the organizational context should facilitate the learning of organizational staff, with this learning in turn sustaining and contributing to the ongoing transformation of the organizational context.

One of the articulated organizational advantages of the learning organization framework is that it is appropriate to the contemporary business environment, which is typically characterized as being highly competitive and turbulent (Harrison & Leitch 2000; Salaman 2001). Thus, in such circumstances organizations require to continually adapt and change, with the adoption of the learning organization framework being argued to make this possible. One of the defining characteristics of a learning organization is therefore that it is flexible, and that this provides organizations with the ability to achieve and retain a position of competitive advantage. Implicitly (and sometimes explicitly) the learning organization is regarded as the antithesis of traditional bureaucracies, which are regarded as having highly centralized and hierarchical systems of management and control (Contu *et al.* 2003). Instead, the learning organization is typically conceptualized as having a relatively flat structure, open communication systems, limited top down control and autonomous working conditions (Driver 2002).

Definition   Learning organization (propagandists)

An organization which supports the learning of its workers and allows them to express and utilize this learning to the advantage of the organization, through having an organizational environment which encourages experimentation, risk taking and open dialogue.

However, the advocates such as Pedler are clear that the benefits of utilizing the learning organization framework are by no means confined to the improving organizational performance. Instead, an inherent element of these frameworks is that management and workers alike will benefit from their adoption. In fact one of the articulated consequences of utilizing these frameworks is that the divisions between management and workers are likely to become blurred. As is clear from all eleven characteristics of the learning organization framework (see Table 6.3), workers benefit through the creation of a working environment where levels of participation in major decisions are high, where the opinions of all are valued, and where there are opportunities for workers to be creative and develop themselves. These features of learning organizations present them in a

---

TIME TO REFLECT LEARNING AND BUREAUCRACIES

To what extent are bureaucratic organizational structures antithetical to organizational learning? Are other types of flexible organizing more conducive to and supportive of organizational learning?

very positive light, as a '*visionary ideal*' (Shipton, 2006, 240), and as a '*utopia of democracy*' (Contu *et al.* 2003, 939).

One element, which is argued to be necessary and central to the creation of such a working environment, is a particular type of leadership style (Sadler 2001; Snell 2001). For example leaders in learning organizations are required to be learners as much as teachers, and they should also have roles as coaches or mentors. Such a leadership style is necessary not only to actively stimulate the curiosity and learning of workers, but to

ILLUSTRATION

A learning organization?

Harrison & Leitch (2000) applied Pedler's learning organization framework to a knowledge intensive company, a small software development company which employed a large proportion of graduates. The company had a flat organizational hierarchy, and structured work around flexible, temporary project teams. Harrison & Leitch used a survey to identify whether the company demonstrated the characteristics of a learning organization. The survey was sent to three levels of workers: the Managing Director (MD), senior managers and project team members. Each respondent was asked questions on both how they perceived the company to be, and how they would like it to be, with the difference between these scores representing what Pedler *et al.* called a dissatisfaction index. One of the most interesting findings was that a consistent difference existed, across all three levels of the hierarchy, in terms of the dissatisfaction index. Thus the MD had a negative average score of −1.2%, indicating that he thought the company exceeded his expectations in terms of supporting staff learning. By contrast, the average score for senior managers was 18.2%, while that for project staff was 38.1%. Thus senior managers, and more specifically project staff, had different perceptions regarding the extent to which the organization supported their learning. However, there was evidence that the company displayed the characteristics of a learning organization as the MD addressed some of these concerns, despite his own feelings. One area where this was done was 'reward flexibility' (see Table 6.3), where issues raised by staff were dealt with. However, there were other areas of disagreement, such as in relation to 'structures' where no conclusive resolution was achieved. Harrison & Leitch (2000, 113) conclude by suggesting that the consistency of difference in satisfaction levels, 'raise the possibility of substantial differences in internal policy-making and prioritization, which will bring into play issues of conflict and power relations'.

This case study suggests that even in an organization aspiring to be a learning organization employees felt that the organization didn't adequately support their learning.

1. Does this suggest that the learning organization vision is too idealistic and that there are likely to be few true learning organizations?

also make leaders sensitive and responsive to the opinions of workers. However, the contradictions of the learning organization advocates regarding the role and style that organizational management should have is discussed later when looking at the critique of this perspective. Before doing this it is useful to illustrate its application in practice, in one of the few empirical evaluations of this perspective.

The learning organization: the sceptics perspective

The arguments of the learning organization advocates have produced an enormous amount of debate (Easterby-Smith 1997; Tsang 1997). This section examines the critique put forward by those who have been labelled the pessimists, or sceptics. The critique is structured into three broad, but inter-related areas: the nature of the employment relationship, the need to account for power, and how individual factors, such as emotion, shape people's willingness to learn.

Learning and the employment relationship

Central to Coopey's (1995, 1998) critique of the learning organization rhetoric is that there is a fundamental contradiction that is not addressed, regarding the power and authority of management. On the one hand, as outlined previously, Pedler's vision of the learning organization—characterized by the support and encouragement given to open discussion and risk free critical debate, as well as the importance of democratic decision making processes—requires organizational managers to share power much more than in traditional organizations. However, on the other hand, Pedler takes for granted the legitimacy of both shareholder rights, enshrined in company law, as well as management's authority and right to manage in their shareholders' interests (Coopey 1995, 195). Thus, while the learning organization rhetoric suggests that more democratic decision making is necessary, it doesn't explain how this can be effectively achieved. Given that empirical evidence suggests that organizational management are often unwilling to share power, it is arguably unlikely that such a process will occur voluntarily (Boeker 1992; Dovey 1997; Kets de Vries 1991).

Coopey's argument, a perspective also taken by Contu & Willmott (2003), is that within the socio-economic context of capitalism, power is structurally embedded in the employment relationship, and that this typically places workers in a subordinate position to management. This is an issue that is returned to in both Chapters 9 and 12. Such institutional arrangements are argued to produce a 'democratic deficit' where the values, ideas and interest of workers are largely downplayed and where the authority and knowledge of management is privileged and taken for granted (Coopey 1998). In such situations it is arguable that the vision of the learning organization articulated by its propagandists is unlikely to be achieved. The relevance of these arguments for the topic of

TIME TO REFLECT AUTHORITY, LAW AND DEMOCRACY

If management's authority to manage is enshrined in company law, does this limit the extent to which organizational decision-making can be made democratic?

ILLUSTRATION

Power and the employment relationship of Orr's (1996) copier technicians

Contu & Willmott (2003) illustrate these issues in their reinterpretation of Orr's (1996) widely known anthropological study of some copier technicians. The popular vision of these workers is as 'heroic troubleshooters' who have a reasonable degree of autonomy over their work practices and who use this autonomy to innovatively develop ways of solving problems with their customers' copier machines which transcend the limits of the repair procedures codified in their repair manuals. Further, through interaction between technicians these 'stories' are shared, and a collective sense of identity developed. However, Contu & Willmott (2003) suggest that this understanding of their work fails to adequately account for how their work is shaped by the context of the capitalist employment relationship they work within. In the context of the technician's work, the best way for the company to keep costs down, keep profits up and keep customers satisfied is via repairing machines in situ, rather than the more expensive and disruptive option of replacing machines. This results in the technicians facing strong pressures to always repair machines. Further, management also attempt to reduce the occasions when machines have to be replaced through increasing their levels of control over the technicians and reducing their level of autonomy through encoding their improvised practices into new standardized operating procedures and documentation. While the technicians appear to largely accept the ideology of keeping customers satisfied via the in situ repairing of machines, Contu & Willmott (2003) suggest that organizational efforts at standardizing work practices creates an antagonism and conflict with the desire of the technicians to have interesting and creative work and some level of autonomy over how they carry it out.

learning is that these features of the employment relationship are likely to significantly shape the nature of organizational learning processes.

Power, politics and learning

Neglecting to adequately take account of power, politics and conflict is another critique made against the learning organization propagandists. However, such neglect was typical of the majority of the learning literature until the mid-1990s (Berthoin Antal *et al.* 2001). Further, the propagandists not only downplay such issues, but are typically unwilling to even acknowledge that they are relevant to the analysis of learning processes (Driver 2002). However, since the mid-1990s, issues of power and politics have been given a greater level of attention (LaPolombara 2001; Easterby-Smith *et al.* 2000; Vince *et al.* 2002). The need to account for power and politics in learning processes flows from three closely inter-related factors (see Figure 6.2).

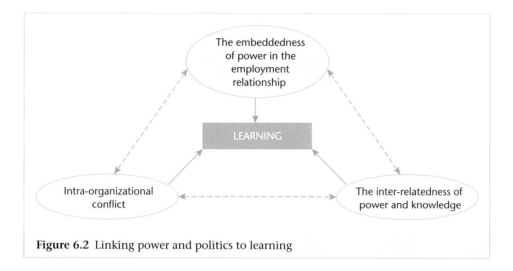

Figure 6.2 Linking power and politics to learning

Firstly, as will be discussed more fully in Chapter 12, power and knowledge are either intimately inter-related, or totally inseparable (the precise way that the power-knowledge relationship is understood depends on how power is conceptualized). Thus if learning is about the development and use of knowledge, then account needs to be taken of issues of power (Vince 2002). Coopey (1998) for example, drawing on Foucault, suggests that managerial authority relates to the inseparability of power and knowledge, where management's power is reflected in the privileging of their knowledge, and vice versa. Secondly, as discussed in the previous section, the need to account for power in learning processes relates to the embeddedness of power in the employment relationship. Thirdly, and finally, some argue that power and politics need to be accounted for due to the typical lack of value consensus which exists in most organizations, and the potential for conflict and disagreement this creates (Huzzard & Ostergren 2002; Salaman 2001). This is another issue that was discussed more fully in Chapters 9 and 12.

The critics of the learning organization rhetoric argue that taking adequate account of these factors means the vision of the advocates is unrealistic, and that there are likely to be some stark contradictions between their rhetoric, and the way the adoption of learning organization practices impact on organizational relations. Thus, rather than workers having a greater potential for creativity and self development, the use of learning organization practices may mean they are subject to greater levels of control. Further, rather than empowering workers, learning organization practices have the potential to bolster and reinforce the power of management (Armstrong 2000; Coopey 1995, 1998; Driver 2002; Easterby-Smith 1997).

The adoption of the rhetoric and practice of the learning organization can be perceived as increasing the potential to control workers, because, as with the use of culture based management practices generally (Kunda 1992), it involves a form of socially based control, where goal alignment between worker and organization is achieved through persuading workers to internalize the organizational value system (Driver 2002). Such control systems are more subtle, less visible and have the potential to be more effective than traditional bureaucratic methods (Alvesson & Wllmott 2001).

> **Definition**   Learning organization (sceptics)
>
> An organization where socially based control systems are used to create value alignment around the benefits to all of learning, which has the potential to reinforce management power, and contradict the logic of emancipation embodied in the learning organization rhetoric.

Some writers however, conclude that conflict is not necessarily detrimental to learning processes, and that if conflict and differences of opinion are managed and negotiated through a certain type of dialogue, they can actually facilitate learning (Coopey & Burgoyne 2000; Huzzard & Ostergren 2002). For example conflict can facilitate learning if it is dealt with in a communication process which does not privilege any particular point of view, where people are able to communicate without fear, where the communication is a two way process, and where ultimately the objective of the process is not to achieve a consensus, but for people to develop a greater understanding of the viewpoint of others. Such processes therefore have much in common with the processes of perspective making and taking outlined in Chapter 3, which are an important element of the practice-based perspective on knowledge.

Emotion and attitudes to learning

The final factor that the learning organization advocates inadequately account for is the role of emotion in shaping attitudes and behaviours towards learning processes. However, a growing number of writers now acknowledge how emotion importantly affects the dynamics of learning processes (Brown 2000; Scherer & Tran 2001; Vince 2001). At the individual level, learning can be regarded as potentially positive and exciting—discovering new knowledge, improving levels of understanding, developing more effective ways of working, etc. But, there is also a potential negative side—giving up the familiar, embracing some level of uncertainty—which may be anxiety inducing for people (Kofman & Senge 1993). Learning is therefore likely to induce conflicting emotions for people. Learning and changing can also be understood to affect an individual's sense of self-identity (Child 2001), which may be regarded positively or negatively. Arguably, the attractiveness of defensive routines (Argyris 1990) is that they provide people with a sense of security and self-identity (Giddens 1991). Thus, a potentially frightening side of learning is that it can be felt to involve giving up that which makes people feel competent and secure. For example, in the case of MacMillan Bloedel examined earlier, part of the reason why senior management resisted change was because they felt that acknowledging the legitimacy of the protester's arguments raised questions about the morality of their actions and the company's strategy (Zietsma *et al.* 2002).

Learning can also be understood to have an emotional component due to the dynamic between individual and group or organizational level learning. Primarily, learning and

ILLUSTRATION

Conflict, emotion and learning at Hyder

Vince (2001) analysed the dynamics of learning at Hyder, a multi-utility and infra-structure company, which had evolved considerably from its origin as Welsh Water. Hyder actively supported individual learning, and believed that this would create organizational learning. However *no* organizational learning occurred, which was explained by the intra-organizational dynamics which were shaped by issues of power and emotion. Hyder's evolution from Welsh Water into Hyder had resulted in two broad perspectives emerging over what the values underpinning the company should be. One camp saw the company as being primarily a Welsh utility, and that it should be driven by values of public service. The other camp saw the company as a global corporation that should be driven by commercial values. People in both camps used a range of methods in attempting to make their view of the company accepted. One of the main political tactics used was to develop change initiatives, which resulted in two competing initiatives being developed simultaneously. One was a corporate re-branding exercise to create the idea of one company driven by commercial values. The other change initiative, which used the rhetoric of employee empowerment, attempted to develop support around the public service perspective. Very little communication occurred between the camps and what was described as an 'iron curtain' developed between them. This reinforced the sense of competition, increased the level of anger and suspicion in both camps at the motivations of the other, and created a sense of entrenchment and defensiveness which ultimately reinforced their isolation. Individual learning was not able to contribute to orga-nizational learning as it couldn't/didn't challenge the existing dynamics. This was partly shaped by emotions of defensiveness, as part of the dynamic was the fear of the consequences of challenging the status quo. As a consequence of this, open and acrimonious disputes were avoided (people publicly pretended they didn't exist), but simultaneously were attempting to defend their interests. Thus these organiza-tional dynamics actively inhibited organizational learning.

This represents an example where conflicting viewpoints actively inhibited organizational level learning.

1. What could management at Hyder have done to make use of these different perspectives to actively facilitate organizational level learning?

change will inevitably involve, to some extent, challenging the existing balance of power, interests, practices and values. Thus, learning may induce hostility and defen-siveness because of its (potential) implications: people may be scared of challenging the existing norms (Salaman 2001). As Coopey & Burgoyne (2000) argue, the character of the organizational context will crucially affect the extent to which people will feel anxious

This paradox represents what they characterize as a 'learning boundary', which is a boundary to learning that is itself a product of learning.

1. Does the 'learning boundary' effect mean that the transferral of intra-project learning to the wider organization will always be difficult?

2. What, if anything, can be done to deal with and minimize this effect?

Source: Scarbrough, H., Bresnan, M., Edelman, L., Laurent, S., Newell, S., & Swan, J. (2004a). 'The Process of Project-Based Learning: An Exploratory Study', *Management Learning*, 35/4: 491–506. With kind permission from Sage publishers.

 For further information about this journal article visit our Online Resource Centre at www.oxfordtextbooks.co.uk/orc/hislop2e/

Review and discussion questions

1   The advocates of the learning organization suggest that critical self-reflection and open debate on norms and values are fundamental to learning organizations. However, Coopey and Burgoyne (2000) suggest few organizations provide the 'psychic space' where such reflection can occur. Do you agree with this analysis? If so, what factors are key in stifling such processes?

2   Compare the two definitions of the learning organization outlined in the chapter. Which do you most agree with, and why?

3   One of the main critiques of the learning organization literature is that management are typically unlikely to 'give up' and share power in the way necessary to facilitate proper learning and self reflection. Do you agree with this? If so, what, if anything, can be done to persuade such managers that sharing power with workers has potential advantages for all?

Suggestions for further reading

1   C. Zietsma, M. Winn, O. Branzei, & I. Vertinsky (2002). 'The War of the Woods: Facilitators and Impediments of Organizational Learning Processes', *British Journal of Management*, 13: S61–74.

A fascinating case study that examines the dynamics of organizational learning processes and provides a useful modification of the Crossan framework.

2   R. Vince (2001). 'Power and Emotion in Organizational Learning', *Human Relations*, 54/10: 1325–1351.

A useful examination of the relationship between individual and organizational level learning, which considers issues of emotion and power.

3   J. Coopey (1995). 'The Learning Organization, Power, Politics and Ideology', *Management Learning*, 26/2: 193–213.

One of the earliest and best critiques of the propagandists' perspective on the learning organization.

4   G. Grabher (2004). 'Temporary Architectures of Learning: Knowledge Governance in Project Ecologies', *Organization Studies*, 25/9: 1491–1514.

Uses the concept of ecologies to understand the relationship between project level learning and learning at other levels such as the firm, the epistemic community and the personal network.

Take your learning further: Online Resource Centre

Visit the supporting Online Resource Centre for resources which will extend your understanding of knowledge management in organizations. As well as web links to sites of interest, the author has provided case studies looking at knowledge management in virtual and knowledge intensive firms, and in global multinationals. These will help you with your research, essays and assignments; or you may find these additional resources helpful when revising for exams.

 www.oxfordtextbooks.co.uk/orc/hislop2e/

PART 3

Knowledge Creation and Loss

While most chapters in this book take a general approach to knowledge management and don't focus specifically on particular types of knowledge process, the two chapters in this brief section are different. Thus Chapter 7 is concerned narrowly with processes of knowledge creation, while Chapter 8 has an exclusive focus on processes of organizational forgetting and unlearning.

These processes deserve particular attention for a number of reasons. Firstly, as is highlighted in both chapters, the turbulent and dynamics business environments that many companies compete in means that the ability to change and adapt is a crucial organizational competence. For different reasons, the extent to which organizations are able to both create new knowledge, and give up or forget old knowledge, are crucial to their ability to effectively compete in such circumstances. Knowledge creation is important in dynamics contexts as organizations require to regularly innovate and develop new products and/or services, with the risk of not doing so being that organizations lose their competitive edge, with their ways of working and products/services becoming outdated.

Forgetting or unlearning is also crucial to an organization's ability to adapt and survive. Arguably, the ability to innovate and create new knowledge is to some extent predicated on the ability of an organization to know when existing competences, ways of work, products and services are becoming out of date and require to be adapted. An inability to do so reflects a blinkered viewpoint, stuck in routines which may have been successful previously, but whose contemporary relevance may be becoming increasingly questionable. Thus the ability to deliberately forget and give up knowledge requires organizations and workers to have the ability to critically reflect on the ongoing relevance and utility of their knowledge and ways of working.

There are two other reasons for examining processes of knowledge creation and forgetting. The importance of examining processes of knowledge creation relates to the importance and popularity of Nonaka's work, and in particular the model of knowledge creation that he, along with a number of collaborators developed. Thus, one of the key objectives of Chapter 7 is to provide a critical review of Nonaka's work.

The other reason for examining processes of forgetting is due to the opposite—its general neglect in the knowledge management literature. While, as will be seen in Chapter 8, processes of forgetting and unlearning have been examined in the literature on organizational learning, it represents a topic that is rarely addressed in the knowledge management literature. Thus, part of the reason for examining processes of organizational forgetting is to suggest that it is a topic which requires greater levels of attention by those interested in the topic of knowledge management.

Innovation Dynamics and Knowledge Processes

Introduction

Organizational innovation is concerned with deliberately designing and implementing changes to an organization's products, services, structures or processes. The importance to organizations of such changes, and learning in general, is that the business context faced by most organizations requires it. This business context, shaped by a variety of factors such as rapid and profound change in computer and communication technologies, as well as processes of globalization and internationalization, can be characterized as being highly turbulent. Thus, for a significant number of business organizations the continuous development and implementation of innovations is necessary to remain competitive.

At a common sense level, innovation is often characterized as being primarily a knowledge creation process. Thus, from this perspective, whether developing a new product, or transforming an organization's working practices, innovation is concerned with going beyond the realms of existing knowledge, and developing new knowledge and insights. This idea is challenged here. As will be seen, much organizational innovation is relatively incremental in nature, involving the modification rather than transformation and replacement of existing knowledge. Further, while knowledge creation is an important aspect of innovation processes, so is the ability to search for and identify relevant external knowledge, apply existing knowledge to new contexts, understand and absorb unfamiliar external knowledge, and blend and integrate different bodies of knowledge together. Thus innovation processes are much more than knowledge creation processes.

The general character of innovation processes (if it's possible to talk about the general characteristics of such a diverse phenomenon) have evolved since the early 1980s. In general, innovation processes appear to be becoming more complex in nature and increasingly innovating organizations no longer possess all relevant knowledge internally. Thus, the importance of developing external networks has increased significantly, as has the need to integrate together diverse bodies of knowledge. Thus, Lam (1997, 973) suggested that, '*firms increasingly build cooperative ventures in order to sustain and enhance their competitiveness.*' Because of these changes, this chapter has many issues in common with Chapter 11.

The next section of the chapter provides an overview on how the literature on organizational innovation has evolved since the 1980s and points to three key elements to innovation processes. These are their increasing interactivity, the role of knowledge and the growing importance of developing and managing diverse networks. While these issues are closely inter-related, the chapter proceeds by examining each one separately.

Characterizing innovation processes

Before the knowledge dynamics of innovation processes can be examined in detail, it is worthwhile making a few introductory comments on the topics of terminology, the diversity in type of innovation that exists, and finally, the evolution in the way that innovation processes have been conceptualized.

As outlined, the central focus of this chapter is on the way organizations systematically develop and change themselves and/or their products/services, with the objective of improving organizational performance. However, this encompasses a wide diversity of organizational activities from investing in large scale, basic scientific research (such as pharmaceutical or chemical companies undertaking research on genetics), through the development and utilization of technology for the creation of new products (such as mobile phone companies incorporating photo and video functions into new generation mobile phones), to modifications in organizational processes (such as changing intra-organizational communication systems or developing knowledge management systems). A diversity of labels can be utilized to refer to these processes including new product development (NPD), research and development (R&D), and innovation. In this chapter the term 'innovation' is used, as it is generic enough to refer to all of the above processes.

> **Definition**   Innovation
>
> The deliberate modification, or transformation, by an organization of its products/services, processes or structures.

As should already be apparent, organizational innovations are extremely diverse in character. For example, they can be incremental, where the scale of change is small, or radical, where the innovation involves large-scale and fundamental change. Further, innovations can be product/service focused (where a new product/service is designed or an existing product/service is modified), or process focused (where organizational processes and/or structures are modified). These represent significant differences, as they importantly shape the character of innovation processes with, for example, incremental and radical innovation processes being significantly different. However, equally, there

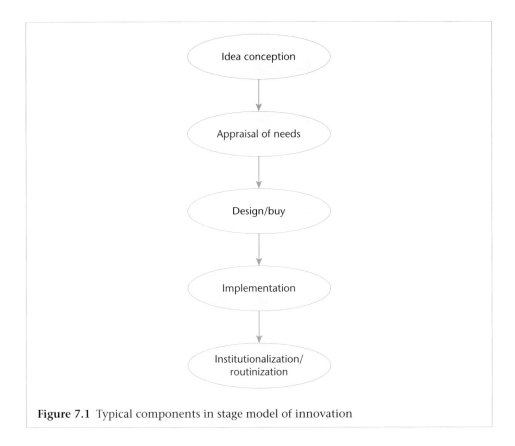

Figure 7.1 Typical components in stage model of innovation

are a number of general characteristics common to all innovation processes, and it is these common features that are examined here.

While the literature on organizational innovation has typically been characterized by a heterogeneity of diverse theoretical perspectives (Slappendel 1996; Wolfe 1994), one of the dominant streams in it is the stage model theory, where innovation is conceptualized as a linear process consisting of a number of discrete stages (see Figure 7.1).

However, since approximately the 1990s this model has increasingly been brought into question. As will be seen later, a number of writers, including Leonard-Barton (1995) argued that the problem with the stage model was that it disguised the extent to which these stages were inter-related (for example, with design modifications occurring during implementation). More broadly, others argued that innovation processes were becoming more interactive in nature, increasingly requiring extensive and repeated interactions throughout the whole innovation process between a diverse range of actors from both within the innovating organization, and from external actors such as customers, suppliers, consultants, universities and public and private sector research institutions (Alter & Hage 1993; Jones *et al.* 2001; Powell 1998; Swan *et al.* 2007). The need for the development and utilization of such networks flows partly from the increasing complexity of innovations, which means that organizations increasingly no longer possess all relevant knowledge internally, and who therefore require to develop networks with individuals

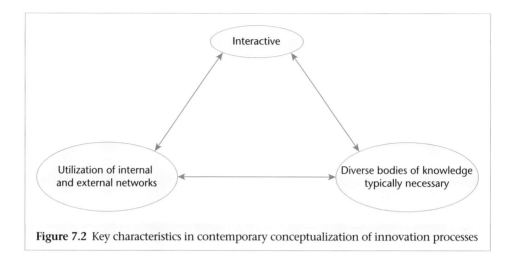

Figure 7.2 Key characteristics in contemporary conceptualization of innovation processes

and organizations in possession of relevant knowledge (Cohen & Levinthal 1990; Lam 1997; Sakakibara & Dodgson 2003; Tidd *et al.* 2001; Perkmann & Walsh 2007; Pittaway *et al.* 2004). Thus, contemporary writers typically conceptualize innovation processes as having three closely inter-related characteristics: they are highly interactive, they require the development and utilization of heterogeneous networks of actors, and they involve the utilization of diverse bodies of knowledge (see Figure 7.2).

Innovation as an interactive process

Meeus *et al.* (2001) define interactive learning as the continuous exchange and sharing of knowledge resources conducive to innovation processes, between an innovating firm and its customers and suppliers. This is a useful definition except for the unnecessarily narrow focus on customers and suppliers.

Whilst the interactivity of innovation processes is not totally new (Lundvall 1988; Pavitt 1984; von Hippel 1976, 1988), a number of factors that emerged during the 1980s mean that the extent and intensity of such interactions has increased significantly. Swan *et al.* (1999), for example argue that advances in ICTs and the move to virtual and network forms of organization mean that innovations are increasingly becoming organization-wide in scope, requiring intra-organizational interactions between different functions, and business units. For example, Carlile (2002, 2004) refers to such cross functional innovation when developing his theory on the role of boundary objects in boundary spanning work contexts (see Chapter 11).

Meeus *et al.* (2001), suggest that the growing complexity of innovations contributes to the increasing interactiveness of innovation processes, as the more complex an innovation, the more likely it is that all relevant knowledge will not be internally possessed. Finally, Jacquier-Roux & Bourgeois (2002), drawing on the influential work of Gibbons *et al.* (1994), suggest that the changing nature of knowledge production in society, from narrow, disciplinary based innovations, to trans-disciplinary innovations helps explain the increasing interactiveness of innovation processes.

The need for extensive and repeated interactions between organizations during innovation processes questions the linearity of the stage model, and suggests that the notion of innovation processes involving discrete, sequential stages is over-simplistic. As innovation processes become more interactive the more likely it is that there will be over-laps

ILLUSTRATION

Interactive innovation in the energy industry

Jacquier-Roux & Bourgeois (2002) investigated innovation activity in the energy production industries and found that in the period between 1985–98, paradoxically, as the R&D spending of the main oil and electricity production companies went down, there was a simultaneous overall increase in the production of knowledge in these sectors (measured in terms of number of patents granted). This was explained by the change in these sectors towards more interactive based innovation processes, where the level of collaboration in innovation activity between the main oil and electricity production companies and equipment suppliers increase markedly.

During the period examined significant changes had occurred in these sectors which encouraged the main producers to reduce their R&D spending. Primarily, deregulation and privatization, combined with a process of globalization in these industrial sectors, significantly increased the pressure on the main oil and electricity production companies to focus on short term economic performance, which encouraged them to reduce their levels of R&D spending. Simultaneously, these companies started developing innovation partnerships with equipment suppliers as a way to sustain their R&D efforts and outputs. Prior to this, the main oil and electricity production companies had undertaken virtually all their R&D activity totally in-house. Thus the strategy change undertaken by the main oil and electricity production companies resulted in the level of interaction between users and suppliers during innovation activities increasing significantly, and with equipment suppliers playing a greater role in such activities than had historically been traditional. These changes were visible in the evolving number of patents granted to these companies, with the patent activity of the main oil and electricity production companies declining, while the number of patents granted to equipment suppliers increased significantly. While these changes gave equipment suppliers a more important role in innovation activities a power asymmetry still existed which favoured the main oil and electricity producers. This was related to both their size (they were typically large multinational companies), and also their ability to be able to switch their business to different equipment suppliers if so desired.

between different stages. One of the most visible ways in which this occurs is in the blurring of the boundary between design and implementation activities. Thus a number of writers suggest that the implementation of innovations can produce important changes to the characteristics of the innovation being implemented (Badham *et al.* 1997; Leonard-Barton 1995; Swan *et al.* 1999).

In conclusion, this section has shown that one of the key characteristics of contemporary innovation processes is their typically interactive nature, requiring innovating companies to intensively work with a wide and diverse range of organizations, groups and individuals. This characteristic of innovation processes thus links closely with the other key elements of innovation processes examined: the importance of networks and knowledge processes. However, this type of working relationship is by no means straightforward to manage. Firstly, there is a need for some common knowledge to exist (or be developed) between collaborating partners. Second, such work can involve collaboration between communities that may have distinctive and divergent cultures or values. Thirdly, the type of trust based social relations that are conducive to knowledge sharing may not initially exist. Finally, the tacit, context specific, structurally and contextually embedded character of much organizational knowledge makes it difficult to share. These issues will be examined in detail in the following two sections, and will also be returned to in Chapter 11 which examines the social dynamics of knowledge processes in cross-community, boundary spanning contexts.

Knowledge creation and Nonaka

While, as has been outlined, innovation processes involve more than just the creation of knowledge, knowledge creation is a fundamentally important aspect of innovation. In examining the topic of knowledge creation it is virtually impossible to ignore Nonaka's[1] theory of knowledge creation as it represents the single most influential and widely referenced theory in the knowledge management domain (Guldenberg & Helting 2007; Nonaka *et al.* 2006). For example, Gourlay (2006) found that Nonaka & Takeuchi's 1995 book, *The Knowledge-Creating Company*, had been cited 1093 times between 1994 and 2004. This theory has been developed and written about in a large number of publications both by Nonaka individually (Nonaka 1991, 1994) and in collaboration with a number of others (Nonaka & Takeuchi 1995; Nonaka & Konno 1998; Nonaka *et al.* 2000; Nonaka *et al.* 2001; Nonaka *et al.* 2006).

As it has developed, this theory has become broad in scope, linking to a wide range of issues including leadership styles, organizational forms, and strategy. However, the focus here is narrowly on the SECI knowledge creation processes which lie at the heart of Nonaka's theory, and which have remained relatively constant and unchanged as Nonaka's knowledge creation theory has developed (Gourlay 2006; Nonaka *et al.* 2006). However, before outlining the SECI model it is necessary to articulate the epistemological

---

1. This knowledge creation theory has been developed by Nonaka in collaboration with a number of others. However, for simplicity it is referred to here as Nonaka's theory.

assumptions underpinning Nonaka's theory, as they are highly germane to how knowledge conversion processes are conceptualized.

For Nonaka, knowledge, defined as 'justified true belief', refers to the individual knowledge people develop based on their particular experiences and work practices. Thus, in this respect it has resonances with the practice-based perspective on knowledge articulated in Chapter 3. Further, it is a highly subjective and relative definition of knowledge, as knowledge constitutes what an individual believes to be true. Thus, Nonaka *et al.* (2006, 1182) say that, '*knowledge is never free from human values and ideas*'. However, simultaneously, Nonaka's epistemology further distinguishes between tacit and explicit knowledge as being fundamentally different. Thus, '*knowledge that can be uttered, formulated in sentences, captured in drawings and writing, is explicit*', while, '. . . *knowledge tied to the senses, movement skills, physical experiences, intuition, or implicit rules of thumb, is tacit*' (p. 1182). In this respect, Nonaka's epistemology is closer to the objectivist perspective articulated in Chapter 2. Thus, Nonaka's theory of knowledge creation can't easily be characterized as embedded in either the objectivist or practice-base perspectives on knowledge, as it embodies elements of both.

The distinction Nonaka makes between tacit and explicit knowledge is fundamental to his model of knowledge creation, as it is via the continuous interaction between tacit and explicit knowledge that knowledge is created. In Nonaka's knowledge creation spiral (Figure 7.3) there are four modes of knowledge conversion (see Table 7.1), with knowledge being created via the conversion of tacit knowledge into new forms of tacit knowledge (referred to as socialization), the conversion of explicit knowledge into tacit

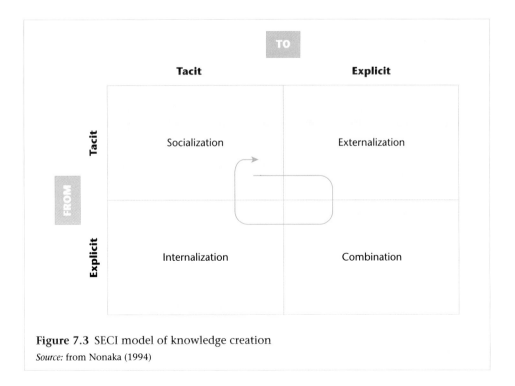

Figure 7.3 SECI model of knowledge creation
Source: from Nonaka (1994)

	Socialization	Externalization	Combination	Internalization
Knowledge conversion type	Tacit to tacit	Tacit to explicit	Explicit to explicit	Explicit to tacit
Illustrative example	Where a new member of a work group acquires the tacit knowledge possessed by other group members through dialogue, observation or co-operative working.	Where an individual is able to make their tacit knowledge explicit, for example through a process of communication and dialogue with others.	The linking together of discrete bodies of knowledge, to create a more complex body of knowledge.	Where an individual converts explicit knowledge into tacit knowledge, through applying it to their work tasks.

Table 7.1 Nonaka's four modes of knowledge conversion
Source: from Nonaka (1994)

knowledge (referred to as externalization), the combination of different forms of explicit knowledge to create new forms of explicit knowledge (referred to as combination) and finally, the conversion of explicit knowledge into tacit knowledge (referred to as internalization). Thus the SECI mnemonic which has evolved to represent Nonaka's knowledge creation model, utilizes the first letter of the four knowledge conversion processes. For Nonaka, socialization is typically the starting point of knowledge creation processes, with knowledge creation then occurring in a spiral, developing and evolving through the different modes of knowledge conversion.

The creation of knowledge through its conversion from one form to another involves the collective validation by groups of a person's individual knowledge (their personal justified true beliefs), and the integration of this knowledge with other group level knowledge. Thus knowledge creation involves a process of amplification, whereby individual knowledge is communicated and made available to others, and where it connects to and becomes integrated within wider organizational knowledge systems. Thus knowledge creation can be conceptualized as 'moving' knowledge up from an individual to a group or organizational level, where it changes from being individual knowledge to being validated group/organizational level knowledge.

The limitations of Nonaka's knowledge creation theory

While Nonaka's theory is widely cited, and highly influential, it has also been the subject of a number of criticisms. Three considered here are that the empirical evidence supporting the theory is unconvincing, secondly that the model has conceptual problems, and thirdly that its universal applicability is limited as it is only relevant to companies

ILLUSTRATION

The application of Nonaka's SECI model to understanding knowledge creation in new product development projects

Hoegl & Schulze (2005) carried out a survey of participants in new product development projects in Germany, Switzerland and Austria to investigate the extent to which a range of knowledge management tools supported knowledge creation processes. The survey investigated both which knowledge management tools were utilized, and the respondents level of satisfaction with them. The paper then used Nonaka's SECI framework to explain how the different knowledge management tools examined facilitated processes of knowledge creation.

The survey found that the most commonly used knowledge management tools were informal social events (used in the organizations of over 80% of respondents), experience workshops (80% of organizations), experience reports, databases, project briefings and communities of practice (all used by just under 75% of organizations). Further, the knowledge management methods that were most commonly used, were also the ones that were regarded as being most effective.

In explaining why these knowledge management methods facilitate knowledge creation processes, Hoegl & Schulze make use of Nonaka's SECI framework by linking each of the knowledge management methods examined to one particular form of knowledge conversion. For example, informal events which encourage conversation and open communication between work colleagues are argued to facilitate processes of socialization (the conversion of tacit knowledge into new forms of tacit knowledge) through the way they allow the development of strong interpersonal relations between people. By contrast experience workshops, which allow people to share their experiences with colleagues, are argued to facilitate the process of externalization. This is because the process of talking about and reflecting on experiences facilitate the explicit articulation and codification of knowledge and understanding.

1. In Hoegl and Schulze's analysis there is a one-to-one relationship between the knowledge management practices and the forms of knowledge conversion in Nonaka's model, with each form of knowledge management being linked to a particular form of knowledge creation. However, to what extent is it possible that particular knowledge management methods may facilitate more than one form of knowledge conversion? For example, as well as experience workshops facilitating processes of externalization, to what extent can they also facilitate processes of socialization, combination and/or internalization?

Type of collaboration	Duration	Character
Subcontract relations	Short–medium term	Can vary from short term, market based contractual relations, to longer term relations such as collaborative innovation development
Licensing	Fixed term	Fixed term, contractual agreement between companies, where one company provides specific technologies, skills and knowledge to another
Strategic alliances	Medium term	A medium term relationship, which can involve two or more companies, with a specifically defined remit, such as the development of a specific product
Joint ventures	Long term	Long term collaborative relationship between two or more companies, which can be wide in scope, and for relatively open-ended time periods

Table 7.2 Forms of collaboration

people articulating and attempting to justify and validate their individual knowledge at group level through communicating and interacting with others. However, everyone involved in such processes possess their individual knowledge, views and values, thus attempts by individuals to have individual knowledge accepted at group level is never a straightforward or automatic process. Nonaka argues that, from a managerial point of view, the way to facilitate such processes is to create and sustain a social environment which facilitates the development of trust-based social relations.

Tacit knowledge and the social dynamics of innovation processes

The importance of tacit knowledge to innovation processes is well recognized (Hislop *et al.* 2000; Powell 1998; Senker & Faulkner 1996; von Krogh *et al.* 2000), with some writers suggesting that the ability to effectively utilize tacit knowledge represents a measure of an organization's innovativeness (Leonard & Sensiper 1998; Subramaniam & Venkatraman 2001). For Leonard & Sensiper (1998) innovation occurs through interactions between people. This is because when an appropriate form of communication exists, people are able to gain an insight into the knowledge of others. When such insights are linked to a person's existing knowledge base, new knowledge and insights can be created. Thus, innovation involves a process of creative knowledge integration, which occurs when a '*creative abrasion*' between contrasting viewpoints and knowledge bases occurs (Leonard & Sensiper 1998, 118).

The typically tacit nature of much organizational knowledge means that the sharing and communication of such sticky knowledge requires detailed and extensive social interactions to occur in a context of typically trust based, social relations (Leonard & Sensiper 1998; Subramaniam *et al.* 1998; Subramaniam & Venkatraman 2001).

ILLUSTRATION

The role of tacit knowledge in new product development processes

Subramaniam & Venkatraman (2001) examined new product development processes in a number of large multinational companies and found that their ability to share and utilize important tacit knowledge was key. Specifically they looked at the development of transnational products. These are products that are developed simultaneously for multiple markets, which contain both standardized features, and features that are responsive to individual local markets. Knowledge of consumer preferences in different local/national markets was thus important to such innovations. This knowledge was found to be largely tacit, being developed by people over time, through experience of working within a particular country/market. The transferral and sharing of such knowledge was an important aspect of these innovation processes. Subramaniam & Venkatraman found that the effective sharing of such knowledge required the use of rich communication mediums. Three particular ways which were examined, and all of which were found to be effective included: the use of face-to-face communication among teams with members drawn from different countries; the use of face-to-face communication among teams with members who had some overseas work experience; and the use of extensive communication amongst project teams which were not co-located. Thus, of the three methods examined two involved face-to-face interaction, while the third involved extensive communication via ICTs.

1. Is knowledge of local market conditions and preferences the sort of knowledge that is always likely to be tacit and which can only be developed over time, through experience?

2. Can such knowledge be codified and communicated more easily?

The complexity of innovation related knowledge

Hansen (1999) found that the complexity of knowledge could have a significant impact on the social dynamics of innovation processes. Hansen defined complexity in terms of both the degree of tacitness and inter-dependence of knowledge. If knowledge is highly inter-dependent, a full understanding of it is not possible without some understanding of related knowledge. Thus complex knowledge is knowledge that is both highly tacit, and simultaneously interdependent. As with tacit knowledge, the sharing of complex knowledge was found to be most effective when strong trust based relations existed between people involved in the innovation process, as the sharing of such knowledge required extensive interactions.

De Holan *et al.* (2004), whose analysis is focussed purely on forgetting at an organizational level define learning as a process of adding to and enhancing an organization's memory, while by contrast, forgetting is about memory loss, and the reduction of organizational memory through losing or giving up knowledge whereby an organization becomes unable (either intentionally or unintentionally) to do something it was previously able to do.

Definition   Organizational forgetting

The reduction in an organization's memory that occurs when an organization becomes unable to do something it was previously able to do.

Another way to conceptualize the relationship between organizational forgetting and learning is via considering their related and overlapping roles in processes of change. The model of change which most explicitly utilizes the concepts of forgetting and learning is Lewin's (1951) three stage change model, which Akgün *et al.* (2007) explicitly draw on in defining unlearning (the deliberate and conscious process of forgetting). The first stage of Lewin's change model is the process of 'unfreezing', where there is an explicit acknowledgement that existing knowledge, values and/or practices have their limitations and require to be changed. The second stage involves a process of transition, whereby the planned adaptations and changes are made. Finally, in the third stage a process of 'freezing' occurs, whereby new knowledge, values and/or practices become stabilized and institutionalized. Thus with this model, forgetting and unlearning are a necessary and intrinsic element of the change process which have to occur before learning and change can take place.[2]

Typology of forgetting

While it has been suggested thus far in the chapter that, in general terms, the ability to forget and give up knowledge is a useful organizational capability, it is important to make clear that not all forms of forgetting are functional for organizations. For example the loss of a key source of knowledge, which can occur when specialist staff who possess important tacit knowledge leave an organization, may have quite negative organizational implications (Massingham 2008—see also Chapters 5 and 14).

Distinguishing between what constitutes useful and positive forgetting and what constitutes dysfunctional forgetting requires defining and differentiating between specific and distinctive forms of forgetting. One of the most fundamental distinctions that can be made is between accidental versus deliberate forgetting. Accidental forgetting is where

---

2. Lewin's change model is relatively dated, and has been subject to much criticism. It has also been revised and adapted by a number of writers (for reviews of how Lewin's model has been criticized and adapted see Burnes 1996, 2004). However, it is beyond the scope of this book to engage more fully with the range of potential ways in which organizational change can be conceptualized. For a useful review of the range of contemporary perspectives on change, see Armenakis & Bedeian (1999) and Burnes (2004).

knowledge and capabilities are lost inadvertently, while deliberate forgetting involves a conscious process of giving up and changing knowledge, values and/or practices which are deemed to have become outdated. Thus, in general terms, unintentional or accidental processes of forgetting are typically understood as having generally negative and dysfunctional consequences, while deliberate processes of forgetting are regarded as having positive consequences for the organizations which undertake them (de Holan & Phillips 2004; de Holan *et al.* 2004; Akgün *et al.* 2006). Thus, organizations need to get the balance right between retaining knowledge which is useful and important, while simultaneously being able to discard, forget or give up knowledge which has become outdated and of limited contemporary use.

De Holan *et al.* (2004) develop a typology which distinguishes between four specific forms of forgetting (see Figure 8.1) which combines the distinction between accidental versus deliberate forgetting, with a distinction between newly acquired/developed knowledge and established knowledge which constitutes a part of the organizational memory. Each form of forgetting is described below, and illustrated subsequently in the boxed example.

The first form of forgetting is the accidental forgetting of existing or established knowledge, which de Holan *et al.* (2004) define as memory loss. This form of forgetting is typical when knowledge is used infrequently. In such situations organizations may forget knowledge through the loss to the organization of the people who possess it, or where an organization loses the ability to carry out long unused, informal and uncodified work routines because the capability to carry them out has been forgotten through lack of use. MacKenzie & Spinardi (1995), based on a detailed study of nuclear weapons development in the USA suggest that such a situation could occur with the capability to develop

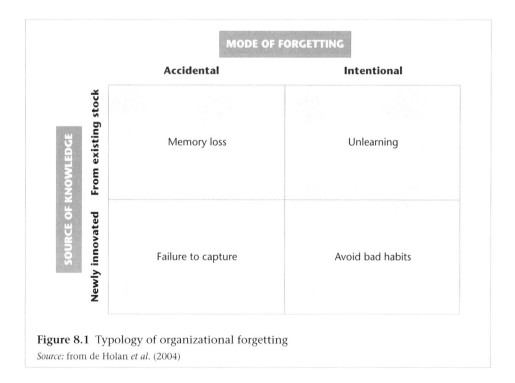

Figure 8.1 Typology of organizational forgetting
Source: from de Holan *et al.* (2004)

This form of forgetting will be the main one focussed in the remains of this chapter, with the following section examining the barriers to unlearning which help explain why processes of deliberate unlearning are typically so challenging, with the final section outlining what can be done to address these barriers and facilitate processes of unlearning.

Barriers to unlearning

As outlined previously, this section focuses purely on the form of forgetting that de Holan & Phillips (2004) defined as unlearning, the deliberate forgetting of established organizational knowledge. This is because it is not only one of the most common and important forms of forgetting that organizations can benefit from, but as will be seen, it is a process which organizations find hard to undertake and manage effectively. The reasons for these difficulties are that there are a number of factors which can make people and organizations unwilling to unlearn and which thus act as barriers to unlearning. Here they are divided into individual level factors, related to people, organizational level factors, related to features of organizational processes which can act as barriers to unlearning, and the role of organizational crisis in inhibiting unlearning.

Individual level barriers to unlearning

Individual level barriers to unlearning are here divided into two broad types, those which are generic, and relevant to all people, and those which are specific to particular types or categories of employee.

General individual barriers to unlearning

The first generic, individual level barrier to unlearning is the negative emotions that learning in general, and more specifically, admitting to and learning from failure, can generate. As was highlighted in Chapter 6, learning of any type, while being potentially positive and enjoyable, can also stir up negative emotions in people. The feelings of fear and anxiety that unlearning can generate relate to admitting the limitations to, and giving up, knowledge and practices which may have provided a person with a sense of competence, self-identity and self-esteem.

Research also suggests that admitting to and learning from failure can be an even more difficult process for people to undertake. For example, one of the general conclusions of the Baumard & Starbuck (2005) study examined at the end of the chapter is that people generally don't like admitting to failure. This is partly due to the stigma that can be attached to being involved in or responsible for failure. Thus, Wilkinson & Mellahi (2005) suggest this typically means that failure is a brush to be tarred with rather than something to be admitted and learned from. Cannon & Edmondson's (2005) research suggests that deep psychological factors related to the importance people attach to both sustaining feelings of self-competence and the importance attached to how people's esteem and competence is judged by others help explain why people are unwilling to admit to and learn from failure. Thus they suggest that, *'being held in high regard by other people, especially those with whom one interacts in an ongoing manner, is a strong fundamental human desire, and most people tacitly believe that revealing failure will jeopardize this esteem'*, and that as a consequence, *'most people have a natural aversion to disclosing or even publicly acknowledging failure'* (Cannon & Edmondson 2005, 302).

TIME TO REFLECT ADMITTING TO AND LEARNING FROM FAILURE

In your own experience, is admitting to failure and using it as a positive learning experience uncommon? Can you think of examples of where failure has been regarded in this way and where people have been willing to admit responsibility for failure?

Another general factor which can act as an individual level barrier to unlearning relates to how people may perceive undertaking a process of unlearning as threatening and undermining their self interest through the way it may impact not only their status and esteem, but also the power they possess, and the interests they are trying to pursue. Fundamentally, if people perceive that unlearning threatens to reduce the power they possess, this may inhibit them from doing so. This links to the point made in Chapter 11, in relation to cross-community knowledge processes that was made by Carlile (2002, 2004). Carlile, adopting a practice-based perspective on knowledge, suggested that the way in which people's knowledge is *'invested in practice'* means that they may be reluctant to participate in processes they perceive will threaten their interests through requiring them to adapt and change their knowledge and practices.

The final generic level factor considered here is the way in which cognitive level factors can act as a barrier to unlearning, through blinkering thinking and creating a sense of cognitive myopia and inertia. Nystrom & Starbuck (2003) suggest that unlearning can be conceptualized as a process of cognitive reorientation, in which people need to give up traditional and accepted ways of understanding and embrace the need to develop and utilize new ones. However, people's cognitive structures shape how they see, interpret and understand events. If particular views, values, ideas and practices have been successful in the past people can become (unconsciously) quite attached to them and be unwilling to give them up, and may become unaware how they blinker and constrain how they understand and interpret events. In the vocabulary of the learning literature, this can result in what may have previously been core competencies, evolving into 'competency traps' (Shipton 2006), which trap people in past-focussed ways of understanding the world.

Specific individual barriers to unlearning

This section discusses barriers to unlearning related to particular types or categories of worker. One group of people that are argued to being responsible for organizations creating conditions where people are unwilling to unlearn are top/senior management in organizations (Nystrom & Starbuck 2003; Baumard & Starbuck 2005). Ultimately if an organization has a culture where people are unwilling to admit to failure for fear of being punished, where the questioning of existing ideas is frowned upon, or where experimentation is discouraged, senior management are the ones who are responsible for creating and sustaining these conditions.

Cannon & Edmondson (2005) further suggest that middle management can act as a barrier to unlearning with regard to the analysis of failure. They found that being able

ILLUSTRATION

Blaming others as a defensive routine and barrier to unlearning

Tranfield *et al.*'s (2000) research involved nine qualitative case studies of UK manufacturing companies, all of which had gone through some significant change in the recent past. The main source of research data was semi-structured interviews with a range of staff from different hierarchical levels, and business areas in each company. A critical incident interviewing technique was used, where interviewees were asked to identify and describe their feelings about and understandings of particular change incidents which they regarded as important and/or significant. The analysis of this data identified four defensive routines which acted as barriers to unlearning/learning, and three enabling routines which facilitated unlearning/learning. Two of the defensive routines, diverting upwards and diverting downwards, created a barrier to unlearning/learning by particular groups of workers passing the blame for problems to other groups of workers.

Diverting upwards was a defensive routine utilized by workers or middle managers to blame senior management for problems that could not be dealt with. One specific example related to the introduction of teamworking by a managing director. Part of the objective of doing this was argued to have been explicitly about allowing people to challenge the MD's authority, but in contradiction with this, the teamworking initiative was introduced without consultation. This defensive routine was used by middle managers and workers as a justification for never attempting to change as it was argued the MD would never introduce any change he didn't initiate. The diverting downwards defensive routine, by contrast, was utilized by senior and middle management and provided them with a justification for never attempting to implement change by suggesting that any such attempts would be futile as the workers in their organizations were intransigent and unwilling to embrace any form of change.

1. Based on any work experience, or organizational knowledge you have, are these finger pointing, 'blaming of others' type defensive routines a common barrier to unlearning in organizations?

to facilitate and manage open and positive group discussions on what can be learned from failure is difficult, and requires the utilization of particular inter-personal skills which are frequently lacking in middle managers.

Finally, Tranfield *et al.* (2000), based on an empirical study whose analysis built on Argyris's (1990) work on defensive routines, found that different groups of workers utilized particular defensive routines which acted as barriers to unlearning. Tranfield *et al.* (2000) define routines as 'habits', repetitive patterns of behaviour, which are often unconscious and which have cognitive, behavioural and structural elements to them. Argyris (1990) defined a defensive routine as, 'any policies or actions that prevent organizational players from experiencing embarrassment or threat while preventing the organization from uncovering the causes of the embarrassment or threat in order to reduce or get rid of them.' Defensive routines are thus repeated behaviours which allow people to avoid admitting to and dealing with any limitations that exist in their thinking and/or actions. Tranfield *et al.*'s study identified four specific defensive routines that acted as barriers to unlearning, two of which, as illustrated in the boxed example, relate to particular types of worker.

Organizational level barriers to unlearning

A number of barriers to unlearning, while fundamentally being related to the individual behaviours of workers and managers in organizations, manifest themselves in organizational processes, and thus can be argued to constitute organizational level barriers to unlearning.

Institutional inertia as a barrier to unlearning

Nystrom & Starbuck (2003) suggest that the embedding and institutionalization of knowledge, values and practices in standard operating procedures and specific work practices can create an inertia which makes them difficult to change. Typically, the longer that work practices have been institutionalized, the more they become taken for granted and unquestioned, and the more difficult they become to change as people become unused to questioning the assumptions on which they work, and new staff members become socialized into particular ways of working. The reluctance to accept that such practices may be outdated, and that a process of unlearning and subsequent learning of new routines and practices is necessary is due to a number of the individual level factors just discussed. Fundamentally, people's power, interests, and sense of self-esteem may be embedded in such traditional practices, and accepting that they require adaptation can represent a threat that people attempt to avoid dealing with.

The difficulty of changing established norms, values and practices was an issue discussed in Chapter 6 when the Crossan/Zietsma model of learning processes was examined where it was suggested that exploration based learning (concerned with the development of new knowledge) may conflict with exploitation based learning (concerned with the utilization of existing and established organizational knowledge) as they can challenge and undermine the norms, values and assumptions on which exploitation based learning is founded.

lateral thinking has the potential to endow workers with the capability to contemplate ideas that challenge their existing norms and values. Secondly, Cannon & Edmondson (2005) suggest that investing in training for middle managers in the areas of managing group dynamics, facilitating collaborative learning, and how to carry out blameless discussions can facilitate an organizations ability to unlearn through improving the organization's ability to reflect on and learn from failure.

Changing organizational processes

The third and final general means of enhancing an organization's ability to unlearn is through organizing a range of work practices and processes in particular ways. Firstly, Nystrom & Starbuck (2003) suggest that senior management staff should not surround themselves with 'yes-sayers' and in contrast should encourage staff to express dissenting views. However, they acknowledge that in hierarchically based communications it can be difficult to persuade subordinates to feel comfortable enough to express such views to management. Cannon & Edmondson (2005) also acknowledge that this issue is a potential barrier to unlearning as it can inhibit people from admitting to (and thus learning from) failure and suggest that for staff to feel comfortable and happy doing so, organizations need to create a sense of 'psychological safety' among staff. Two ways they suggest this can be achieved is through not automatically punishing failure, and utilizing 'blameless reporting systems'.

Yet another way of encouraging and facilitating unlearning is deliberately encouraging experimentation amongst staff (Cannon & Edmondson 2005). This involves a willingness on the part of people to deviate from their norms and to try things that they believe may produce sub-optimal results.

Conclusion

One of the key conclusions of the chapter is that despite forgetting and unlearning being neglected topics in the knowledge management literature, they are crucially important to an organization's ability to adapt, change and survive, as well as to its ability to access, develop and utilize new knowledge. Without being able to acknowledge the limitations of existing knowledge, values, norms and practices, and without being prepared and able to give up established knowledge which may have become outdated, organizations are unlikely to be able to change and acquire or develop new knowledge. Thus, arguably, forgetting or unlearning is as important an element of knowledge management as knowledge creation, codification or knowledge sharing processes are.

While the chapter highlighted the different forms of forgetting that can occur in organizations, the central focus was on unlearning, the deliberate forgetting and giving up of established organizational knowledge. While the ability to unlearn is a capability that is extremely useful for organizations to possess, there are a number of reasons which can make people unwilling to do so which can limit an organization's ability to unlearn. These range from the threat to a person's self-esteem that can be associated with having to give up established forms of knowledge, to organizational systems that punish failure, and thus discourage workers from admitting to being involved in and thus potentially learning from failure. Despite these challenges, the chapter concluded by highlighting the range of methods that organizations can utilize to improve their ability to unlearn.

Case study

The inability to learn from failure

Baumard & Starbuck's (2005) analysis of why organizations typically do not learn from failure is based on the analysis of 14 separate failures (seven large and seven small) that occurred within a single European telecommunications company over a period of over 20 years. The data presented in their paper is based on the personal experiences of one of the authors (who had worked for the company) as well as a number of interviews with senior managers.

In general, there was little evidence that much learning had occurred from either the small or large failures that had been experienced. However, more learning was derived from the small failures than from the large ones. The typical reason for this was that people had more individual interests 'at stake' with the small failures. The scale of the large failures meant that they occurred and unfolded over a reasonable time period and involved lots of different people and departments. This meant that it was generally difficult to allocate blame for the failures to any particular people or departments, and that people generally found it easy to avoid learning from such failures by blaming others for them. The large-scale failures were typically regarded as having been caused by either external environmental conditions that no one had control over or who could be blamed for creating, or by external partners involved in collaborative relationships. Further, the large-scale failures were always analysed in isolation, and no connections were made or found between different large failures.

With the small failures that were analysed, the people involved in them were more identifiable, and thus had more 'at stake' in justifying their actions and attempting to avoid taking responsibility for failure. Typically, failures were analysed in ways which did not challenge core beliefs. For example, small failures which challenged core beliefs were often dismissed as unimportant, and evidence contradicting core beliefs was often simply ignored. Finally sometimes failure was attributed as being due to deviating from core beliefs which provided justification for continued maintenance of core beliefs. Fundamentally they argued that there was a 'reciprocal reinforcement' between the core values people possessed and the way failure was interpreted. For example one of the core beliefs in the company was that it should focus on the hardware rather than software aspects of telecommunications technologies. When a new (software-based) business initiative aimed at developing on-line games failed and went bankrupt this was interpreted as reinforcing the core belief that the companies expertise and core competencies were in the area of hardware rather than software.

1. How unique is this case?
2. Is this an example of an organization that is particularly bad at learning from failure, or are these findings relevant to a wide range of organizations?

Source: Baumard, P. & Starbuck, W. (2005). 'Learning from Failures: Why it May Not Happen', *Long Range Planning*, 38/3: 281–298.

 For further information about this journal article visit our Online Resource Centre at www.oxfordtextbooks.co.uk/orc/hislop2e/

Author	Survey details	Survey results
Ruggles (1998)	431 respondents in USA and Europe, conducted in 1997	1. Biggest problem in managing knowledge: 'changing people's behaviour' (56% of respondents) 2. Biggest impediment to knowledge transferral: 'culture' (54% of respondents)
Management review (1999)	1600 respondents in the USA, conducted 1998/99	Three most common problems: 1. 'Getting people to seek best practice' 2. 'Measuring results' 3. 'Getting people to share their knowledge'
KPMG (2000)	423 large organizations from USA, UK, France and Germany	Two most important reasons for the failure of knowledge management initiatives to meet expectations: 1. 'Lack of user uptake due to insufficient communication' (20% of respondents) 2. 'Everyday use did not integrate into normal working day' (19% of respondents)
Pauleen & Mason (2002)	46 respondents in New Zealand from organizations (public and private)	The single largest barrier (identified by 45% of respondents) to knowledge management was culture
Edwards et al. (2003)	25 academics and practitioners involved in KM field	'People' and 'culture' are the most important issues organizations should emphasize in their KM initiatives
KPMG (2003)	Survey of knowledge management practices in 500 companies from the UK, France, Germany and the Netherlands.	Two of the main difficulties with effectively implementing knowledge management initiatives are that: 1. Knowledge management is not a 'daily priority' for people 2. There was a lack of a knowledge sharing culture in organizations

Table 9 Obstacles to the success of knowledge management initiatives

teams, or knowledge processes which span functional or organizational boundaries. Chapter 12 focuses on the topics of power, politics and conflict, which, as will be seen, are under-researched areas in the knowledge management literature. Chapter 13 examines the impact and role of technology in knowledge management initiatives. Chapters 14 and 15 conclude this section and consider the role that culture management, human resource management practices, and the actions and behaviours of leaders in organizations can have in encouraging workers to participate in organizational knowledge management processes.

The Influence of Socio-Cultural Factors in Motivating Workers to Participate in Knowledge Management Initiatives

Introduction

As the topic of knowledge management has matured and evolved, interest in human, cultural and social questions has grown significantly. Thus, the earliest literature (what Scarbrough & Carter 2000 refer to as the 'first generation' literature) typically assumed people would be willing to share their knowledge, and as a consequence neglected to adequately look at how human and socio-cultural factors can influence knowledge sharing attitudes and behaviours. This chapter provides an overview and introduction to these issues through examining the crucial role that a diverse range of social and cultural factors play in shaping the character and dynamics of organizational knowledge management processes.

The importance of their role in shaping knowledge management processes is visible in both survey evidence (see Table 9) and a significant amount of case study evidence on knowledge management initiatives (see, Empson 2001b; Flood *et al.* 2001; Kim & Mauborgne 1998; Morris 2001; Robertson & O'Malley Hammersley 2000). These analyses found that human, social and cultural factors were key determinants of the success or failure of knowledge management initiatives, and that a reluctance by workers to share their knowledge was not uncommon. For example, Lam's (2005) analysis of an Indian software development company's intranet-based knowledge management initiative found that the primary cause of its failure was the nature of the organizational culture, which was highly individualistic and which acted to inhibit workers from sharing knowledge with each other (see more detail on this example in Chapter 14).

What is suggested here is that whatever approach to knowledge management an organization adopts, the motivation of workers to participate in such processes is key to their success. The importance of human agency to the success of knowledge management initiatives flows largely from the character of organizational knowledge. Primarily much organizational knowledge, rather than being explicit in a disembodied form is personal, tacit and embodied in people. Thus, Kim & Mauborgne suggest, *'knowledge is a resource locked in the human mind'* (1998, 323). The sharing and communication of knowledge therefore requires a willingness on the part of those who have it to participate in such processes. Or, as Flood *et al.* (2001, 1153) suggest, *'the tacit knowledge . . . employees possess may be exploited only if these workers decide to part with this knowledge on a voluntary basis.'*

In exploring this topic the chapter begins by conceptualizing the decision workers face regarding whether to participate in knowledge management initiatives as being comparable to a 'public good dilemma'. After this, the next two sections examine how the context in which most knowledge management initiatives occur shapes workers' attitudes to knowledge management processes by influencing the nature of the relationship between employers/managers and workers, and also inter-personal relations between workers. The fourth and fifth sections look at the role of inter-personal trust and how a worker's sense of belonging to and identity with work groups shapes their willingness to codify and share knowledge with colleagues. The chapter closes by examining the (at this time inconclusive and limited) evidence which suggests that personality can shape a person's general proclivity to share knowledge with others.

The share/hoard dilemma

The decision workers face regarding whether to participate in knowledge related activities has been compared to a classical public good dilemma, with the knowledge workers have access to in their organizations being considered a public good (Dyer & Nobeoka 2000; Cabrera & Cabrera 2002; Fahey *et al.* 2007; Renzl 2008). A public good is a shared resource which members of a community, or network can benefit from, regardless of whether they contributed to it or not, and whose value does not diminish through such usage. Collective organizational knowledge resources are thus a public good as anyone can utilize them whether they have contributed to their development or not. In such situations there is thus the potential for people to 'free-ride', by utilizing such resources but never contributing to their development. The dilemma for the worker is that there are potentially positive and negative consequences to both sharing knowledge and contributing to the public good, and hoarding knowledge and acting as a free-rider. Thus in deciding how to act in such situations workers are likely to attempt to evaluate the potential positive and negative individual consequences of sharing or hoarding knowledge.

TIME TO REFLECT KNOWLEDGE AS A PUBLIC GOOD?

If a public good is a shared resource whose value does not diminish through use, to what extent can knowledge be considered a public good? Does the use of shared knowledge diminish or affect its value? Is there a risk that sharing it with large numbers of people may reduce its value?

Knowledge sharing	Advantages	• Intrinsic reward of process of sharing • Group/organizational level benefits (such as improved group performance) • Material reward (financial or non-financial) • Enhanced individual status
	Disadvantages	• Can be time consuming • Potentially giving away a source of power and expertise to others
Knowledge hoarding (free riding)	Advantages	• Avoids risk of giving away and losing a source of power/status
	Disadvantages	• Extent of knowledge may not be understood or recognized

Table 9.1 The potential advantages and disadvantages to workers of sharing their knowledge

Some of the main potential benefits to workers of knowledge sharing are that doing so may be intrinsically rewarding, that there may be benefits at the group level (such as enhanced team or organizational performance), that there is some material reward (such as a pay bonus, or a promotion), or that a person's status as an expert becomes enhanced (see Table 9.1). However, the negative consequences of contributing knowledge are that, firstly, doing so may be time consuming. Secondly, there is the risk that workers are 'giving away' a source of individual power and status. Finally, there are also the rewards/benefits of hoarding to be accounted for. While the benefit of hoarding knowledge (free-riding) is that the worker avoids the risk of giving away knowledge, and the power and status that may accompany it, a potential negative consequence is that by doing so they never receive full recognition for what they do know.

There is some evidence in the knowledge management literature that people consider such issues and that their knowledge behaviours are shaped by such factors, with a number of studies finding that people's concerns about negative consequences from knowledge sharing actively inhibited them from participating in knowledge management initiatives (Empson 2001b; Lam 2005; Ardichvili *et al*. 2003; Martin 2006; Mooradian *et al*. 2006; Renzl 2008).

More specifically, how workers' considerations of the potential power and status effects of participating in organizational knowledge management initiatives shape their willingness to do so can be illustrated by the following two examples, one where workers were willing to share their knowledge, and one where they were not. Morris (2001) examined a knowledge management initiative in a management consultancy firm, which is examined in more detail later in the chapter. He found that the consultants examined were happy to contribute some of their knowledge to their employer's knowledge codification project as they perceived that doing so would not jeopardize crucial elements of their specialist knowledge and expertise, and that they could thus contribute knowledge to the project yet simultaneously retain the status/power they derived from the part of their knowledge which remained tacit. Willman *et al*.'s (2001) analysis of the knowledge sharing behaviours of some traders in London's financial markets by contrast found evidence of knowledge hoarding, where traders often refrained from codifying elements of their tacit knowledge, due to the financial benefits and status they believed they could derive from personally retaining, or 'hoarding' it.

A potential limitation of this way of conceptualizing worker's knowledge sharing/hoarding decisions is that it presents an over-rational view of how people think and act. Fundamentally, workers' behaviour and decisions are not only shaped by rational calculation. Spender (2003) develops an analysis which suggests that issues of emotion also shape people's decision making processes. For Spender, emotions affect how people think and act when they have to deal with situations beyond their control and when uncertainty exists. The importance of the linkage between emotion and uncertainty is

ILLUSTRATION

Fear inhibiting knowledge sharing

Empson (2001b) studied knowledge sharing behaviours in the immediate aftermath of some mergers. She examined three mergers involving accounting and management consultancy firms in the UK. She found that in all three merged organizations there was a strong unwillingness among staff to share knowledge with new colleagues, with the emotion of fear having a significant influence. In all three mergers staff typically retained a strong identity with their pre-merger organizations and colleagues. Further, they also had negative opinions on the character and quality of the knowledge possessed by new colleagues from what had prior to the merger been competitor organizations. In this context people's unwillingness to share knowledge with new post-merger colleagues was shaped by the twin fears of exploitation and contamination. The fear of exploitation was that due to the perceptions that new colleagues possessed knowledge of an inferior quality any knowledge exchange would involve people giving away valuable knowledge and receiving something of limited value in return. The fear of contamination was that not only would such knowledge exchanges result in the acquisition of knowledge of inferior quality, but that any attempt to integrate it with their existing knowledge would result in their knowledge and expertise becoming contaminated. However, importantly, these fears were not based on any objective analysis of the knowledge of new colleagues, it was a purely subjective, emotional reaction to having to collaborate with people who had until the merger been regarded as competitors in possession of inferior expertise. Empson concluded by suggesting that greater account requires be taken of how such factors shape the way people act and think in organizations.

1. How typical or untypical is this situation?

2. How important is the role of subjective factors in workers' decision-making processes?

that uncertainty is argued to be a fundamental feature of organizational life. Spender suggests that the idea of emotion, uncertainty and the limits to a person's knowledge are less compatible with the objectivist epistemology, which emphasizes objective knowledge, and is more compatible with the practice-based epistemology, which acknowledges and emphasizes the tacit, personal and subjective nature of knowledge (see Chapters 2 and 3). From this perspective, there is always a subjective and personal element to a worker's knowledge, with it being impossible for workers to possess purely objective knowledge isolated from personal opinion.

In studies of knowledge management initiatives, the emotion of fear has been highlighted by a number of writers as inhibiting people from participating in knowledge management initiatives, with the workers studied fearing a number of things including a loss of status and power, the loss of their jobs, and a fear of ridicule, related to concerns that sharing knowledge may reveal its limitations to others (Ardichvili *et al.* 2003; Newell *et al.* 2007; Renzl 2008).

In understanding the socio-cultural factors which shape workers' willingness to participate in organizational knowledge management initiatives it is also important to take account of the context in which such action takes place, as this shapes workers' relations with colleagues and their managers/employers, and as a consequence influences workers' knowledge sharing/hoarding decisions. The next section looks at the worker–manager relationship in the context of the employment relationship.

The context of the employment relationship: employer–employee relations in business organizations

The focus in this section is narrowly on one specific type of organization: private business organizations operating in capitalist markets. While the analysis here is of limited use in understanding the manager/employee relationship in other types of organization, such as public sector or voluntary organizations, it is arguable that the vast majority of knowledge management initiatives occur within private business organizations.

Much analysis in the knowledge management literature portrays the knowledge possessed by an organization's workforce as an economic asset which is owned by the employing organization, and which they have the power to manage. However, the knowledge that workers have can also be conceptualized as belonging to them rather than their employer. From this perspective, while workers may apply, develop and use their knowledge towards the achievement of organizationally directed goals and objectives, the knowledge is fundamentally the workers, to use as, when, where, how and if they want. This highlights the potential tension between workers and the organizations they work for over who owns and controls their knowledge, and points towards an important factor which may inhibit the willingness of workers to share their knowledge. This tension is neatly summed up by Scarbrough, who suggests that,

> '*knowing* as an active, lived experience is in a constant state of tension *with knowledge* as a commodity within firms and markets.' (1999, 6, emphasis in original)

Arguably, the origin of this tension is the intrinsic character of the employment relationship in private business organizations. Firstly, the employment relationship involves organizational management acting as the mediating agents of shareholders and typically places workers in a subordinate position, having no ability to shape corporate objectives and with one of management's key roles being to achieve their shareholder's objectives (for profit, market share etc.) through controlling and directing workers' efforts (Contu & Willmott 2003; Coopey 1998; Tsoukas 2000). The issue of power in the employment relationship is returned to and examined in more detail in Chapter 12. Secondly, embedded in the employment relationship is the potential for conflict between the interests of managers/shareholders and workers.

In the context of workers' knowledge this tension relates not only to who 'owns' an employee's knowledge, but how and for what purposes such knowledge is used (see Table 4.1). For example, while management may perceive that it is the interests of the organization to encourage workers to codify their knowledge, workers may be reluctant to do so if they feel that such efforts will negatively affect them through diminishing their power and/or status. Such concerns explain the reluctance of some experienced middle and senior managers in the UK based pharmaceutical company studied by Currie & Kerrin (2004) to participate in their organization's knowledge management efforts (which took place in the context of a downsizing initiative) as they were concerned that doing so would make it easier for their employer to get rid of them and replace them by younger, less experienced staff. These feelings were expressed by one manager as follows,

> 'The experience I have built up over the years is knowledge the organization needs. They have to keep me if they want to benefit from my years of experience. They can't replace me with a young kid and I'm certainly not going to help them do so by giving away to a young kid what I've learned through my years of experience.' (p. 21)

Such concerns by workers therefore mean that they may not automatically participate in organizational knowledge management processes if they perceive there to be negative personal consequences from doing so.

One further indication that worker can perceive there to be differences between their interests and opinions, and those of their managers relates to occasions/situations where they have been reluctant to express particular views. Both Hayes & Walsham (2000) and Ciborra & Patriotta (1998) found that concerns held by a number of workers about the visibility of their opinions to senior management actively inhibited them from participating in electronic knowledge exchange forums. These concerns were related to how this information/knowledge might be used, or interpreted by senior managers. For example, Ciborra & Patriotta (1998, 50) showed that in one of the groupware systems they studied contribution levels changed dramatically following comments put on the system by a *'very senior manager'*. Their research showed that *'[t]his "intrusion" . . . provoked a panic reaction amongst employees and contributed to a freeze in the use of the system for some months.'* Primarily in both studies, workers were loath to express opinions which

ILLUSTRATION

Tensions over the ownership of knowledge

Morris (2001) examined a knowledge codification project undertaken by a management consultancy. He found the codification project was significantly dependent on the consultants taking an active and willing part in the codification process. Morris suggests that this project represented an attempt by the company to assert its 'property rights' over the knowledge of its workers, to establish a sense of organizational ownership over it. In this case the workers were willing to participate in the project, but this was because they considered the codification project to have significant limitations. Ultimately the workers perceived that any attempt to codify their knowledge was likely to be partial and that they could thus participate in the project while simultaneously retaining key aspects of their knowledge that sustained their power and importance in the organization.

1. If the workers had perceived that it may have been possible for the organization to codify significant and important elements of their knowledge, would their attitude to participating in the project have been different?

might be seen as not complying with managerial perspectives in forums which were transparent and widely used.

It is also useful to acknowledge that factors other than the employment relationship affect a worker's relationship with their employer and can shape their knowledge sharing attitudes. Kim & Mauborgne (1998) suggest that 'procedural justice' represents one such factor. Procedural justice represents the extent to which organizational decision making processes are fair, with fairness being related to how much people are involved in decision making, the clarity of communication regarding why decisions are made, as well as a clarity of expectations. Kim & Mauborgne (1998), based on a small study of some senior managers in American corporations, suggest that the willingness of workers to share their knowledge can be related to whether they perceived a sense of '*procedural justice*' to exist in their organization. They suggest that when all these factors are in place workers will feel valued for their intellectual capabilities and skills. Kim & Mauborgne argue that making workers feel valued can impact on attitudes towards knowledge sharing, '*when*

TIME TO REFLECT 'VISIBILITY' AND BEHAVIOUR

How typical are the findings of Hayes & Walsham and Ciborra & Patriotta? If workers are aware that their knowledge and values will be visible to senior management are they likely to censor or modify how they act and what they say?

What level of equity do workers expect from the organizations they work in? For example, with regards to involvement in decision-making, what type of decisions, and what levels of involvement do workers regard as fair?

they felt that their ideas and person were recognized through fair process, they were willing to share their knowledge and give their all . . .' (1998, 332). Conversely they argue that when workers do not believe procedural justice exists, workers are likely to hoard their knowledge, and be less willing to participate in team based cooperative work.

The ubiquity of conflict in business organizations and its impact on knowledge processes

A general weakness of the mainstream knowledge management literature is that issues of conflict, power and politics are generally neglected (exceptions being Contu & Willmott 2003; Currie & Kerrin 2004; Marshall & Rollinson 2004: Storey & Barnett 2000; Willem & Scarbrough 2006; Yanow 2004). However, such factors arguably can have a significant influence on the character and dynamics of knowledge processes in organizations. The previous section has highlighted how the potential for conflict between workers and their managers/employers can shape people's willingness to participate in organizational knowledge processes. This section shows how inter-personal and inter-group conflict in organizations also shapes these processes.

The purpose of this section is to highlight the important role that inter-personal and inter-group conflict can have on knowledge processes in organizations. Primarily, the actual or perceived differences of interest between individuals or groups in knowledge management projects may affect attitudes to participating in such activities. The analysis of how such factors influence organizational knowledge processes is returned to and developed in Chapter 12 by adding the issue of power into the analysis.

The contemporary knowledge literature is full of examples of where such conflicts have affected attitudes to knowledge sharing (Currie & Kerrin 2004; Empson 2001b; Hislop 2003; Newell *et al.* 2000). The Empson (2001b) example presented earlier showed how conflict and differing perspectives in a post-merger situation between staff from the pre-merged companies significantly shaped the dynamics of knowledge processes, with people being unwilling to share knowledge with their new colleagues. Hislop (2003) examined a number of case studies where organizational change was inhibited by a lack of willingness among staff to share knowledge across functional boundaries. This unwillingness to participate in cross functional knowledge sharing was suggested to be partly due to a history of inter-functional conflict and rivalry (a similar situation is examined in the end of chapter case study). Other studies illustrate how issues of power and politics are intimately linked with processes of knowledge sharing. For example, Willem & Scarbrough (2006) in looking at the relationship between social capital and knowledge

Can you think of an example from your own experience where there was inter-personal, or inter-group conflict with regards to the sharing and utilization of some knowledge? What was the basis of the conflict?

sharing found that what they referred to as 'instrumental social capital' was often used politically through a very selective form of knowledge sharing. Further Hislop *et al.* (2000) in the case study analysis of some innovation processes found that knowledge, and personal networks were used by many people as political tools in support of particular objectives. However, as outlined earlier, the relationship between conflict, knowledge, power and politics is explored in Chapter 12.

The typical neglect of conflict (and power and politics) in the mainstream knowledge management literature is largely due to the assumptions of consensus and goal congruence in business organizations that exist in the majority of the knowledge management literature. For example, as outlined in Chapter 1, Schultze & Stabell (2004), borrowing from Burrell & Morgan's (1979) paradigms of social science framework, suggest that one dimension against which the knowledge management literature can be characterized is the extent to which consensus in society and organizations predominates, with their analysis suggesting that the consensus perspective represents the mainstream perspective in the knowledge management literature. This perspective has echoes of Fox's unitarist framework on organizations, where everyone in an organization is assumed to have common interests and shared values (Fox 1985).

However, such a perspective on organizations can be challenged by evidence and analysis which suggests the opposite, that conflict is an inherent and unavoidable feature of business organizations. A radical version of this argument, similar to that developed in the previous section, can be found in knowledge management literature adopting what Schultze & Stabell (2004) label a dissensus perspective (see Figure 1.3) and suggests that the potential for conflict between management and workers is an inevitable part of the employment relationship. A less radical version of this argument aligns with what Fox (1985) labelled the pluralist perspective on organizations, where organizations are regarded as a coalition of different interest groups acting in a coordinated way. Marshall & Brady (2001, 103), reflecting such a perspective, refer to the '*frequent organizational reality of divergent interests, political struggles and power relations*'. Empirical support for this perspective can also be found in the work of Buchanan (Buchanan 2008; Buchanan & Badham 1999), where political behaviour has been found to be a common feature of organizational life.

However, the importance of taking account of how conflict (and power and politics) shapes people's willingness to participate in knowledge management processes is not just due to the fact that conflict is an inherent/common feature of organizational life. As will be shown in Chapter 12, it is also because the close inter-relationship that exists between power and knowledge means that knowledge can be used in a highly political way and is a resource people commonly make use of in dealing with situations of conflict.

Inter-personal trust

This section highlights the crucial role that inter-personal trust can have in shaping people's attitudes to participating in organizational knowledge processes. As will be seen, it has been generally found that the lower the level of trust a person has in someone else, the less willing they will be to share knowledge with them. However, this section also highlights the complexity of the concept of trust, and thus after providing a general definition of it and outlining how levels of trust affect attitudes to knowledge sharing, the concept will be unpacked through considering both the distinction between trust and a person's 'propensity to trust' as well as the typologies of distinctive types of trust that have been developed.

Interest in the topic of trust is not restricted to the knowledge management literature. In fact there has been an enormous amount of interest in it in a number of areas, for example, with trust being argued to underpin effective group working, and inter-personal interaction (Jarvenpaa & Leidner 1999; Maznevski & Chudoba 1999; Meyerson *et al.* 1996; Nandhakumar 1999; Newell & Swan 2000). The crucial role of trust in shaping people's willingness to participate in knowledge related processes has also been recognized by a growing number of writers (Abrams *et al.* 2003; Andrews & Delahaye 2000; Ardichvili *et al.* 2003; Davenport & Prusak 1998; Levin & Cross 2004; Mooradian *et al.* 2006; Newell *et al.* 2007; Roberts 2000). Fundamentally, a lack of trust between individuals is likely to inhibit the extent to which people are willing to share knowledge with each other. To understand why this is the case it is useful to formally define what trust is and how it shapes the character of inter-personal relationships.

Trust can be defined as, '*the willingness of a party to be **vulnerable** to the actions of another party based on the expectation that the other will perform a particular action important to the trustor*' (Mooradian *et al.* 2006, 524, emphasis added). Therefore, if trust exists a person is likely to act on faith by the unilateral provision of resources, information etc. (in this context giving knowledge), with the expectation that this action will be reciprocated at some point in the future. Thus trust involves an element of risk, where a person makes themselves vulnerable to another by providing knowledge prior to receiving anything in return (with one risk being that a person acts opportunistically and doesn't provide anything in return). The existence of trust in a person helps mediate and reduce the perception of risk people experience, and provides a level of confidence that their action will be reciprocated.

Definition   Trust

Trust refers to the belief people have about the likely behaviour of others, and the assumption that they will honour their obligations (not acting opportunistically). A trusting relationship is based on an expectation of reciprocity, or mutual benefit.

However, sharing knowledge on the basis of trust arguably involves an unavoidable element of uncertainty, and can thus be a process which produces and is shaped by emotion (see earlier section in this chapter for a discussion on the relationship between uncertainty and emotion). Knowledge sharing can be a time consuming and uncertain process. Not only is there uncertainty whether someone will reciprocate a trust-based action, but even when there is reciprocation there will be an element of uncertainty regarding the utility of the knowledge received. Acting on the basis of trust, due to the uncertainty involved, can therefore generate and produce strong emotions, both positive and negative, with for example, someone feeling anger when their trust has been betrayed, or where someone feels a sense of happiness and joy when a trust-based action is effectively reciprocated.

Research has found trust to be a complex concept. One aspect of this is the distinction that can be made between a person's general propensity to trust others and specific

ILLUSTRATION

The role of perceived trustworthiness in shaping the knowledge sharing decisions of bio-medical scientists

Andrews & Delahaye (2000) conducted a study into what shaped the decisions of some bio-medical scientists from Australia to share knowledge with each other. These scientists were involved in cross-organization collaborative research projects in the bio-medical technology field. They found that the scientist's perceptions of trustworthiness played a key mediating role influencing what knowledge they shared with whom. In the context of their work, knowledge was regarded as a valuable commodity, and thus sharing it casually was regarded as risky, and being cautious about who to share knowledge with was regarded as wise rather than selfish. They found that due to the importance of their personal knowledge and experience to their work, all the scientists undertook a process of conscious reflection prior to sharing knowledge with people, and that without trust existing they were unlikely to share knowledge. One interviewee articulated these feelings by saying,

'If you haven't got trust and confidence then it doesn't matter what else you've put in place, or what other structures you put in place to try and encourage co-operation, it's not going to happen.' (p. 804)

The risks that concerned the scientists from unwise knowledge sharing connected with issues of visibility and ownership. Fundamentally the risk was that in providing someone else with knowledge the receiver may claim ownership of it, and the provider would thus potentially lose both ownership of the knowledge, and visibility in relation to how it was used. The scientist's perceptions of trustworthiness in colleagues mediated such concerns through creating a confidence by the people they shared knowledge with that they would not act in such ways.

instances where trust exists in particular people (Mooradian *et al.* 2006). Mooradian *et al.* conceptualize a person's propensity to trust as being a relatively enduring predisposition they have which is a facet of the personality trait, 'agreeableness', one of the five dimensions in the five factor personality model (see later section in this chapter on the five factor model). Thus the propensity to trust is a *'general willingness to trust others'*, (Mooradian *et al.* 2006, 525) which can vary significantly between people. In contrast, the act of trusting is a specific instance in a particular context and at a particular time, where trust is extended to or developed in a particular entity (person, group, organization . . .). Mooradian *et al.* argue that the greater a person's propensity to trust, the more likely they will be to extend trust to others in specific contexts. As will be discussed later, they examine how a person's propensity to trust is related to knowledge sharing attitudes and conclude that this personality variable can influence people's general willingness to share knowledge with others.

A number of analyses introduce another layer of complexity by suggesting that trust has multiple dimensions and that there is more than one type of trust. For instance Lane (1998) distinguishes between calculative, norm-based and expectation-based trust, Zucker (1986) distinguishes between process-based, characteristic-based and institutionally-based trust, while Wang *et al.* (2006) distinguish between calculus, knowledge and identification-based trust. Further, Meyerson *et al.* (1996) develop the concept of 'swift trust'. Further, this work suggests that each type of trust is developed in quite different ways, and have a complex, mutually interdependent relationship. However, there is inadequate space here to fully describe, compare and contrast these different typologies. Instead, one typology alone is examined to highlight one particular way of conceptualizing trust into different types.

In Newell & Swan's (2000) three-dimensional typology (see Table 9.2), companion-based trust represents typically the strongest form of trust that can exist. This form of trust is developed over time and is built up gradually based on perception of acts of goodwill and generosity. Thus this form of trust cannot develop quickly, and requires extensive interaction to occur between people. Competence-based trust is the second of Newell & Swan's trust types and relates to trust in a person's ability to carry out work tasks. Finally, the third form of trust in Newell & Swan's typology is commitment-based trust, which relates to trust stemming from contractual obligations that a person has

Type of trust	Description of trust
Companion	Trust based on judgments of goodwill or friendship, built up over time
Competence	Trust based on perception of others' competence to carry out relevant tasks
Commitment	Trust stemming from contractual obligations

Table 9.2 Newell and Swan's three types of trust

Source: from Newell and Swan (2000); see also Newell *et al.* (2007)

made. For example, if someone has made an explicit commitment to help someone, or has committed to a formal contract to provide some resources or services, this can result in a form of commitment-based trust developing (based on the expectation that if an explicit promise has been made this means there is a reasonable chance the person is likely to keep it).

Typically, inter-personal relations at work with colleagues will involve elements of all three forms of trust. Thus, if two colleagues who have known each other for a number of years have to collaborate in a particular project team there may be an element of companion and competence based trust due to firstly the personal relationship that may exist between them, and their confidence in each others ability from knowing how they have performed on previous projects. Further, there may be an element of commitment-based trust due to promises that may have been made to do particular tasks within particular timescales. However, inter-personal trust may also be based on one element alone.

The final issue touched on here is the fact that trust can be developed not only in individual people, but also in groups, teams or organizations, and that these types of trust can have an equally important influence on a person's willingness to share knowledge with others. For example, Renzl (2008) found evidence that the greater the extent to which workers trusted their managers the more likely they would be to have a positive attitude to sharing knowledge with colleagues. Ardichvili *et al.* (2003) reached similar conclusions based on their analysis of what factors shaped workers willingness to contribute knowledge within a virtual community of practice. They talked about institution-based trust, which referred to the extent to which people trusted the organization to provide a working environment conducive to positive knowledge sharing and where people were unwilling to act opportunistically or excessively selfishly. They found that workers were likely to contribute knowledge to the virtual community of practice when this form of trust existed, as they were confident that others wouldn't use this knowledge opportunistically. Finally, Usoro *et al.* (2007)—see following section, and the communities of practice literature more generally (see Chapter 10)—suggest that the greater a person's level of trust in and identification with a particular work group or community, the more likely they will be to be willing to share knowledge with others in that community/group.

The issue of trust links to themes examined in a number of the remaining chapters in this section of the book. Firstly it is relevant in Chapter 10 on communities of practice where the nature of inter-personal relations in communities of practice, where groups of people have shared identity and values, facilitates the development of high levels of trust among community members, which has positive consequences for intra-community knowledge sharing. Trust is also examined in Chapter 11 which examines group based working where people do not have shared values and identity, which makes the development of trust more difficult. Finally, issues of trust are also engaged with in Chapter 13 on the role of information technology in knowledge management processes, where it is suggested that in situations where people have to collaborate and communicate extensively via electronic means, and where opportunities for face-to-face interaction are limited, that the development of high levels of inter-personal trust may be difficult.

Group identity

This section examines how issues of personal identity can affect the extent to which and ways in which workers participate in organizational knowledge processes. As will be seen, research has shown that the extent to which people feel a part of and identify with their organization, a project team, a work group or a community of practice can significantly shape their willingness to participate in knowledge processes. For example, Chapter 6 showed how knowledge intensive workers can identify strongly with the clients they work for, with Ravishankar & Pan (2008) presenting an example from an Indian IT consultancy firm of where the sense of identity some staff had with the client firm made them unwilling to participate in their employer's knowledge management initiative due to concerns that they would give away valuable client knowledge to colleagues.

Further, the extensive literature on communities of practice (Roberts 2006) suggests that when people feel a sense of identity with a community this facilitates the development of trust with other community members and is likely to create a positive attitude towards sharing knowledge with other community members. For example, Usoro et al. (2007), who examined a virtual, IT-mediated community of practice in a Fortune 500 global IT company found that people's level of community trust was positively related to knowledge sharing.

Finally, a number of studies have shown how worker's identity with the particular functional group or business unit that they work in can influence their knowledge sharing patterns, with it being common for people who have a strong sense of identity with their function or business unit being relatively unwilling to share knowledge with people from outside of these areas (Hislop 2003; Newell et al. 2000). For example, Currie & Kerrin's (2003) study of the sales and marketing business of a UK based pharmaceutical company found that the existence of strong sub-cultures within the sales and marketing divisions created an unwillingness among staff to share knowledge across these functional boundaries (see more details on this case in the end of chapter example).

All this research thus suggests that one of the key effects of a worker's sense of identity is to influence who they are and are not willing to share knowledge with. An issue that connects with the theme of trust, and which is examined in more detail in Chapter 11 is how a lack of shared identity and values between people can inhibit the development of trust, and thus make knowledge sharing between such people more complex and difficult. The issues touched on here will be examined more extensively in Chapter 10 which looks at the characteristics of knowledge processes within communities of practices, where people have a strong sense of shared identity, and in Chapter 11, which examines knowledge processes where people do not have such a strong sense of shared identity, such as in cross functional, or multi-disciplinary team working.

Personality

The final factor considered which may shape workers' attitudes to participating in knowledge management processes is not related to the socio-cultural characteristics of the work environment, and is concerned with personality. Fundamentally, some research suggests that people with certain personality traits may have a more positive attitude to knowledge sharing than others. However, in general, this is a very under-explored topic in the knowledge management literature.

There are a couple of studies in this area that have concluded that certain personality traits did appear to be positively related to knowledge sharing attitudes. Both the studies in this area (Cabrera & Cabrera 2005; Mooradian *et al.* 2006) make use of the five factor personality model. This personality model, which is becoming the dominant way of conceptualizing personality, suggests that human personality can be understood to be made up of five broad traits: openness, conscientiousness, extraversion, agreeableness, and neuroticism (see Table 9.3).

However, despite both these studies using this model they came to different conclusions about which personality traits are related to positive knowledge sharing attitudes. Thus, Cabrera & Cabrera's (2005) research found that the 'openness to change' personality variable was related to a positive knowledge sharing attitude. By contrast, Mooradian *et al.*'s (2006) study found a link between 'agreeableness' and positive knowledge sharing attitudes. Further, both these studies are based on surveys conducted in a single company, thus their findings cannot be regarded as generalizable. Therefore research in this area is in its infancy and is inconclusive regarding exactly how personality relates to a person's propensity to share knowledge or their willingness to participate in any organizational knowledge processes.

Trait	Characteristics
Openness (or openness to change)	The extent to which someone is imaginative, creative and curious
Extraversion	The extent to which someone is sociable, talkative, enthusiastic and assertive
Neuroticism	The extent to which someone experiences negative emotions such as anxiety, anger or guilt
Conscientiousness	The extent to which someone is careful, self-disciplined, hardworking, dependable and reliable
Agreeableness	The extent to which someone is generous, trustful, cooperative and forgiving

Table 9.3 Characteristics of the traits in the five factor personality model

3   Have you found trust to be an important factor underpinning attitudes to knowledge shar-
    ing? Have you had any experiences where a lack of trust has inhibited knowledge sharing,
    or where the existence of trust has facilitated it?

4   To what extent is people's behaviour at work (whether concerned with knowledge sharing
    or not) shaped by rationality and decision making, and to what extent is it shaped by
    emotion and subjective feelings?

Suggestions for further reading

1   **W. Lam (2005). 'Successful Knowledge Management Requires a Knowledge Culture:
    A Case Study',** *Knowledge Management Research and Practice,* **3: 206–217.**

    Analyses a failed knowledge management initiative in a case study organization, illus-
    trating the role that organizational culture can play in inhibiting workers from sharing
    their knowledge with each other.

2   **H. Scarbrough (1999). 'Knowledge as Work: Conflicts in the Management of
    Knowledge Workers',** *Technology Analysis and Strategic Management,* **11/1: 5–16.**

    Considers the issues and dilemmas involved in organizations attempting to motivate
    knowledge workers to share their knowledge.

3   **D. Hislop (2003). 'The Complex Relationship Between Communities of Practice
    and the Implementation of Technological Innovations'.** *International Journal of
    Innovation Management,* **7/2: 163–188.**

    Presents a number of case studies illustrating how cross-functional conflicts and antago-
    nisms can inhibit cross-functional knowledge sharing.

4   **S. Newell, G. David, & D. Chand (2007). 'An Analysis of Trust Among Globally
    Distributed Work Teams in an Organizational Setting',** *Knowledge and Process
    Management,* **14/3: 158–168.**

    Highlights the crucial role of inter-personal trust (of different types) in shaping attitudes
    to knowledge sharing within geographically dispersed and culturally diverse work teams.

5   **L. Empson (2001b). 'Fear of Exploitation and Fear of Contamination: Impediments
    to Knowledge Transfer in Mergers Between Professional Service Firms',** *Human
    Relations,* **54/7: 839–862.**

    Detailed case study examining reluctance of workers to share knowledge with new col-
    leagues following a merger.

Take your learning further: Online Resource Centre

Visit the supporting Online Resource Centre for resources which will extend your
understanding of knowledge management in organizations. As well as web links to sites
of interest, the author has provided case studies looking at knowledge management in
virtual and knowledge intensive firms, and in global multinationals. These will help you
with your research, essays and assignments; or you may find these additional resources
helpful when revising for exams.

www.oxfordtextbooks.co.uk/orc/hislop2e/

Communities of Practice

Introduction

In the vast literature on knowledge management that has been produced, the concept of 'communities of practice' has been one of the most popular. For example, Edwards *et al.* (2003), in a survey of KM academics and practitioners, found that it represented the second most important concept developed in this literature. The popularity of the term is largely because communities of practice are argued to both facilitate inter-personal knowledge sharing (for example, allowing women education managers to increase their opportunities to gain promotion through developing their knowledge and networks—see Roan & Rooney 2006), and can support and underpin innovation processes in organizations (Cross *et al.* 2006). Thus, a growing number of writers suggest that developing communities of practice can be key to the success of knowledge management initiatives (for example Bate & Roberts 2002; Ward 2000; Wenger 1998; Wenger *et al.* 2002).

Communities of practice are informal groups of people who have some work related activity in common. As will be seen, the communities of practice literature is most closely associated with the practice-based perspective on knowledge, as it assumes that the knowledge people have is embedded in and inseparable from the (collectively based) activities that people carry out. The informality of these communities stems from the fact that they emerge from the social interactions that are a necessary part of the work activities that people undertake. Further, while most of the literature on communities of practice focuses on organizationally specific communities, communities can span organizational boundaries (Brown & Duguid 2001). For example, Gittelman & Kogut (2003) conceptualize the researchers involved in the biotechnology industry in the USA as constituting a community of practice.

This chapter has a very specific focus, discussing and analysing the *internal dynamics* of communities of practice. The character and dynamics of inter community knowledge processes are explored in Chapter 11. Chapters 10 and 11 can therefore be read together, as they both examine the dynamics of group based knowledge processes. The reason for doing this in two chapters rather than one is that, as will be discussed more fully in Chapter 11, the character and dynamics of intra and inter community knowledge processes are qualitatively different. Further, the dynamics of knowledge processes within 'virtual'

Communities of practice: origins, features and dynamics

The community of practice concept is based on two central premises: the practice-based perspective on knowledge, and the group based character of organizational activity. The primary relevance of the practice-based perspective on knowledge stems from the assumption in the communities of practice literature that knowing and doing are inseparable, as undertaking specific tasks requires the use and development of embodied knowledge. Thus, Brown & Duguid (1991, 43) argue that *'learning-in-working is an occupational necessity'* and that carrying out work activities also involves the *'situated production of understanding'* (1991, 44).[2]

The second major premise is that organizational activities are typically collective, involving the co-ordinated interaction of groups of workers (see for example, Barnes 1977; Brown & Duguid 1998; Gherardi *et al.* 1998; McDermott 1999). Thus, one common feature of virtually every type of work imaginable, from office cleaning to management consulting, is that they involve an element of co-ordination and interaction with co-workers, subordinates and/or supervisors.

Therefore, while the knowledge that members of a community of practice have and develop is highly personal, there is an extent to which much of this knowledge is simultaneously shared within a community. From an objectivist perspective on knowledge, the common knowledge shared by the workers in a community of practice is collective/group knowledge (with both tacit and explicit elements—see Table 2.3 earlier).

Lave & Wenger (1991), who are typically acknowledged as being instrumental in the development and elaboration of the community of practice concept, define them as a community of practitioners within which situational learning develops, which results in the community developing '. . . *a set of relations among persons, activity and the world'* (p. 98). Extrapolating from this definition communities of practice can be seen to have three defining characteristics, all of which flow from the community members involvement in some shared activities (Table 10.2). Firstly, participants in a community possess, and develop a stock of common, shared knowledge. Secondly, communities typically also develop shared values and attitudes, a common 'world-view'. Boland & Tenkasi (1995) referred to the process of developing and communicating such views, *'perspective making'*

Characteristics of a community of practice
1. Body of common knowledge/practice
2. Sense of shared identity
3. Some common, or overlapping values

Table 10.2 Generic characteristics of communities of practice

---

2. Brown & Duguid take this quotation from Orr (1990).

(see Chapter 3). Finally, and equally importantly, members of communities also possess a sense of communal identity (Brown & Duguid 2001). These elements of a community develop not only through the physical activities involved in collectively carrying out the communities tasks, but also through language and communication. Thus, for example, stories, or specialist jargon can be regarded as a part of the collective knowledge of the group, whose use by group members contributes to their sense of collective identity and shared values.

A useful way to illustrate these characteristics is through an example. Trowler & Turner (2002) illustrate how the deaf studies group of an English university constitutes a community of practice. This group consisted of three hearing academics (who are fluent in sign language) and three deaf academics. The shared practice of this community constituted both the teaching of the deaf studies curriculum, as well as research conducted by the group on a range of issues affecting deaf people. This group had a strong sense of collective identity, as well as a belief in a common goal (contributing to the education of deaf people and their integration in society, raising awareness of the social issues affecting deaf people, and furthering knowledge on the issues which affect deaf people through carrying out research). While the group communicated both internally and externally in both sign language and English, the shared language of the group was arguably sign language. The study also showed how the use of English language, and the English language protocols embedded in certain formal meetings and group forums, represented a form of power that significantly disadvantaged the deaf members of the working group.

Communities of practice are highly dynamic, evolving as new members become absorbed into a community, as existing members leave, and as the knowledge and practices of the community adapts with changing circumstances. Learning, and knowledge evolution are therefore inherent and fundamental aspects of the dynamics of communities of practice, which helps explain why one of the main contexts in which the community of practice concept originated and developed was in the organizational learning literature.

Lave and Wenger (1991) used the term 'legitimate peripheral participation' to characterize the process by which people learn and become socialized into being a member of a community. This process is based on 'triadic' group relations involving masters (or 'old timers'), young masters (or 'journeymen') and apprentices (or 'newcomers'). Apprentices learn from watching and communicating with the master and other members of the community, and start as peripheral members, participating initially in relatively straightforward tasks. However, over time, as the apprentices become competent with these basic skills, they gradually become introduced to more complex tasks. Legitimate peripheral participation is thus the process by which newcomers to a community acquire the

TIME TO REFLECT LANGUAGE AND COMMUNITIES OF PRACTICE?

Are you or have you ever been a member of a community of practice? What role, if any, did language, in the form of specialist jargon and shared stories play in the development and reinforcement of the community?

ILLUSTRATION

Legitimate peripheral participation among naval quartermasters

Hutchins (1993) describes the process of learning and socialization that apprentice naval quartermasters undergo (this study is also described and analysed by Fox 2000). Naval quartermasters are responsible for maintaining a continuous log of a ship's position. While much of this work is relatively solitary, key aspects (such as entering and leaving port) require a team of quartermasters to work together. Learning to be a quartermaster typically takes about one year. The preferred way that established quartermasters like to train new ones is through on the job learning. Over the year that it takes to learn to be a quartermaster, newcomers begin by doing relatively routine and straightforward tasks (such as taking bearings). Once such skills have been mastered, apprentices gradually become allowed to do more complex tasks, such as integrating all the different readings together, and interpreting the information. By the end of the year they will have become more central, experienced and established members of their community, and will be in a position to train other new apprentices.

1. What is the potential for conflict between the established quartermasters and the apprentices?

2. Is it possible that the established quartermasters may feel resentful towards and threatened by the apprentices, who they may regard as providing a potential challenge to their status and authority? Further, can such tensions be managed and minimized?

knowledge required to be a community member, through gradually increasing levels of *participation* in community activities, during which time they simultaneously move from being *peripheral* members of the community to become more central and *legitimate* members of it. Informal learning from other group members is a key element of this process, or as Trowler & Turner (2002, 242) suggest,

'learning to become an organizational member is far more a question of socialization than of formal learning . . .'.

Communities of practice and the organizational knowledge base

The communities of practice literature, building from insights developed using the practice-based perspective on knowledge (see Chapter 3) suggests that the knowledge base of organizations can be conceptualized as a '*community-of-communities*' (Brown &

Duguid 1991), or more poetically, a *'constellation of communities'* (Gherardi & Nicolini 2002; Ward 2000). Thus, rather than the organizational knowledge base being a coherent and unitary body of knowledge, it can more accurately be conceptualized as fragmented, being constituted by a diverse range of localized bodies of specialist knowledge possessed by specific communities. While the knowledge base of these communities is overlapping and interdependent, with an element of common knowledge existing (Kogut & Zander 1992), much of the knowledge contained within these organizational communities is localized and specialized in nature, having limited relevance beyond its specific context of application.

However, the character and structure of organizational knowledge bases varies significantly between organizations (see for example Empson 2001b; Lam 1997). This is because, as Brown & Duguid suggest (1998, 98), *'the distribution of knowledge in an organization . . . as a whole, reflects the social division of labour.'* Thus the way in which work activities are structured within organizations will affect the character of the organizational knowledge base.

ILLUSTRATION

Communities of practice and the structuring of work

Business in UK-Pension, one of the UK's largest and most recognizible pensions companies had traditionally been structured around their two main product areas, pensions and life assurance. These divisions were run as separate businesses, with their own, distinct management structures, staff, business processes, IT systems and customer bases. Further, there had historically been little interaction between them. Communication only occurred within the divisions, and never between them. This resulted in the development of two separate and specialized knowledge communities, which only had knowledge of their own customers, IT systems and working practices.

One illustration of the extent of this was in the fact that there was no sharing of customer information. Neither division had any straightforward way of finding out whether any of their customers had business in the other division, and it was impossible for customers with products in both divisions to get a single, summarized statement of their total portfolio. Further, the autonomy of these divisions was such that the evolution and development of their working practices, the upgrading of their IT systems etc., was done purely on the basis of intra-divisional considerations. For example, each division had its own separate IT systems and working practices for using them. These systems and working procedures were so different that administrative staff in the pensions division would not have been able to use the IT systems in the life assurance division without substantial training, and vice versa.

ILLUSTRATION

A scientific community resisting culture change

Breu & Hemingway (2002) studied a large European scientific research organization, Alpha, which had recently been privatized. Following this privatization the scientists had been highly resistant to the introduction of a new, commercially focussed business culture. The scientists in Alpha constituted a community of practice as they had the three constituent elements of a community. Firstly, there was a shared, common practice (conducting 'blue sky' research in specialist disciplinary teams). Secondly, the scientists had a common set of values (a belief in the value of scientific research driven by scientific inquiry and the advancement of knowledge). Finally, the scientists in Alpha also had a collective sense of identity (as being professional scientists who were members of both a local and global research community).

The resistance by the scientists in Alpha had a number of sources. One factor was the particular change implementation strategy adopted (introducing large scale change rapidly with only limited consultation). However, a large part of the scientists' resistance stemmed from the fact that they interpreted the values of the new economic culture (pursuing research driven by economic goals) as being antithetical to the values of their research community. Further, the scientists refused to change their values, and were able to quite effectively resist the changes through a range of strategies including continuing to pursue work driven by scientific values, recruiting new scientists in ways which perpetuated the existing culture, and developing independent and informal networks for the resourcing of research projects.

Gittelman & Kogut (2003) identified similar tensions in the Unites States biotechnology industry, between producing knowledge for scientific purposes, and knowledge for economic gain.

1. Does this mean that there are inevitable and unavoidable tensions between the commercialization of knowledge for profit, and the development of knowledge for more abstract, scientific purposes?

The diversity of these communities is such that their social and cultural characteristics, and their knowledge sharing dynamics are likely to vary. However, the community of practice literature has only just started to examine and acknowledge this diversity, and thus far, there have been few attempts to systematically compare and contrast the characteristics of different types of community.

The misuse of the community of practice concept

The third issue examined is the potential misuse or misapplication of the community of practice concept. As it has grown in popularity and importance, the concept has been applied and used in a diverse range of contexts. However, in some cases the work groups examined do not appear to possess the attributes of a community of practice. Arguably, fundamental characteristics of communities of practice are their self-initiating, *ad hoc*, organic and non-hierarchical features, however not all the work groups examined that have been described as communities of practice possess them.

For example, Chua (2006) charts the 'rise and fall' of a 'community of practice'. However, the details of the article reveal that the work group which is characterized as a community of practice firstly wasn't self-initiating (it was set up as part of a top down management initiative), secondly, its membership didn't develop and evolve organically, as it was set up by a senior manager who approached various people to join it, and finally, it wasn't a non-hierarchical community of equals as there was a senior manager who managed and controlled it. Cross *et al.* (2006) present an analysis designed to help management improve the performance of the communities of practice in their organizations. However, the advice given, which involves moving communities away from being informal and *ad hoc*, arguably eliminates the features of the work groups which make them a community of practice. Thus, increasingly caution is needed in reading analyses of what are articulated as communities of practice, as whether some of the work group examined constitute communities is open to dispute.

Blinkered and inward looking communities

While the collective sense of identity and values that exist between members of a community can create a bond that may facilitate the development of trust, and knowledge sharing, there are potential negative consequences if such bonds are too strong. For example where too strong a sense of community identity exists this may provide a basis for exclusion, where those not part of the 'community' are ignored, and their knowledge not considered to be relevant or important to the community (Alvesson 2000; Baumard 1999). This can cause communities to become inward looking, and unreceptive to ideas generated outside the community (Brown & Duguid 1998). In such circumstances a community's search processes may be limited rather than extensive, with consequent negative implications for the community's innovativeness (Leonard & Sensiper 1998). See for example Starbuck & Milliken's (1988) examination of the Challenger Space Shuttle disaster, outlined earlier in Chapter 3.

Such communities may not only neglect external ideas, but also people. Communities with a strong sense of identity may become exclusive clubs or 'cliques' (Wenger *et al.* 2002), where membership is tightly controlled, and the factors that define a community's identity may be used to exclude entry to others. Just as with the neglect of external ideas, such practices can result in communities becoming poor at absorbing new, external knowledge and ideas.

TIME TO REFLECT 'NOT INVENTED HERE' SYNDROME

Have you worked as part of a team or community where there has been a hostility or blindness to ideas generated outside of it? If so, did this have any effect on group or organizational performance?

Conclusion

Communities of Practice have been defined as informal groups that have some work activities in common. As a consequence, these communities develop a shared body of common knowledge, a shared sense of collective identity and some overlapping values.

The mainstream knowledge management literature portrays communities of practice as being effective vehicles for knowledge sharing and knowledge creation. Consequently, the existence of effectively operating communities of practice is typically argued to underpin individual and organizational level learning processes, as well as supporting high levels of organizational innovativeness. The effectiveness of communities of practice in this respect occurs for two reasons. Firstly, the existence of common knowledge and a shared system of values makes sharing tacit knowledge easier, as group members have insights into the implicit assumptions and values embedded in each others knowledge. Secondly, the shared knowledge, values and identity which exist also facilitate the development and maintenance of trust based relations, which, as outlined in Chapter 9, creates social conditions conducive to knowledge sharing.

However, the chapter also concluded that the mainstream literature on communities of practice portrays an overly optimistic image of them. To understand why communities of practice have the potential to inhibit as much as facilitate knowledge processes, account needs to be taken of issues of power and conflict within communities, as well as the way that too strong a sense of community identity may inhibit inter-community processes of knowledge sharing. This final conclusion points towards the dynamics of inter-community interaction, which is the topic dealt with in Chapter 11.

Case study

The emergence and disintegration of a community of practice in a web design company

Thompson (2005) analysed the emergence, evolution and disintegration of a community of practice within a small web design company (e-future) that was created as a stand alone company by a global software company. E-future operated as a completely independent entity, with quite distinctive and different norms, values and behaviours to the rest of the corporation. When it was formed it initially had 10 staff, but this grew organically to 40. Thompson's research was a qualitative case study which was based on both interviews with e-future staff, and observations of their workplace.

Thompson conceptualizes communities of practice as having two types of element which help create and sustain a sense of community. These are structural and epistemic elements. Structural elements are boundary objects or artefacts that community members collectively work with and which to some extent symbolize the existence of a community. These objects play a dual role in simultaneously allowing members of a community to develop a sense of collective identity and secondly allowing such communities to differentiate themselves from others. Non-work related examples of such boundary objects are the music, haircuts and clothes that young people can use to symbolize their membership of a particular youth sub-culture. The second core element of communities of practice for Thompson are epistemic elements such as knowledge, ideas, values and norms that are developed in and sustained by a community.

While e-future was set up as a formal organization, staff in it had the autonomy to develop their own ways of working, and it evolved a set of working relations and sense of identity akin to a community of practice. For example, while work within e-future was organized around project teams, people in e-future had a sense of identity as being part of e-future which transcended any project-based identities they had. This sense of group identity was facilitated by the open plan nature of the office space that e-future used, and was developed through and sustained by open and extensive communication between people irrespective of what project teams they worked on.

A number of structural elements also existed which symbolized the values of e-future (which were of fun and creativity) and which further helped cement a sense of community identity amongst e-future staff. These included a very casual dress code, the development and use of non-traditional job titles (such as 'creative spark', 'producer', and 'director'), a physical environment full of leisure equipment such as pool tables, computer games and casual furniture that could be used at any time, artistic installations which symbolized the creativity of the work and the existence of artists in residence.

However, equally importantly in creating the sense of community were the development and existence of some epstemic elements. Primarily, there was an openness and willingness amongst staff to share knowledge with each other, whether they worked on the same projects or not. Creativity was regarded as key, and this was facilitated via extensive interpersonal interaction. This was symbolized by the fuzzy boundary that existed between chargeable project time, and non-chargeable activities, as apparently non-chargeable activities such as discussions among staff often produced ideas that could be utilized on projects. The most visible manifestation of the open culture of knowledge sharing was the 'Doorway' tool. This was a repository for ideas and knowledge that was regarded as a collective, group resource and which all community members were willing and happy to both contribute to and draw upon in doing their work.

However, the community began to dissolve, ironically due to structural interventions by corporate management which were concerned with expanding e-future to build on and maximize the benefits that could be derived from it. However, most of these structural interventions upset and damaged the 'delicate relations' that had sustained e-future's community of practice. One of these changes was the rapid and non-organic growth of the company from 40 to 170 staff, which resulted in a large number of new staff starting to work for e-future at virtually the same time. This produced a sense of them and us with the original staff who constituted the community not accepting the new staff as legitimate members of their community. Other structural interventions had an equally negative impact on community relations. Firstly, e-future's workspace was made accessible to corporate visitors and outsiders which disrupted the ability of e-future staff to continue working in the way they had done traditionally (for example with it becoming difficult to play loud music, which was something that had occasionally been done). Finally, individually based performance targets were introduced when group based targets had been the norm, with these individualized targets undermining people's willingness to share knowledge collectively.

1. How important was the non-organic growth of e-future to the dissolution of its community of practice?

2. Is it possible in such circumstances to preserve and sustain community relations? If so, how?

Source: Thompson, M. (2005). 'Structural and Epistemic Parameters in Communities of Practice', *Organization Science*, 16/2: 151–164.

 For further information about this journal article visit our Online Resource Centre at
www.oxfordtextbooks.co.uk/orc/hislop2e/

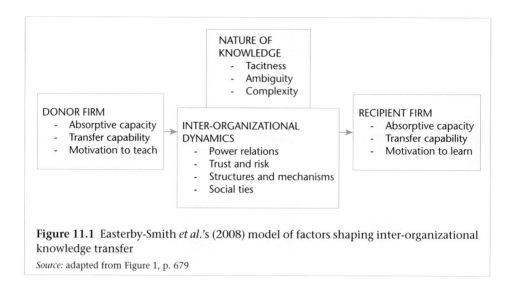

Figure 11.1 Easterby-Smith *et al.*'s (2008) model of factors shaping inter-organizational knowledge transfer

Source: adapted from Figure 1, p. 679

This topic has been addressed by people adopting both objectivist and practice-based epistemologies. For example, Easterby-Smith *et al.* (2008), and all the contributors to the special issue of the *Journal of Management Studies* on knowledge sharing in intra and inter-firm knowledge transfer processes, broadly adopt an objectivist perspective. This is visible in the way Easterby-Smith *et al.* model the character of inter-firm knowledge processes (see Figure 11.1), which utilizes the transmitter–receiver model of knowledge sharing outlined in Chapter 2. By contrast, other writers, such as Carlile (2002, 2004) examine this topic utilizing a practice-based epistemology.

In looking at this topic, the chapter has a relatively narrow and specific focus, being concerned with how the nature of knowledge and the character of inter-personal dynamics shape the character of micro-level knowledge processes in cross community contexts. Thus, the chapter has some, but only limited, engagement with the vast literature that exists on joint ventures and inter-firm alliances. Much of the writing in this area has adopted an organization level analysis, looking at how firm performance is affected by participation in such alliances, and how the structuring of these alliances at the firm level shapes their likelihood of success. Such issues are not considered here. What this volume is engaged with is interest in how inter-personal factors such as trust (see Figure 11.1) shape the character of knowledge sharing in inter-firm alliances.

The chapter begins in the following section by considering why cross community knowledge processes are so important. After this, the chapter examines the character of cross community knowledge processes outlining how the lack of common knowledge and shared identity shape their dynamics. After this the chapter uses Carlile's (2002, 2004) work to distinguish between the different type of boundaries that can be involved in cross community working, before considering the way that cross community knowledge processes can be facilitated and managed, partly with the use of boundary objects and the management of cross boundary social relations.

The significance of cross community knowledge processes

Consider the following situations:

- Inter-organizational collaboration on the development and/or production of complex and high technology products (Harryson *et al.* 2008; Lam 1997; Powell *et al.* 1996; Tallman & Phene 2007)

- Collaborative working that spans significant cultural boundaries (Inkpen & Pien 2006; Pauleen & Yoong 2001; Peltokorpi 2006)

- Cross project knowledge sharing processes (Prencipe & Tell 2001)

- Multi-disciplinary working (Newell & Swan 2000).

- Cross occupational/functional collaboration (Bechky 2003; Carlile 2002, 2004)

- Inter-organizational supply chain based collaboration (Dyer & Nobeoka 2000; Mason & Leek 2008)

- Cross business collaboration *within* multinational corporations (Jonsson & Kalling 2007).

All these situations, while being diverse in character, have one thing in common: they all represent cross community, boundary spanning situations as they involve the sharing or joint utilization and development of knowledge among people who do not typically work together, and who have substantially different knowledge bases. One of the reasons why examining the dynamics of cross community knowledge processes is so important is that the type of working practices outlined in these examples are becoming more and more common. For example, evidence suggests that the use of network based form of organizing, involving inter-organizational collaboration have become widespread (for example, see Castells 1998; Cravens *et al.* 1996; Fulk 2001; Pettigrew & Fenton 2000; Powell 1990).

Another factor that signals the importance of cross community knowledge processes is the growing acknowledgement that the knowledge bases of all organizations are to some extent fragmented into separate, specialized knowledge communities. As outlined in Chapter 3, this led Brown and Duguid (1991, 53), to refer to organizations as being comparable to a '*community-of-communities*'. Carlile (2002, 2004), utilizing a practice-based epistemology, makes a similar argument in talking about the localized nature of knowledge that develops within particular functions of organizations (due to their focus on specific, distinctive problems, and the use of particular, localized practices), and argues that cross functional collaboration constitutes a boundary spanning process. Thus, the knowledge base of all organizations can be considered as being made up from a diversity of localized communities which have some overlapping knowledge in common, but which also possess much specialized and specific knowledge.

From this perspective, one of the general tasks of management is to co-ordinate these diverse internal communities, integrating, diffusing and combining fragmented internal knowledge as necessary (Blacker *et al.* 2000; Brown & Duguid 2001; Grant 1996; Tsoukas 1996). Thus, if the knowledge base of all organizations is constituted by a diverse collection of specialized knowledge communities, intra-organizational processes

Is the level of fragmentation in an organization's knowledge base likely to be proportional to organizational size? Further, if so, are the difficulties of managing such a fragmented knowledge base likely to be greatest for large, global multinationals?

which require collaboration between people possessing different specialized knowledge can be conceptualized as cross community, boundary spanning situations as much as inter-organizational collaborations (Easterby-Smith *et al.* 2008; van Wijk *et al.* 2008).

Thus, the importance of cross community, boundary spanning knowledge processes stems both from the fact that the contemporary restructuring of organizations is placing a greater emphasis on such forms of working than has been traditional, and also because intra-organizational co-ordination can be conceptualized as involving cross community interaction.

Characterizing cross community knowledge processes

As illustrated by Figure 10.1 in the previous chapter, knowledge processes within communities of practice are facilitated by the high degree of common knowledge, overlapping values, and shared sense of identity that community members typically possess. This is because in such circumstances it is likely that the tacit assumptions underpinning people's knowledge, which are key to effective knowledge sharing, are likely to be well understood, or commonly shared. Also, the level of trust and mutual understanding between people in this context is also likely to be conducive to effective knowledge sharing. Hansen (1999), in the context of product innovation and development processes, argues that effective knowledge sharing requires two key elements to exist. Firstly, people must be willing to share their knowledge, and secondly, people must have the ability to share knowledge. Both these elements typically exist within communities of practice, as due to the shared knowledge and values there is enough mutual understanding to make the sharing of knowledge possible, while the sense of shared identity and values makes it probable that people will be willing to share their knowledge.

However, in cross community knowledge processes, as has been outlined, the situation is somewhat different (see Table 11.1). In these circumstances people will have much

Weak shared identity or different sense of identity

Knowledge-related differences

1. Lack of common knowledge
2. Tacitness and context specificity make transferability difficult
3. Epistemic differences—based on different assumptions, values and world-view

Table 11.1 Factors making cross community knowledge processes difficult

less shared, common knowledge, they may only have a weak sense of shared identity, or may even have distinctive and separate identities, and finally, may have fundamentally different value systems. Thus, the social relations between people who are not members of the same group/community are much less conducive to effective knowledge sharing. For example, Hansen (1999) found that when weak ties existed between people this was likely to impede the transfer of complex knowledge (knowledge which was highly tacit, and which had a high level of inter-dependence with other knowledge).

The following two sub-sections consider in detail how the lack of a shared identity, and/or differences in knowledge can inhibit knowledge processes in cross community contexts.

Identity

People from different groups or communities who work together may have either a weak sense of common identity, or may have distinctive and separate identities. For example, consider the situation described by Lam (1997) in Chapter 3. In the electronics corporation she examined, the Japanese and UK staff who were required to collaborate had a weak sense of shared identity as being members of the same organization. Instead, their identity was more closely linked to the divisions they had historically worked within.

This potentially weak sense of common identity arguably complicates knowledge processes through the potential for conflict this creates, as people with differing senses of identity may perceive differences of interest to exist between themselves and others. As was made apparent in Chapter 9 via a number of different examples, conflict, or perceptions that differences of interest exist between people/groups, have been found to play a crucial role in shaping whether, with whom, and how, people are prepared to share knowledge. The following example presents another such case where functional-based identities inhibited corporate level knowledge sharing.

This example, and those presented in Chapter 10 show how people can identify with organizational groups such as particular business units (as immediately above), organizations (Empson 2001b) or functions (Currie & Kerri 2003). However, another type of identity that requires to be considered is more culturally based—national forms of identity, as such forms of identity can affect the character and dynamics of cross community knowledge processes. For example, van Wijk *et al.*'s (2008) meta-analysis of research on the antecedents of knowledge sharing in cross organizational alliances found that the degree of culture distance that existed typically inhibited the level of knowledge sharing that occurred.

Most fundamentally, as was outlined in Chapter 3, those adopting a practice-based epistemology build from the assumption that all knowledge is culturally embedded, and that everyone's knowledge thus to some extent reflects the values, assumptions and worldviews which predominate in the cultures they were socialized into (Jonsson & Kalling 2007; Weir & Hutchings 2005). For example, Inkpen & Pien's (2006) analysis of the collaboration between Chinese and Singaporean organizations in the development of the Suzhou Industrial Park (SIP) found that cultural differences significantly inhibited knowledge sharing. Specifically, Chinese workers found it difficult to understand the intent and rationale underpinning the actions of the Singaporean workers, because the Singaporean workers couldn't articulate them as they were so deeply embedded in their cultural values that they were subconscious and impossible to articulate.

ILLUSTRATION

Conflicting identities inhibiting knowledge sharing in Globalbank

Globalbank is a Dutch bank researched by Newell, Swan, Scarbrough and Hislop (Hislop 2003; Newell *et al.* 2000) that grew aggressively by acquisition. By the late 1990s it had divisions in over 70 countries worldwide. At this point corporate management decided it was necessary to improve levels of co-ordination and knowledge sharing between divisions. A key element of this strategy was the development of a global intranet, a project developed and managed by corporate IT staff. However, Globalbank had a strong historical culture of divisional autonomy, with divisions having typically operated completely independently from each other. Thus each division had controlled how it was organized, with the consequence that each division had its own working practices, IT systems etc. For example, each division had its own intranet site, with its own specific style, level of functionality, etc.

Staff thus typically had a strong sense of identity with their division, and possessed specialist knowledge related to their division's particular customers, products, market conditions and internal ways of working. The global intranet project experienced significant problems however, as management staff from most divisions were hostile to the idea, primarily because they perceived the objectives of the project to be incompatible with their desire to retain divisional autonomy. Thus one of the main obstacles to the project's progress was the stronger sense of identity that key divisional management staff typically for their specific division rather than the corporate group as a whole.

1. What can be done to overcome the narrow sense of divisional identity that staff had, which was acting as a brake on the progress of the global intranet project?

At a more basic level, cross cultural communication and knowledge sharing can also be inhibited by a lack of a shared language, or misinterpretations due to variable language skills. For example, Peltokorpi (2006), found that knowledge sharing between some Nordic managers working in Japan and the Japanese people they worked with were inhibited by the lack of a shared language to communicate. Peltokorpi further found that the knowledge sharing behaviours of the Japanese workers were heavily influenced by their cultural values, with for example the strong respect they had for status hierarchies inhibiting lower level workers from interacting with the Nordic managers.

A further way in which national culture has been found to shape knowledge sharing in cross community contexts is that the strong collectivist nature of culture in many Asian countries, while facilitating in-group knowledge sharing, can act as a significant brake on cross community knowledge sharing (Michailova & Hutchins 2006; Peltokorpi 2006; Weir & Hutchings 2005).

Knowledge

The difficulties of cross community knowledge sharing, as outlined, are related to more than just the sense of identities that individuals possess. Another, equally important factor complicating such processes, is the nature of the knowledge possessed by people in these situations. These difficulties stem from three inter-related factors (see Table 11.1).

Firstly, as in any context, the sharing of knowledge may be inhibited by its tacitness. However, the sharing of tacit knowledge in cross community contexts is made more difficult and complex by two other knowledge related factors. Firstly, people may share only a limited amount of common knowledge, and second there may be significant epistemological differences in the knowledge people possess (i.e. their knowledge is based on different underpinning assumptions and values). Thus, for example, Newell & Swan (2000) found that the difficulty of knowledge sharing between different members of the cross disciplinary research project they examined were related to epistemological differences in their knowledge, which stemmed from the different disciplinary backgrounds they came from.

The issue of epistemological differences is worth elaborating on, as such differences can have a profound effect on attempts to share or collectively utilize knowledge. Brown & Duguid (2001, 207) argue that while the advantage of communities of practice is that '*common . . . practice . . . creates social-epistemic bonds*', conversely, '*[p]eople with different practices have different assumptions, different outlooks, different interpretations of the world around them, and different ways of making sense of their encounters.*' Thus, in cross community, boundary spanning contexts people may not only have limited amounts of common, shared knowledge, but the knowledge they possess may be based on a fundamentally different system of values and assumptions. Carlile (2002), in a similar vein, and adopting a practice-based epistemology argued that the reason that such epistemic differences will always exist in cross community contexts is that people's knowledge is localized, being developed around and focussed on the particular problems and issues that their day-to-day work is concerned with. Carlile's analysis also suggests that the scope for conflict in such situations can be related to such knowledge-based differences. This is because he suggests that people's knowledge becomes '*invested in practice*'. People's sense of competence relates to the knowledge they possess and the way it allows them to do their work. Thus, people can become committed and attached to particular types of knowledge and ways of doing things, and may be reluctant to adapt and change them due to the negative impact such change may have on their sense of individual competence.

Such issues may arise in multi-disciplinary work (Newell & Swan 2000), where staff from different organizational sub-units require to collaborate (Hansen 1999), in international collaborations involving people with significantly different cultures working together (Pauleen & Yoong 2001), where people from different occupational communities require to share knowledge (Bechky 2003; Carlile 2002, 2004), or where different organizational functions require to collaborate (see the illustration on France-Co below). The complexity of knowledge sharing in such circumstances stems from the fact that epistemological differences between people or groups can inhibit the development of even a fundamental understanding of the basic premises, and values that the knowledge

Trust and knowledge sharing in a globally distributed work team

Newell *et al.* (2007) utilize Newell & Swan's (2000) typology of trust (see Chapter 9 and Table 9.2) to analyse how the evolution of trust affected work relations and knowledge sharing in globally dispersed software development teams in a company called GLOBALIS. The company examined had offices in a number of cities in the USA, but also in Ireland and India. Project management and strategic elements of the work were typically done in the USA, with more routine work being done in the 'offshore' offices in India and Ireland. In the context studied the development of trust based working relations was inhibited not just by the cross cultural nature of the project teams, but also because most communication was electronic, with opportunities for face-to-face interaction being limited.

Working relations in the teams were also negatively affected by the perception among many of the American workers that their jobs were threatened by the use of offshore sites, due to the rapid rise in the use of 'offshoring' that had been undertaken. There was therefore a strong sense of 'us' versus 'them' in the project teams, rather than people identifying strongly with the project they worked on. This sense of 'them' and 'us' was reinforced by the strategy of knowledge hoarding adopted by many American workers, who believed this provided a way of protecting their position and knowledge with the perception being that sharing knowledge would make it easier for the company to get rid of them. Because of these factors, levels of commitment trust, the extent to which people feel committed to the goals of their joint endeavour, were limited. For example, levels of commitment based trust among the Irish and Indian workers was low as they felt excluded from the more interesting work, and didn't like the lack of knowledge sharing by American workers. Further, the extent of the knowledge hoarding that was undertaken by the American workers meant that the Irish and Indian workers often found it difficult to do their jobs effectively, which inhibited the extent to which the American workers developed a sense of competence based trust in them. Finally, the professional rather than collegiate way in which work-related interactions were carried out, and the lack of opportunities for face-to-face interaction between Irish, Indian and American workers made the development of companion based trust difficult as well.

1. Given the cost and difficulty of organizing face-to-face meetings among these workers, what, if anything, could management in GLOBALIS have done to address the lack of trust that existed in their software development teams?

in the written contracts, which was greater than they were typically used to. However, over time, through face-to-face interaction, and close collaboration between Chinese and Singaporean workers, levels of companion and competence based trust developed significantly as these workers developed not only personal relationships (companion based trust) with each other, but also a confidence in each other's abilities (competence based trust).

Harryson *et al.*'s (2008) study of the development of new Volvo C70, which involved intensive collaboration between Swedish and Italian engineers found that informal socialization provided another means via which trust based working relations could be developed. The types of events that project team members participated in included attending football matches together, having wine tasting events, regularly going out to dinner together and weekend snowboarding trips. Thus trust based working relations can be developed via both collaboration on work-related activities and through interacting and socializing at non-work events. However, as the boxed illustration in this section shows, the development of trust based working relations is by no means easy or straightforward, especially when the groups collaborating perceive that their interests may be conflicting.

A classification of boundary types

Thus far, while cross community boundary spanning contexts have been acknowledged as being highly diverse, no effort has been made to systematically differentiate between the different types of boundary that exist, and how the character of these boundaries influences the nature and dynamics of cross community knowledge processes. This topic is addressed here, through using Carlile's (2002, 2004) framework of boundary types which differentiates between three distinctive types of boundary. The empirical focus of Carlile's work is predominantly on cross functional working within single organizations. Adopting a practice-based perspective Carlile characterized such situations as involving boundary spanning as the knowledge possessed by staff working in different functional areas, even within the same organization, is understood to be quite different. For Carlile this is because the knowledge of staff in these functional areas is localized, being concerned with addressing the particular problems, and being embedded in the particular work practices that each function is involved in and responsible for.

Carlile developed a typology of boundaries distinguishing between three distinctive types of boundary: syntactic, semantic and pragmatic (see Table 11.2) with the degree of novelty of the collective tasks being undertaken varying from low (syntactic boundaries) to high (pragmatic boundaries). Syntactic boundaries are assumed to be the easiest to work across as people share a common logic, set of values and worldview. Thus, working across a syntactic boundary involves the relatively straightforward process of transferring knowledge and information from one community to the other. Semantic boundaries are more difficult to work across, as with them people do not have a shared logic or set of values. Instead, in such contexts people will have different understandings and interpretations of the same knowledge. In such contexts, successfully working across a semantic boundary involves people developing an understanding of and sensitivity to other people's understandings and interpretations.

Boundary object type	Boundary object characteristics
Repository	Common data or information that provide shared reference point for groups involved in cross boundary work.
Standardized forms/methods	Shared forms and methods of working allow differences of opinion across a boundary to be acknowledged, accounted for and understood.
Objects/models	Complex representations (such as drawings, computer simulations) which can be observed and shared by groups involved in cross boundary situations.
Maps	Representation of dependencies between groups involved in cross boundary working.

Table 11.3 Carlile's boundary object types
Source: from Carlile (2002, 2004)

between people from different communities, and thus can be utilized to help develop and improve the working relationship between people, and the mutual understanding they have of each other. One of the most common type of boundary objects mentioned by Brown & Duguid are contracts, which typically provide a focus for cross community negotiation, and which can help provide an initial stimulus to a process of perspective making and taking. The boundary object concept has proved popular and has been used by an increasing number of analysts to understand change processes (Fenton 2007) and the sharing of project-specific knowledge (Sapsed & Salter 2004; Swan *et al.* 2007)

A more systematic analysis of the concept of boundary objects is developed by Carlile, as alluded to earlier. Carlile (2002) outlined a typology of distinctive types of boundary objects, that was adapted from Star's (1989) work (see Table 11.3), and links this to his typology of boundary types (see Table 11.2) to suggest that successfully working across boundaries requires the use of boundary objects appropriate to the type of boundary being crossed (see Table 11.4). In the space available here it is only possible to briefly sketch out a complex model that is developed over two papers (Carlile 2002, 2004).

To successfully span syntactic boundaries, the fact that people have a shared syntax and language, means repository type boundary objects, in the form of common data and infor-mation can facilitate cross boundary working. Thus, the primary knowledge process involved in spanning syntactic boundaries is knowledge sharing, where repository type boundary objects are developed via the transferral and sharing of knowledge to allow the develop-ment of a common knowledge base, agreed upon and understood by all communities.

Successfully spanning semantic boundaries, where people do not have a shared syntax and language, and where people may have divergent interpretations and understandings is more complex. To do this involves the development and use of boundary objects which facilitate a process of perspective making and taking, where people develop an increased understanding of the perspective of others. Carlile suggests that this can be achieved via the use of three types of boundary object. Firstly, standardized forms and models can be used, where people gain insights into the perspective of others via understanding the

Type of boundary	Characteristics required for cross boundary collaboration	Boundaries objects that allow successful cross boundary working
Syntactic	Shared system and common set of data/information	• Repository
Semantic	Provide a means for people to specify and learn about cross boundary differences and dependencies	• Standardized form and methods • Objects/models • Maps
Pragmatic	Provide a means whereby people develop a common sense of shared interests and a willingness to transform their knowledge to achieve them	• Objects/models • Maps

Table 11.4 Carlile's boundary types and appropriate boundary objects
Source: from Carlile (2002, 2004)

different ways that common forms are used. Secondly, objects/models can be used, as the use of shared drawings etc. provides a means via which people's differences in perspective can be communicated and discussed. Finally, maps, which outline the inter-dependencies between communities can also be used, as they allow groups to understand how people's perspectives are shaped by their community interests and co-dependencies. Thus, with the spanning of semantic boundaries, the primary knowledge process is one of translation.

Finally, pragmatic boundaries are the most difficult and complex to span, due to the differences of interest that exist between communities, with Carlile arguing that both object/models and maps are appropriate boundary objects for this context. This is because the development and use of maps allow people to better understand and appreciate the differences of interest that exist, while the use of objects/models can provide a resource which not only allows people to develop a sense of shared interests and common endeavour, but which also allows people to transform their knowledge to achieve a collective goal. Thus, with the spanning of pragmatic boundaries, the primary knowledge process is one of transformation.

Carlile (2002) illustrated the role of boundary objects in facilitating boundary spanning via the analysis of a specific issue that developed and was eventually resolved in his ethnographic study of the development of a new car valve. While the development process involved collaboration among staff from four functions/communities (sales, manufacturing engineering, production and design engineering), the focal issue examined involved the manufacturing and design engineering functions. A manufacturing engineer, who was responsible for transforming the design engineers' work into a manufacturable product had a concern with the design that would potentially require a significant redesign to be undertaken. Thus, the boundary being spanned was a pragmatic one, requiring the transformation of knowledge. The manufacturing engineer's initial efforts at communicating his concerns to the design engineers failed, largely because, Carlile argued, the

TIME TO REFLECT THE POWER OF KNOWLEDGE WORKERS

How unique is the situation of knowledge workers? Are they the only type of workers whose knowledge is important and valued? Can you think of other types of workers who have important knowledge that provides them with a source of power?

As also outlined in Chapter 9, for those adopting a dissensus-based perspective on social order the potential for conflict in organizations emanates from more than just the nature of the employment relationship. This potential flows from the different interests which exist within organizations between both individuals and groups. Thus from this perspective the social dissensus, conflict and antagonism that is assumed to exist within societies also exists within organizations. Thus, both the dissensus-based perspectives on knowledge management adopt, as outlined in Chapter 9, what Fox (1985) labelled a pluralist perspective, which assumes organizations can be conceptualized as being made up of coalition of different interests groups acting in a co-ordinated way. This divergence of interests may come from individuals/groups competing over scarce organizational resources, or through clashes between the personal objectives and strategies that individual employees may pursue in order to sustain and develop their careers, such as receiving recognition for particular efforts/knowledge, receiving financial rewards or gaining promotions.

As outlined in Chapter 9, despite the general neglect of issues of power, politics and conflict in much knowledge management literature, there is a significant and growing body of empirical evidence which reinforces this perspective, as conflict, or perceived conflict, between individuals and groups has been found to play an important role in shaping the character and dynamics of organizational attempts to manage knowledge.

Power/knowledge and the dialogical discourse on knowledge management

It is impossible to examine the relationship between power and knowledge without taking account of the work of the French philosopher Michel Foucault, as arguably he is the single most influential author in this area. Further, in both the general business and management literature and in the area of human resource management his work and ideas have become relatively influential (Barratt 2002; McKinlay & Starkey 1998; Townley 1994). As will be seen, Foucault's (1980) conceptualization of power, and characterization of the relationship between power and knowledge, is quite different from that elaborated by Hales. This section begins by giving a brief overview on the way Foucault theorizes power and its relationship with knowledge before subsequent

TIME TO REFLECT THE NATURE OF ORGANIZATIONS

What does your own experience say about the nature of organizations? Is conflict inevitable? Are power imbalances inherent?

sub-sections elaborate some of the key ways in which his work is relevant to the topic of knowledge management. As has been alluded to earlier in the chapter, only a small amount of writing on the topic of knowledge management draws on Foucault's work and adopts what Schultze & Stabell (2004) label the perspective of the dialogical discourse. The two pieces of work most closely aligned with this perspective are Sewell's (2005) conceptual paper, and Marshall & Rollinson's (2004) analysis of the dynamics of a problem solving situation (which is examined here as the extended end of chapter example). A number of other studies which make use of Foucault's panopticon concept are also examined.

Conceptualizing power/knowledge

In understanding Foucault's particular way of conceptualizing power it is worth quoting him in full,

> 'the power exercised on the body is conceived not as a property, but as a strategy. . . . this power is exercised rather than possessed; it is not the "privilege", acquired or preserved, of the dominant class, but the overall effect of its strategic positions—an effect that is manifested and sometimes extended by the position of those who are dominated.' (Rabinow 1991, 174, quoting from Foucault's *Discipline and Punishment*)

Thus Foucault suggests that power, rather than being a discrete resource that social actors can utilize, is something which is produced and reproduced within and through the dynamics of evolving social relationships. This therefore resonates with the practice-based epistemology's conceptualization of knowledge as being embedded in particular contexts and work practices. Thus, power isn't a resource that can be utilized at will by an actor, but is instead something that is embedded in the way people act, talk and interact with others. In more simple terms, power isn't a resource that actor 'a' can use autonomously to influence actor 'b' (as with the resource based view of power), but is instead something that is constituted by actors 'a' and 'b' through how they interact with each other. Both actors play an equally fundamental role in the constitution of power.

Further, Foucault suggests that power and knowledge are so inextricably inter-related that they are fundamentally inseparable, and coined the phrase power/knowledge to symbolize this (Foucault 1980). Further, the term power/knowledge symbolizes that not only are power and knowledge mutually constituted, but also that neither element should be privileged over the other. To properly appreciate Foucault in this respect, it is again worth quoting him in full,

> 'Power produces knowledge . . . power and knowledge directly imply one another; that there is no power relation without the correlative constitution of a field of knowledge, nor any knowledge that does not presuppose and constitute at the same time power relations.' (Rabinow 1991, 17, quoting from Foucault's *Discipline and Punishment*)

TIME TO REFLECT ICTs AS PANOPTICONS

Based on your own experience, do ICTs represent technologies with significant disciplinary power? Can their gaze be avoided, resisted or subverted?

a particular impression. This, it was argued, would lead to a process of '*homogenization*' where diversity would be damaged. Thus, based on this analysis, a potentially negative effect of the use of ICTs for knowledge management is that because of such factors they may not reflect the diversity of knowledge and attitudes which typically exist in organizations.

McKinlay (2000, 2002) presents an alternative analysis, which suggests that the disciplinary power of ICT based knowledge management systems has been somewhat exaggerated. McKinlay's analysis, based on a case study of the UK divisions of an American pharmaceutical corporation, suggests that ICT based knowledge management systems have a limited ability to capture highly tacit knowledge. Further, workers have the ability to resist the disciplinary gaze of such systems through creating and communicating within '*unregulated social processes*' (2002). This debate and disagreement reflects a wider debate in the business and management literature on the effectiveness of panopticon style, surveillance-based managerial control systems and the extent to which they disempower workers (Button *et al.* 2003; Thompson & Ackroyd 1995).

Conclusion

While two contrasting perspectives on power have been examined, they both point to the conclusion that to analyse and effectively understand the full dynamics of organizational knowledge processes power requires to be accounted for. The chapter has identified two key reasons why this is the case. From a resource-based perspective the importance of taking account of power is due to the extent to which conflict shapes organizational knowledge processes, and the role that power and politics play in shaping them. From a Foucauldian perspective power requires to be accounted for in knowledge management processes, as power and knowledge are inseparable and mutually constituted.

As a consequence, one of the most general conclusions of this chapter is that the centrality of power to knowledge processes means that any analyses of such processes that neglects to account for power are relatively impoverished. For example, taking account of power helps to explain and understand the human/social dimension of knowledge processes, such as whether people are willing or reluctant to participate in organizational knowledge processes. Thus, Walsham suggests (2001, 603):

'what we know affects how influential we are [thus] . . . there may be good reasons why individuals may not wish to participate in, or may modify some aspect of their sense-giving activities, for reasons related to organizational politics.'

Knowledge management was also shown to be concerned with more than simply managing all the knowledge that exists in organizations. Taking account of power helps reveal and make visible how knowledge management processes involve certain claims to knowledge becoming legitimated (and others marginalized), which often involves disputes and negotiations over competing knowledge claims. Thus, taking account of power helps address the typically neglected topic of why certain types and forms of knowledge become the focus of knowledge management initiatives.

Case study

The negotiation of meaning in a problem solving context

Marshall & Rollinson (2004) utilize Foucault's power/knowledge concept to analyse the dynamics of a dispute that developed regarding the diagnosis of a fault that occurred in a cross organizational project concerned with the upgrading of a telephone exchange. Effectively there was a dispute related to what the cause of the fault was and how it should be remedied. This dispute occurred during the later stages of a £21m two year project concerned with upgrading the functionality of some UK telephone exchanges via the design and implementation of new software. Data was collected via the direct observation of project meetings, interviews conducted with some project team members, and the analysis of relevant documentation.

Marshall & Rollinson argue that the occurrence of faults such as the one they examined represent an appropriate social context in which to examine power and politics, as such situations typically allow the questioning and possible renegotiation of meaning, providing people with an opportunity to put forward particular knowledge claims, which are based on particular assumptions, beliefs and values. These situations often involve what Marshall and Rollinson refer to as a 'struggle over meaning', which is a collaborative social process of negotiation in which actors draw on and enact different power/knowledge claims which actors involved in the dispute negotiate over. However, crucially, the power/knowledge claims made by actors are not stable/discrete resources that people draw on but are open to dispute/negotiation/challenge/affirmation, and whose legitimacy only emerges as an outcome of these negotiation processes. Thus these 'struggles over meaning' constitute political disputes regarding the legitimacy of the different power/knowledge claims that are enacted and drawn upon.

After the fault being analysed was discovered there was a period of 12 days until it was rectified, during which a dispute had evolved over its cause. During this period the dispute was discussed in a number of face-to-face project team meetings at which some participants often participated via phone conference. The main political tactic utilized during the dispute involved different actors making particular discursive claims which enacted and sought to legitimate particular power/knowledge claims, with the dispute being centred around two particular power/knowledge claims.

One power/knowledge claim, which drew on a discourse of expert knowledge, was utilized largely by the software company who designed and implemented the software updates. The legitimacy for this claim was sought in the alleged expert technical status of the company's engineers, which was partly demonstrated via their fluent use of specialist technical jargon. However, the expert status of these engineers was not automatically regarded as legitimate and unquestionable by those in the project team who worked for the network company which owned the telephone exchange. Thus during the dispute the software company had to bolster their argument by involving increasingly more senior and experienced engineers.

The second power/knowledge claim, which was largely utilized by staff from the network company drew on a discourse of formal authority, as staff from the network company occupied positions of formal seniority on the project team. One example of how this authority was used was to threaten withdrawal from and hold up progress with the implementation timetable until the problem had been diagnosed and resolved to their satisfaction. Again, as with the discourse of expert knowledge utilized by staff from the software company, such claims to authority were not automatically regarded as legitimate, partly due to perceptions of questionable project management skills emanating from a significant problem that had occurred in a previous phase of the project.

1. Can you think of other situations and/or events apart from the emergence of problems, such as the departure of an important member of staff from an organization, which create circumstances in which taken for granted knowledge claims become open to dispute and renegotiation?

Source: Marshall, N., & Rollinson, J. (2004). 'Maybe Bacon had a Point: The Politics of Collective Sensemaking', *British Journal of Management*, 15, Special Issue: s71–86.

 For further information about this journal article visit our Online Resource Centre at www.oxfordtextbooks.co.uk/orc/hislop2e/

Review and discussion questions

1   In general, how compatible are the interests of workers and their employers over how workers' knowledge is used? Does the requirement by organizations to derive economic value from it mean conflict is likely or inevitable?

2   The chapter assumed that power and knowledge are closely related, if not inseparable. Can you think of any ways in which knowledge can be used in organizations which do not involve the use of power?

3   Compare the two conceptualizations of power examined. Can you relate either/both of them to your own experience?

Suggestions for further reading

1   **A. Mckinlay (2002). 'The Limits of Knowledge Management',** *New Technology, Work and Employment*, **17/2: 76–88.**

Critiques the ICT as panopticon perspective by illustrating the limitations of ICT based knowledge management practices.

2   **N. Marshall & T. Brady (2001). 'Knowledge Management and the Politics of Knowledge: Illustrations from Complex Product Systems',** *European Journal of Information Systems*, **10: 99–112.**

Provides theoretical and empirical support for the argument that issues of power and conflict require to be accounted for in analysing organizational knowledge management initiatives.

3   **A. Willem & H. Scarbrough (2006). 'Social Capital and Political Bias in Knowledge Sharing: An exploratory Study',** *Human Relations*, **59/10: 1343–1370.**

Case study analysis of two Belgian companies which examined how politics moderates the relationship between social capital and knowledge sharing and can produce a very selective form of self-interested knowledge sharing.

4   G. Sewell (2005). 'Nice Work? Rethinking Managerial Control in an Era of
     Knowledge Work', *Organization*, 15/5: 685–704.

     A conceptual paper which outlines a Foucauldian perspective on knowledge manage-
     ment and suggests that with the increasing importance of knowledge in work, manage-
     rial control systems require to change.

5   A. Contu & H. Willmott (2003). 'Re-Embedding Situatedness: The Importance of
     Power Relations in Learning Theory'. *Organization Science*, 14/3: 283–296.

     Uses re-analysis of Orr's study of copier engineers to argue that situated learning theory
     needs to better account for how relations of power in capitalist work organizations
     shape worker action and learning practices.

Take your learning further: Online Resource Centre

Visit the supporting Online Resource Centre for resources which will extend your
understanding of knowledge management in organizations. As well as web links to sites
of interest, the author has provided case studies looking at knowledge management in
virtual and knowledge intensive firms, and in global multinationals. These will help you
with your research, essays and assignments; or you may find these additional resources
helpful when revising for exams.

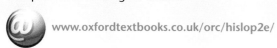

www.oxfordtextbooks.co.uk/orc/hislop2e/

13

Information & Communication Technologies and Knowledge Management

Introduction

One of the dominant themes in the early knowledge management literature was the importance of the role accorded to information and communication technologies (ICTs hereafter). This is visible in two ways. Firstly, ICTs had a central place in much of the early knowledge management literature (see Table 13.1). Secondly, ICTs had a prominent role in many of the earliest knowledge management initiatives. Thus, Ruggles (1998), reporting on a 1997 survey, found that the four most popular types of knowledge management projects involved the implementation of intranets, data warehouses, decision support tools and groupware (groupware refers to technologies that support collaboration and communication). A common assumption which accompanied these early initiatives was that simply implementing such systems could allow organizations to effectively manage their knowledge. However, while this assumption has been widely criticized, this has *not* led to a position where ICTs are regarded as having no useful role in knowledge management initiatives. Instead, there has been an enormous evolution in how the relationship between ICTs and knowledge management processes is conceptualized. This chapter examines these changes.

Definition   Information and communication technologies (ICTs)

ICTs are technologies which allow/facilitate the management and/or sharing of knowledge and information. Thus the term covers an enormous diversity of heterogeneous technologies including computers, telephones, e-mail, databases, data-mining systems, search engines, the internet and video-conferencing equipment.

The chapter begins by providing an overview of the diversity of ways that ICTs can be used to facilitate knowledge management initiatives, which is done via linking back to

Thematic category	Number	%
Information technology	73	40
Information systems	51	28
Strategic management	35	19
Human resources	9	5
Consultancies	8	4
Other	8	4

Table 13.1 Thematic focus of early knowledge management literature
Source: adapted from Scarbrough & Swan (2001, 8, Table 2)

the typologies of knowledge management examined in Chapter 4. One of the key conclusions of this section is that the role assigned to ICTs in knowledge management initiatives is significantly shaped by the assumptions about knowledge that are made. Thus, the following two sections separately consider the role ascribed to ICTs in knowledge management initiatives when objectivist and practice-based perspectives on knowledge are adopted. The chapter then briefly considers the importance of taking account of socio-cultural factors in ICT-enabled knowledge management, which, as outlined above, were typically neglected in the earliest knowledge management initiatives. The chapter then concludes by considering three debates regarding the character of ICT-mediated social processes which have implications for the role that ICTs can play in knowledge management processes. These debates centre on: the extent to which ICTs can facilitate the sort of perspective making processes described in Chapter 3; the extent to which communication media have fixed or variable degrees of information richness; and, the extent to which trust can be developed and sustained in social relations mediated by ICTs.

Linking knowledge management and ICTs

As was discussed explicitly in Chapter 4, and what should be apparent implicitly throughout this book is that there are a vast range of ways via which organizations can attempt to manage their knowledge. A specific issue that was touched on in Chapter 4, and that is examined more fully here is how the role that ICTs can play in such activities will vary significantly depending upon the particular approach to knowledge management an organization adopts. The objective of this section is to return to the knowledge management typologies outlined in Chapter 4 to consider the particular roles that ICTs play in them.

Hendriks (2001) described the bringing together of ICTs and knowledge management as involving the clash of two titans, as such an enormous amount of ink has been spilled on examining both topics, and the inter-relationship between them. Attempting to do justice to the scale and scope of the debate on these linkages in the space of one chapter is therefore a difficult task. Fundamentally, Hendriks challenges the assumption that knowledge management can simply be equated with the implementation and use of certain types of technology. Instead Hendriks suggests that there are five dimensions which affect the way ICTs are used to help manage knowledge in organizations including the extent to which knowledge is important to organizational performance and the nature of organizational knowledge (whether it is largely tacit or explicit etc.). However, rather than attempt to articulate the full complexity of Hendriks' model of the ICT–KM relationship, the divergent roles that ICTs can play in organizational knowledge management initiatives are here considered by combining the epistemological distinctions between the objectivist and practice-based epistemologies, with the knowledge management typologies outlined in Chapter 4 (see Table 13.2).

ICT-enabled KM from objectivist perspective		
Purpose	KM strategies linked with	Empirical examples
Libraries of codified knowledge	• Alvesson & Kärreman's extended library • Earl's systems-based school • Hansen *et al.*'s codification-based approach	• McKinlay (2002): the 'warehouse' element of Pharmaco's knowledge management initiative which was a searchable knowledge repository intended to improve drug development times by allowing pharmacists to gain quicker access to relevant knowledge • Gray & Durcikova (2005–06): knowledge repository used by technical support staff in a call centre environment
Task-related codified knowledge embedded in documentation and standard operating procedures	• Alvesson & Kärreman's enacted blueprints • Earl's engineering school	• Hsaio *et al.* (2006): system to support work of engineers in a semiconductor fabrication equipment company—see the example at the end of this chapter • Voelpel *et al.* (2005): Siemens' ShareNet system for sharing knowledge among sales and marketing teams—see the example at the end of Chapter 4
ICT-enabled KM from practice-based perspective		
Purpose	KM strategies linked with	Empirical examples
Mapping of expertise	• Earl's cartographic approach	• Robertson (2002): the employee expertise search facility of the knowledge repository examined
Collaboration tools to facilitate ICT-based communication and knowledge sharing	• Earl's organizational school • Earl's spatial school	• McKinlay (2002): the 'café' element of Pharmaco's knowledge management initiative which was a virtual forum intended to facilitate informal interaction and knowledge sharing • Alavi *et al.* (2005–06): the communication tools and 'knowledge café' element of the knowledge management initiative aimed at facilitating rich and informal communication and knowledge sharing among globally dispersed IT staff

Table 13.2 Divergent approaches to ICT-enabled knowledge management

Table 13.2 illustrates the extent of the role that ICTs can play in knowledge management processes, as they have a significant role to play in a large number of the particular approaches to knowledge management articulated in the three different knowledge management typologies examined in Chapter 4. Specifically, one of Hansen *et al.*'s (1999) two knowledge management strategies, two of Alvesson & Kärreman's (2001) four approaches to knowledge management, and five of the seven schools of knowledge management developed by Earl (2001) all give a significant role to ICTs. It is suggested here that roles allocated to ICTs by these different styles of knowledge management can be classified into four generic types, two of which relate to each epistemological perspective.

The following two sections examine in more detail the different ways that ICTs can be used in organizational knowledge management processes through outlining how the epistemological assumptions of the objectivist and practice-based epistemologies shape the way ICTs are used, examining the four generic roles that ICTs typically have in knowledge management processes, and illustrating the issues raised with examples.

Objectivist perspectives on ICT-enabled knowledge management

The popularity of the objectivist perspective on knowledge management, and the idea that through codification ICTs can play a crucial role in knowledge management processes is visible in the number of organizations that embed their knowledge management initiatives in such assumptions. Consider, for example, the illustration of Globalbank's IT support initiative described in Chapter 2, the ShareNet case study described in Chapter 4, and the illustration of Nortel Networks examined later in this chapter. Further examples include: the knowledge codification project undertaken by the UK consulting firm examined by Morris (2001); the media organization examined by Robertson (2002), whose knowledge management system was in essence a searchable repository of employee expertise and know-how; and, the World Bank, where the objectives of its knowledge management strategy in the late 1990s was to make itself a *'technology broker, transferring knowledge from one place where it is available to the place where it is needed'* (van der Velden 2002, 30).

Epistemological assumptions and ICTs

Chapter 2 outlined in detail both how the objectivist perspective on knowledge conceptualizes knowledge and how it characterizes knowledge sharing processes. However, it is worth briefly restating some of the key assumptions of this perspective, as they help explain the roles that this perspective assumes ICTs can play in knowledge management processes. Firstly, this perspective conceptualizes knowledge in entitative terms, with knowledge being regarded as a discrete object that can exist separately from the people who possess and use it. Secondly, there is an optimism embedded in this perspective that much knowledge either exists in an explicit form, or that it can be made explicit through a process of codification (Steinmueller 2000). Thirdly, this perspective conceptualizes knowledge sharing as being based on a transmitter–receiver or conduit model (see Fig 2.1), and assumes that it is relatively straightforward to share codified knowledge.

Building from these assumptions those utilizing an objectivist perspective believe that ICTs can play a direct role in knowledge management processes. Based on this viewpoint, which Scarbrough & Swan (2001) refer to as the 'knowledge management as technology' perspective, ICTs simply represent one channel/medium through which explicit knowledge can be shared.

Objectivist perspectives on knowledge and the two roles for ICTs in knowledge management

The meta-analysis of the role of ICT systems in the three knowledge management typologies examined in Chapter 4 is articulated in Table 13.2 above. This suggests that despite the diversity of approaches to knowledge management embedded in these typologies, when objectivist assumptions about the nature of knowledge (outlined above) are utilized, there are two specific ways in which ICTs can be utilized to facilitate knowledge management processes. Both of these roles for ICT-enabled knowledge management build from the twin assumptions outlined above that firstly, knowledge can be codified and secondly, once codified can be transferred and shared between people via ICTs.

The first role for ICTs is in creating searchable repositories or libraries of knowledge. As outlined in Table 13.2 this relates to three specific knowledge management strategies including Hansen *et al.*'s codification approach, Earl's systems approach and Alvesson & Kärreman's extended library approach. The rationale of such systems is that if people are looking for knowledge on a particular topic or issue then they can search the repository for it, rather than having to develop their own solutions. For such systems to be successful a number of factors are necessary. Firstly, people must be willing to codify their knowledge. Secondly, a system of categorizing and structuring knowledge must be found which allows people looking for knowledge to find it. Finally, people must be willing to search such systems for knowledge when they require assistance (Bock *et al.* 2006). Gray & Durcikova (2005–06), for example, examine the use of electronic repositories of knowledge in the context of technical support work from the 'demand' side of the users of such systems, rather than is more common, the 'supply sided' process of codification and categorization.

The second role for ICTs is in codified and documented knowledge which is task specific. As outlined in Table 13.2 this relates to both the enacted blueprint approach of Alvesson & Kärreman, and Earl's engineering school of knowledge management. With this approach task-related knowledge is codified into documents like standard operating procedures, troubleshooting checklists, protocols for decision-making etc. The assumption is that once what is regarded as the 'best practice' way of completing a task has been identified, this knowledge can be codified and disseminated to all relevant staff who may need to use it. The end of chapter example by Hsiao *et al.* (2006), which examines a knowledge management system to help engineers installing equipment to manufacture semiconductors, represents one example of such a system.

Practice-based perspectives on ICT-enabled knowledge management

Even over the short space of time that knowledge management has been regarded as an important topic there has been a significant evolution in the role that ICTs are conceptualized as being able to play in such processes. Broadly speaking, this has seen practice-based perspectives on knowledge become more fully embraced. As will be seen, the practice-based perspective regards ICTs as having a less direct, but equally important role in supporting and facilitating the social processes that underpin inter-personal knowledge processes.

Epistemological assumptions and ICTs

Most fundamentally, due to the way those writing from a practice-based perspective conceptualize knowledge, they believe that the codification and storage of knowledge in ICT-based repositories is unlikely to result in useful knowledge. This is because these processes of codification typically produce a denuded form of knowledge, as the tacit assumptions and values which underpin it are lost (Hislop 2002b; Walsham 2001). Thus, effectively, what is codified is only part of the knowledge people possess, whose utility, on its own, is limited.

Further, as outlined in Chapter 3, those adopting a practice-based epistemology assume that the transmitter–receiver metaphor of knowledge sharing is inappropriate, as the sharing of knowledge does not involve the simple transferral of a fixed entity (explicit knowledge) between two people. Instead, the sharing of knowledge involves two people actively inferring and constructing meaning from a process of interaction (Hislop 2002b). This relates to the processes of perspective making and taking which were described in Chapter 3, where those interacting develop an understanding of the values, assumptions and tacit knowledge which underpin each other's knowledge base (Walsham 2001). Communication processes in such interactions, to be successful, require to be relatively rich, open and based on a certain level of trust.

The role which those writing from a practice-based perspective believe that ICTs can play in knowledge processes is thus somewhat indirect, being related to facilitating and supporting the social relationships and communication processes which underpin knowledge processes. Walsham (2001, 599), usefully summarized this by arguing that *'computer based systems can be of benefit in knowledge based activities . . . to support the development and communication of human meaning.'*

Practice-based perspectives on knowledge and the two roles for ICTs in knowledge management

As outlined in Table 13.2, despite the diversity of approaches to knowledge embedded in the three typologies of knowledge examined in Chapter 4, there are two ways that

ILLUSTRATION

Nortel Network: ICTs and knowledge management

Massey *et al.* (2002) examined how Nortel Networks used a 'process oriented' knowledge management strategy to successfully re-engineer its new product development (NPD) process. This was done through the development and implementation of a knowledge management tool called 'Virtual Mentor', which was described as an electronic performance support system (EPSS). This system linked together all relevant 'disparate knowledge resources' that were relevant to their product development process (including internal knowledge and expertise, which was highly dispersed, as well as customer knowledge, and relevant, archived historical knowledge). Virtual Mentor was designed to be of value to the three categories of worker they identified as being key to the NPD process: idea generators, decision makers, and process owners. Process owners being the people responsible for tracking the progress of the evolving NPD process. Massey *et al.* argue that the development and implementation of this system was a significant factor in the economic success that Nortel Networks experienced between 1994–2000. One of the central elements to the success of this project was that while it was a technology based knowledge management project, technological issues did not dominate. Instead, Nortel Networks began by defining the stages in their NPD process, before then considering the people related issues flowing from this process. The technical specification and design of Virtual Mentor was thus the third and final stage in their NPD re-engineering project.

1. The success of Nortel's knowledge management system was that the technology was designed to be compatible with existing work practices, rather than vice-versa. Based on your understanding of organizational knowledge management projects, which approach is most commonly used?

likely to fail. Thus, key to the success of ICT-enabled knowledge management is dealing effectively with the socio-cultural factors which motivate people to participate in knowledge management initiatives that were considered in Chapter 9.

Debates regarding the role of ICTs in knowledge management processes

Within the knowledge management literature there are also debates and disagreements on a number of quite specific issues regarding the role that ICTs can play in knowledge management processes, and the limitations that exist to ICT-enabled communication and knowledge sharing. This section examines three of the key debates and illustrates the issues examined through the use of various examples.

ICTs and perspective making/taking

The first area of debate relates to the question of whether ICTs can facilitate the rich interaction and processes of perspective making and taking that those adopting a practice-based perspective suggest is necessary for inter-personal knowledge sharing to be successful. Walsham (2001) answers this question in the positive, and believes that ICT mediated communication does have the potential to facilitate processes of perspective making and taking. Boland *et al.* (1994) also believe that it could be possible to design IT systems to do this, suggesting,

> 'information technology can support distributed cognition by enabling individuals to make rich representations of their understanding, reflect upon those representations, engage in dialogue with others about them, and use them to inform action.' (p. 457)

However, Boland *et al.* argue that to do this requires a radical transformation in IS design philosophies. DeSanctis & Monge (1999, 696) also take a positive view regarding the ability of ICTs to allow a rich form of interaction, by arguing that rather than the loss of social cues which occurs when communicating via most ICTs being negative, such a loss may in fact facilitate understanding *'by removing the distraction of irrelevant stimuli'*.

However, other writers are more critical, fundamentally arguing that the difficulties of facilitating rich interactions via ICTs should not be underestimated (Hislop 2002b). This is primarily because the loss of social cues (tone & pace of voice, gesture, facial expression) which occurs when using most ICTs significantly degrades the communication process, and limits the extent to which knowledge can be shared via such media (Goodall & Roberts 2003; Roberts 2000; Symon 2000). Further, there may be a limited role for ICTs particularly in the sort of inter-community knowledge processes examined in Chapter 11. That chapter showed how knowledge sharing in such circumstances is complicated by the lack of shared identity and limited overlap in the knowledge base of people. These difficulties are arguably exacerbated when such knowledge sharing is electronically mediated, as the social cues that are important to the sharing of such factors are lost (Walsham 2001). McLoughlin & Jackson (1999) make similar conclusions, arguing that rich knowledge sharing in virtual interactions is most likely to be successful where there is a positive, pre-existing social relationship between people.

TIME TO REFLECT THE ADVANTAGES OF HAVING FEW SOCIAL CLUES

Is a potential advantage of ICT mediated communication that people are less likely to judge others on potentially superficial factors such as looks? How does the process of making initial judgements of strangers vary between face-to-face situations and ICT mediated situations?

Finally, a perspective somewhat intermediate to the above two positions suggests that while ICTs alone may have a limited ability to facilitate a rich form of communication, they can have a role when combined with face-to-face interactions (Nandhakumar 1999). Maznevski & Chudoba (1999) reach such a conclusion in their study of global virtual teams, suggesting that *'effective global virtual teams . . . generate a deep rhythm of regular face-to-face incidents interspersed with less intensive, shorter incidents using various media'* (p. 473).

ICTs and media richness

One related issue that emerges from the above debate is that face-to-face communication has different characteristics to electronically mediated communication processes. Looking in more detail, it can also be seen that different ICTs have different communication characteristics (see Table 13.3). However, the characteristics and degrees of information richness of different communication media are the subject of disagreement, and are the second area of debate examined.

Medium	Communication characteristics
Face-to-face interaction	• Information rich (social cues such as facial expression, voice, gesture visible. Plus, synchronous communication, potential for rapid high quality feedback/interaction) • Most relevant for sharing of tacit knowledge • Spontaneous/informal interactions possible when people geographically proximate • Conditions amenable to development of trust (other factors excluded) • Expensive when people geographically dispersed
Video conferencing	• Information rich (social cues, and virtually real time, synchronous medium) • Expensive to set up • Set up time inhibits spontaneity
Telephone	• Intermediate information richness (tone of voice conveys some social cues, but gesture, expression invisible. Also synchronous, facilitating detailed, immediate feedback) • Cost variable • Spontaneous/informal interactions possible irrespective of geographic proximity • Can facilitate development of trust where face-to-face interaction difficult
E-mail	• Suitable for sharing of highly codified knowledge • Relatively low information richness (all social cues lost) • Inexpensive (cost unrelated to geographic proximity) • Asynchronous, with variable feedback speed • Spontaneous/informal interactions possible irrespective of geographic proximity • Permanent record of interaction exists • Development of trust based on e-mail alone difficult

(left margin, vertical: Increasing information richness?)

Table 13.3 Characteristics of various communication mediums

Information richness theory (IRT) in the information systems literature suggests that different media have fixed and static levels of information richness, where *'communication richness (or leanness) is an invariant, objective property of communication media'* (Ngwenyama & Lee 1997, 147). Further, this theory adopts a rational choice approach to people's selection decisions with regard to the communication media they use, with people being assumed to select the communication medium most appropriate to the task being undertaken. From this perspective, it is possible to rank different media in terms of their 'objective' levels of information richness, with face-to-face interaction being the richest, and e-mail being one of the leanest (Daft & Lengel 1986). Table 13.3 is thus laid out to reflect such a ranking.

However, this theory has been the subject of an increasing level of criticism, which questions the idea that each communication medium has fixed and objective information richness characteristics. This is therefore why there is a question mark in Table 13.3 beside the ranking arrow. Instead of communication media having fixed and objective information richness characteristics, as IRT suggests, others suggest the leanness or richness of any communication process is something which emerges from the *'interactions between the people, and the organizational context'* (Ngwenyama & Lee, 1997, 148). Thus the richness of any communication process will not be determined by the technical characteristics of the communication medium, but will instead be shaped by a range of social and technical factors. Relevant social factors include the degree of mutual understanding which exists between people, the willingness of people to make the effort to communicate and understand, and the abilities of people to effectively use a communication medium. Thus, 'low richness' media like e-mail can be used for complex, information rich interactions if organizations encourages it, or people become adept at using it (Markus 1994; Ngwenyama & Lee 1997; DeSanctis & Monge 1999). Thus, if people are more comfortable and competent using e-mail, compared to 'richer' communication media, such as groupware, this may help explain the preference for e-mail reported in a number of studies (Ngwenyama & Lee 1997; Markus 1994; Pauleen & Yoong 2001; Robertson *et al.* 2001).

Organizational level factors, such as the character of the organizational culture can also affect both the type of medium used, and the way in which it is used. Thus, if an organizational culture places an emphasis on accountability and documentation, this may encourage the use of e-mail, as, compared to other communication media, this provides a good, documented record of conversations and interactions. Alternatively, an organizational culture that emphasizes teamworking, openness and good inter-personal working relations, may encourage the use of face-to-face meetings, and telephone conversations.

ICTs and developing/sustaining trust

The final area of debate and disagreement examined, which links closely to the first topic of debate examined, is the extent to which trust can be developed and sustained in social relations which are mediated by ICT based modes of communication. The literature on this topic shows that the extent of face-to-face interaction that occurs

Suggestions for further reading

1   D. Hislop (2002). 'Mission Impossible? Communicating and Sharing Knowledge via Information Technology', *Journal of Information Technology*, 17: 165–177.

Develops an analysis which favours a practice-based epistemology and which questions the centrality of the role that ICTs can play in knowledge sharing processes.

2   S. Newell, M. Bresnen, L. Edelman, H. Scarbrough, & J. Swan (2006). 'Sharing Knowledge Across Projects: Limits to ICT-led Project Review Practices', *Management Learning*, 37/2: 167–185.

Presents case study evidence suggesting there are limits to the role that ICTs can play in the sharing of project specific knowledge.

3   A. Massey, M. Montoya-Weiss, & T. O'Driscoll (2002). 'Knowledge Management in Pursuit of Performance: Insights from Nortel Networks', *MIS Quarterly*, 26/3: 269–289.

Presents a detailed analysis of a successful ICT based knowledge management initiative, which did take account of social/contextual factors.

4   J. Roberts (2000). 'From Know-How to Show-How? Questioning the Role of Information and Communication Technologies in Knowledge Transfer', *Technology Analysis and Strategic Management*, 12/4: 429–443.

Examines the difficulties of sharing knowledge, particularly tacit knowledge, via ICTs.

5   G. Walsham (2001). 'Knowledge Management: The Benefits and Limitations of Computer Systems', *European Management Journal*, 19/6: 599–608.

Reviews the literature on IT based knowledge management, and concludes that ICTs can facilitate knowledge management efforts, but from a practice-based perspective.

Take your learning further: Online Resource Centre

Visit the supporting Online Resource Centre for resources which will extend your understanding of knowledge management in organizations. As well as web links to sites of interest, the author has provided case studies looking at knowledge management in virtual and knowledge intensive firms, and in global multinationals. These will help you with your research, essays and assignments; or you may find these additional resources helpful when revising for exams.

www.oxfordtextbooks.co.uk/orc/hislop2e/

14

Facilitating Knowledge Management via Culture Management and HRM Practices

Introduction

As the introduction to Part 4, and Chapter 9 detail, social and cultural issues have been found to play a key role in affecting the dynamics and likely success of knowledge management initiatives. This is primarily because such factors have increasingly been recognized as playing a fundamental role in determining whether workers will be willing to actively participate in knowledge management initiatives. Inevitably, this has led to organizations deliberately attempting to manage their cultures to produce appropriate knowledge behaviours and to also use people management, or human resource management practices (HRM thereafter) to support their knowledge management efforts.

The central focus of this chapter is on the ways in which management can use culture management and HRM practices, such as recruitment and reward, to reinforce and support organizational knowledge management efforts through shaping workers' attitudes and behaviours in particular ways. The attitudes and behaviours that are relevant to knowledge management initiatives are outlined in Table 14.1. Thus, the use of culture management and HRM policies can be seen to be concerned not only with attempting to create a positive attitude towards, and a willingness to participate in, organizational knowledge management activities, but also with making workers committed and loyal to their employer, so that valuable knowledge is not lost through staff turnover (Leidner 2000). As was highlighted towards the end of Chapter 5, and as will be reinforced later, problems of knowledge loss through limited levels of staff loyalty are a particular problem in knowledge intensive firms. Thus people management practices concerned with supporting organizational knowledge management efforts should be concerned as much

15

Leadership and Knowledge Management

Introduction

The study of leadership is focussed upon how the actions of those with responsibility over other people in organizations can impact not only on the attitudes and behaviour of subordinates, but also team and organizational performance. A fundamental assumption underpinning the majority of literature on this topic is that leaders can play a pivotal role in organizations and that effective and appropriate leadership can both motivate and inspire subordinates and also positively impact on team and organizational performance. While leadership can be argued to be relevant to anyone with managerial responsibilities over others, the study of leadership has typically been focussed upon relatively senior figures in organizations.

Leadership in business organizations is a topic that has been extensively analysed by writers and academics since the first decades of the twentieth century. Further, an enormous diversity of perspectives on leadership has been developed and empirically evaluated (Northouse 2007; Yukl 2008). No attempt is made here to summarize this diverse literature. Instead, the focus here is narrowly on the sub-category of literature which links leadership behaviour to knowledge management processes.

The location of this chapter immediately after the chapter on the use of HRM processes and culture management practices to facilitate knowledge management activities is deliberate. This is because these topics are related, and are both concerned with the way that deliberate managerial interventions can be used to facilitate knowledge management activities. What distinguishes this chapter from the last one is that while HRM and culture management practices are concerned with using general procedures and practices that are relevant to all workers to facilitate knowledge management activities, the literature on leadership and knowledge management is concerned with the role that the behaviour and actions of key individuals can have in facilitating knowledge management activities. The general underpinning assumption of the literature examining the link between leadership and knowledge management is that effective leadership can positively impact on knowledge management processes, for example increasing the willingness of workers to share knowledge with others.

However, despite the extensive literature that exists on leadership in general, only a relatively limited amount of analysis has been produced on how leadership links to knowledge management processes, and in particular there is a significant lack of evidence which empirically substantiates this relationship (Chen 2007; Güldenberg & Konrath 2006). Further, as will be seen, much of this literature is open to criticism.

The chapter is organized into three discrete sections. In the following section the distinction between leadership and management is examined, and a very brief overview of how thinking on leadership has evolved is presented. However the main focus of this section is on examining the concept of transformational leadership, which is extensively used in the knowledge management literature on leadership. The second major section of the chapter describes the literature on knowledge management and leadership, illustrating the arguments made with some examples. The third and final major section of the chapter then presents a critique of this literature, drawing extensively upon a study by Alvesson & Sveningsson (2003) on leadership in knowledge intensive firms which challenges much of the analysis of leadership in general, and leadership and knowledge processes in particular.

The conceptualization of leadership in the academic business and management literature

Before examining the knowledge management literature which deals with the topic of leadership it is useful to begin the chapter by providing some context to this work through, briefly, engaging with the general academic literature on leadership. Given both the amount of writing that has been produced on the topic of leadership, as well as the diversity of perspectives and theories on leadership that have been developed, it is impossible in the space available here to provide a comprehensive overview of this literature. Thus all that is provided here is the presentation of a schematic outline of how the theorization of leadership has historically evolved and some detail on what represents the mainstream contemporary perspective on leadership.

Serious interest in the topic of leadership in the academic business literature dates back to the early twentieth century. At this time, what is characterized as the 'trait' theory of leadership dominated (see Table 15.1). This perspective suggested that great and successful leaders possess particular personality traits and characteristics which distinguished them from others, such as high levels of charisma. Thus from this perspective, great leaders are people born with particular traits that distinguish them from 'ordinary people'. However, over time, this perspective became subject to a number of criticisms, not least that empirical evidence has provided questionable support for it. Since then a number of different perspectives on leadership were developed (see Table 15.1), which themselves became subject to a number of criticisms. A useful starting point for those interested in gaining a more detailed understanding of how the theorization of leadership has evolved is to read relevant books or book chapters on the topic (see for example Densten 2008; Northouse 2007; Yukl 2008).

Leadership theory	Assumptions about leadership	Contemporary status/ relevance
Trait approach	Great leaders are born, not created, and possess particular inherent characteristics that distinguish them from other people—such as charisma, the ability to communicate effectively, emotional intelligence	Most popular in 1930s and 40s but re-emerged in 1970s. Discredited as empirical studies found no agreed relationship between particular traits and successful leadership. Also criticized for neglecting context
Behaviour-based theories	Focus on what leaders do—attempt to identify behaviours of successful leadership	Developed in 1950s but still utilized by some researchers. Has been criticized for lacking adequate theorization and empirical methodologies used to measure and investigate behaviours
Contingency approach (including Fiedler's contingency theory and path-goal theory)	What constitutes appropriate leadership is shaped by the nature of the organizational context	Developed in late 1960s with general growth in popularity of contingency theory. Has been criticized on a number of issues including lack of consistent empirical support
'New leadership' theories (including charismatic leadership theory, and transformational/trans-actional leadership theory)	Concerned with how leader's action and talk motivates followers to act	Developed in late 1970s and have grown in popularity since. Have been criticized for universalistic assumptions which neglect importance of context

Table 15.1 Historical overview of diverse perspectives on leadership

As suggested in Table 15.1, 'new leadership' theories represent the most popular contemporary perspective on leadership in the academic business literature. It is worth elaborating on this perspective in a little depth, not only because of its contemporary popularity, but also because, as will be seen later, it represents the perspective on leadership most widely used by writers on knowledge management (for example Crawford 2005; Politis 2002; Hinterhuber & Stadler 2006; Vera & Crossan 2004).

Arguably Burns's (1978) development of the concept of transformational leadership represents the starting point of what has subsequently been labelled 'new leadership'. However, various terms such as strategic leadership, charismatic leadership and

TIME TO REFLECT APPLYING LEADERSHIP THEORIES

Think of an example of a high profile and successful leader (either from a business organization or from some other context, such as a sports team or a political party). Which leadership theory best explains their success?

	Leadership	(Micro) management
Timescales focussed upon	Long term	Short term
Primary role	Strategic	Operational
Key task	Development and communication of long term vision	Day-to-day management of people towards work objectives
People management role	Motivate by providing inspiring vision and providing intellectual stimulation	Day-to-day management of people towards short and medium term work objectives through goal setting and reward management
Impact on culture, values and structure	Develop new values and vision with aim of sustaining long term competitiveness	Reinforce existing culture, values and structures through operating within them

Table 15.2 Distinguishing leadership from (micro) management

visionary leadership have been utilized by others to refer to a very similar style of leadership. Thus typically, all these concepts are categorized as together representing 'new leadership' theory (Vera & Crossan 2004). Arguably, one of the key features of transformational leadership (and all 'new leadership' theories) is that it represents a form of leadership and people management that is distinctive from more traditional forms of management. Thus, transformational leadership is often defined in parallel with, and as the virtual opposite of, management (what might be referred to as micro-management, which is referred to by various writers on instrumental leadership, for example Nadler & Tushman (1990), and on transactional leadership, Burns (1978)). As outlined in Table 15.2 transformational leadership is fundamentally concerned with motivating and inspiring followers by developing long term strategic visions and persuading people to buy into them and work towards their achievement. Transformational leaders thus motivate workers through providing them with intellectual stimulation and inspiring them to work towards these corporate visions and values.

Alvesson & Sveningsson (2003) highlight the contemporary popularity and importance of this perspective on leadership in their analysis of leadership practices in a biotechnology company. They argue that leadership discourse, consisting of a repertoire of terms, ideas and concepts provides managers and leaders with insights into what is argued to constitute leadership. The characteristics of the dominant contemporary discourse on leadership they articulate resonates strongly with the characteristics of leadership embedded in 'new leadership' theories. Thus this discourse suggests that the main concerns of leaders should be with developing and communicating long term strategy, vision, and guidelines for future action. A further key assumption of this discourse on leadership is that leadership has a direct link to and impact upon organizational performance and competitiveness, and that for companies to maintain competitiveness in the long term, effective leadership is necessary.

> **Definition**   Transformational leadership
>
> A mode or style of leadership focussed on the development of long term visions, values and goals which also involves persuading workers to become attached to them and to work towards achieving them.

While this literature places a central emphasis on the strategic importance of transformational leadership, there is also an acknowledgement that this form of leadership is not enough on its own for the successful management of workers. Thus, it is usually argued that transformational leadership requires to be used in parallel with other forms of leadership and management which are more focussed on the day-to-day management of workers and operational issues. Thus for example Burns talked of transformational and transactional leadership, and Nadler & Tushman (1990) refer to charismatic and instrumental leadership.

However, while there is an enormous corpus of writing on the topic of leadership, and while it represents a relatively mature subject area, there is a lack of consensus on the questions of what leadership fundamentally consists of and whether and how links can be made between the leadership styles and behaviours of key individuals, and organizational performance (see for example Kelly 2008; Northouse 2007). For example, there is limited agreement on how leadership is differentiated from and related to management (Alvesson & Sveningsson 2003). Further, the mainstream literature on leadership has been criticized on such fundamental issues as making universalist assumptions about the relevance of certain leadership styles which neglect to adequately account for context, being weakly theorized, making use of questionable research methods, and of providing weak empirical support for the claims that are made (Barker 2001; Güldenberg & Konrath 2006; Yukl 2008). Despite this lack of consensus the vast majority of knowledge management literature, as will be seen in the following section, adopts a relatively uncritical stance to contemporary perspectives on transformational leadership.

Knowledge management and leadership

As outlined, the relationship between leadership styles and behaviours and knowledge management processes is relatively under-researched. Of the literature that has been produced on the topic, some explicitly links to existing leadership theories and some does not. The main perspective on leadership adopted by the knowledge literature which does explicitly link to leadership theory is the transformational leadership perspective (see for example Crawford 2005; Politis 2002; Vera & Crossan 2004). The most influential exemplar of work in the area of knowledge management that does *not* make explicit links to leadership theory is the work of Nonaka and his colleagues (see Chapter 7). However, Nonaka *et al.*'s conceptualization of leadership has much in common with the transformational leadership perspective. Thus, within the knowledge management literature on leadership, as will be outlined below, the transformational leadership perspective dominates.

This literature can be characterized by two features. Firstly, the claims it makes with regard to the relationship between knowledge management or learning and leadership, and secondly, the claims made regarding the type or style of leadership necessary to facilitate knowledge management and learning. With regards to the link between leadership and knowledge management this literature typically makes a relatively strong claim that effective leadership can play an important role in facilitating learning and knowledge management activities in organizations. Further, due to the assumptions made in this literature regarding the importance of knowledge processes to organizational performance effective leadership is also assumed to help contribute to competitive advantage and organizational performance. Thus, Hinterhuber and Stadler (2006, 237), argue that *'leadership and strategy are the immaterial competencies which contribute most to a company's value'*.

With regards to the style of leadership argued to be necessary to achieve such performance, as outlined, there is virtual unanimity in the knowledge management literature that transformational leadership is the most appropriate form of leadership. Thus, this literature talks about the importance of leaders who are concerned with developing long term strategy and vision. Secondly, in relation to people management this literature emphasizes the ability of the leader to inspire and motivate rather than to micro-manage workers. For example, Nonaka *et al.* (2006, 1192) talk about leadership as being concerned with *'interpreting, nurturing and supporting the knowledge vision'*, and that in relation to their SECI model of knowledge creation (see Chapter 7) should be about *'enabling knowledge creation—not controlling and directing it'*.

Finally, somewhat in contradiction with the idea of transformational leadership, this literature also suggests that effective leadership is not simply the responsibility of senior management, but that instead responsibility for leadership should be the concern of all workers and managers, and that leadership should be dispersed throughout an organization. For example, Nonaka *et al.* (2006, 1191) talk of 'distributed leadership' (they argue that middle managers in particular have a key leadership role), while Güldenberg & Konrath (2006) talk about organizations creating a 'community of leaders'.

The importance of the role that effective leadership can play in facilitating knowledge management processes is illustrated in the following example, where a particular leader was argued to play a fundamentally important role in the creation of a knowledge sharing culture.

TIME TO REFLECT SUCCESSFUL LEADERSHIP THAT ISN'T TRANSFORMATIONAL

Can you find an example of a successful knowledge management initiative which was facilitated by a form of leadership that was distinctive from transformational leadership?

ILLUSTRATION

Buckman Laboratories

Pan & Scarbrough (1999) argue that appropriate knowledge cultures can be developed, but admit that doing so is a complex, daunting and time consuming process. Their argument is based on a detailed examination of one organization—Buckman Laboratories. This organization has arguably been a pioneer of knowledge management, and was one of the earliest organizations to actively manage and utilize its knowledge base to improve business performance. Buckman Laboratories has been relatively successful in these efforts, and has, in the words of one top manager interviewed by Pan & Scarbrough (1999, 369), 'created a culture of trust encouraging active knowledge sharing across time and space among all of the company's employees across the world.' The initial vision for this culture was a pledge made by Bob Buckman, that knowledge was to become the foundation of its competitive advantage.

Central to Buckman Laboratories' efforts to develop a knowledge sharing culture was the development and implementation of a technological system for codifying and sharing knowledge (K'Netix). However it was also recognized by senior management that to create an effective knowledge sharing culture, that management required to be pro-active in the transformation of the company's culture, who developed a culture change programme to achieve this.

Pan & Scarbrough argue that key to the success of this programme was the role played by the organization's leader, Bob Buckman. He is described as a 'pioneering figure' (p. 369), who initiated and strongly championed the idea of developing a knowledge sharing culture. Further, his style of leadership was described as being very different from that of his father, the company's founder, who was a very hands on micro-manager who 'oversaw every decision, sales order, cheque and memo' (p. 369). Bob Buckman by contrast was argued to be more concerned with and focussed upon the longer term concern of developing a future vision of the company and creating conditions which allow it to be achieved. This was acknowledged by one senior manager who was interviewed who said that the 'climate we create as leaders has a major impact on our ability to share knowledge across space and time' (p. 370). Thus, the skills attributed to Bob Buckman by Pan & Scarbrough—of having a clear vision, a strong commitment to implementing it and an ability to communicate it to others—fits closely with the typical characteristics of transformational leadership outlined above.

Knowledge management and leadership: limitations of existing perspectives

As with the mainstream literature on leadership, the knowledge management literature which examined leadership can be criticized and challenged on a number of important points. Firstly, much of the writing in this area has been concerned with the development of conceptual models which aren't empirically evaluated (such as Bryant 2003; Hinterhuber & Stadler 2006). For example, Vera & Crossan (2004) develop a conceptual model which suggests that both transformational and transactional forms of leadership may play an important role in facilitating learning in organizations. However, the veracity of the model isn't evaluated against any empirical data, thus its accuracy and utility remains open to question.

Secondly, the empirical data presented by many of the studies on this topic which do empirically examine how leadership impacts on knowledge management processes can also be questioned. For example the generalizability of some of the empirical data that is presented can be questioned, as it is either anecdotal or case study evidence related to a single organization case study (such as Nonaka *et al.* 2006; Pan & Scarbrough 1999; Singh 2008). Further, studies which have collected and analysed quantitative, survey based data in an attempt to statistically measure the relationship between leadership and knowledge management processes have largely failed to provide strong convincing evidence (Crawford 2005; Güldenberg & Konrath 2006; Politis 2002; Singh 2008). For example, Politis (2002) developed and tested (via a survey) seven hypotheses concerning the relationship between transformational and transactional leadership and both knowledge acquisition and team performance in an Australian manufacturing company. However, the results didn't support the hypotheses developed, and with respect to the relationship between team performance and transformational leadership concluded that transformational leadership '*may not be the prime impetus for moving team performance forward*' (p. 187).

A third critique of this literature is that in making strong claims regarding the role of leadership on knowledge management processes and organizational performance, it neglects to account for ambiguity (Alvesson & Sveningsson (2003). While suggesting that ambiguity is an inherent feature of all organizations, Alvesson & Sveningsson (2003) argue that ambiguity is a particular feature of work in knowledge intensive firms. Such ambiguities, they argue, bring into question one of the claims of contemporary leadership theory, the link between leadership behaviour and organizational performance.

TIME TO REFLECT HOW CONVINCING?

Find an example of an empirical study which suggests that particular leadership behaviours have contributed to the success of a knowledge management initiative. How convincing and/or generalizible is the empirical data and the analysis?

Fundamentally, Alvesson & Sveningsson (2003) argue that the unavoidable ambiguities that exist in all organizations make it virtually impossible to demonstrate any clear link between the behaviour and actions of particular individuals, and organizational performance outcomes.

A useful way to illustrate what are argued to be the limitations of transformational leadership theory, and its ability to facilitate and enhance knowledge management processes, is through an example. Thus, the remainder of this section presents an extended example from a knowledge intensive firm where the way the managers talked about their work challenged and contradicted the idea of transformational leadership.

ILLUSTRATION

Contradictions regarding the relevance of transformational leadership

Alvesson & Sveningsson (2003) undertook a qualitative empirical study of middle managers in a knowledge intensive firm (a biotechnology company). One of the key empirical findings from their study was that they found a contradiction between how the middle managers interviewed described their leadership roles and what they described as their day-to-day work responsibilities.

In interviews people drew on the idea of transformational leadership in describing their leadership roles, suggesting that leadership was less about day-to-day micro management and more about developing long term vision, values and strategy and ensuring buy in to it, and also providing autonomy and empowerment to workers to make their own decisions about day-to-day matters. Thus one interviewee talked of, *'putting people in the same direction, leadership, there's providing common vision . . . what the direction of that group is going in, you personally as a manager have to live that vision'* (p. 970).

By contrast when interviewees elaborated in more detail on what they did as leaders they gave descriptions of work as involving a significant amount of micromanagement, having significant administrative and operational responsibilities. For example, one interviewee talked about a constant need to get involved in detailed project work, another about a need to be decisive and directive, and a third about often being oriented towards technical rather than strategic issues. While such responsibilities were regarded as unavoidable, the amount of time they devoted to them was a source of conflict and frustration for the interviewees, who appeared to accept the logic that transformational leadership was a positive form of leadership, while day-to-day administration and micro-management represented a bad and inappropriate form of leadership.

Alvesson & Sveningsson (2003) concluded that the contradiction between the rhetoric and actions of the interviewees with regard to leadership was partly caused by the ambiguities of the corporate context they worked within. At one level, there were explicit corporate messages regarding what constituted good and bad forms of leadership, with transformational leadership regarded as good, and micro-management bad. However, this message contradicted pressures the managers experienced to become involved in micro-level management, which was caused by an articulated corporate need for standardization and consistency following a recent corporate merger.

They also concluded that another reason why the interviewees were attracted to ideas of transformational leadership was that they helped them to reinforce their sense of self-identity as leaders. The need to bolster their sense of identity as leaders was argued to be partly due to the declining legitimacy of traditional management roles in knowledge intensive firms.

1. Is the type of ambiguity in the corporate context of the case company likely to be a typical feature in all business organizations?

Conclusion

This chapter has been concerned with providing an overview of how the leadership behaviours of key individuals in organizations can impact on organizational knowledge management activities. As outlined, the assumption that typically underpins much of the literature on this topic is that effective leadership behaviours can have a very positive role in facilitating and supporting knowledge management activities.

While in the mainstream literature on leadership there are a diversity of perspectives, in the knowledge management literature the transformational leadership concept dominates. This perspective on leadership makes a relatively sharp distinction between leadership and management, arguing that while management is focussed upon operational issues and is concerned with the day-to-day management of people and resources, transformational leadership by contrast is more focussed on strategic issues and is concerned with more long term matters such as developing and communicating a future vision that people can be inspired and motivated by.

Overall, the meta-analysis of the literature on leadership and knowledge management literature conducted here suggests that there isn't clear, unequivocal evidence of a direct link between leadership behaviours and knowledge management processes. Thus the numerous claims of such a linkage in the knowledge management literature are relatively unsubstantiated. There is some anecdotal and case study evidence of the role that leadership can play in facilitating knowledge management activities, such as the case study of Buckman Laboratories produced by Pan & Scarbrough (1999). However, much of the writing which claims that leadership behaviours can support knowledge management activities either presents no supporting empirical evidence, or presents evidence which doesn't strongly substantiate the claims being made.

Thus, this is a domain of enquiry that is significantly under-developed, and before more confident claims can be made regarding the impact that leadership behaviours can have on knowledge management activities, more extensive empirical investigation of this area is required.

Case study

The relationship between empowering leadership, knowledge sharing
and the performance of management teams

Srivastava *et al.* (2006) examined the intervening role that knowledge sharing had on the relationship between empowering leadership and the performance of management teams. The study also examined the intervening role of team efficacy, but this aspect of the paper isn't examined here. In studies of leadership these relationships are argued to have never been empirically tested.

Empowering leadership is defined as a form of leadership where power is shared by leaders and managers with subordinates, which is argued to increase subordinates' levels of intrinsic motivation. Specific examples of empowering leadership behaviours are participative decision-making and coaching. While intra-team knowledge sharing can facilitate team performance through helping to effectively utilize a team's cognitive resources, such forms of knowledge sharing in teams do not occur automatically. They have to be developed, encouraged and supported. Empowering leadership, through encouraging subordinates to express and share their opinions, have the potential to play a crucial role in facilitating such knowledge sharing processes. Thus it was hypothesized that knowledge sharing would be positively related to empowering leadership behaviours.

With respect to the relationship between team knowledge sharing and team performance, it was hypothesized that team performance would be positively related to knowledge sharing. This was argued to be the case not only because the sharing of knowledge within teams is likely to improve team decision making, through the effective utilization of a team's cognitive resources, but also because the sharing of knowledge contributes to improved team coordination through to the development of shared mental models within teams.

The hypotheses that were developed were tested via conducting a survey of management teams from various regions in the USA. The surveys were sent to management team leaders, with the team leaders asked to distribute the surveys to their management team members. Responses had to be provided by at least 2 members of a team for a team to be included in the data analysis. Of the 550 management teams that the survey was sent to, data from 102 teams was used. All the variables being examined, including leadership, knowledge sharing and team performance, were measured on the survey via a number of scales made up of specific items. For example, in relation to knowledge sharing, one of the questions/items used was, 'managers in our team share their special knowledge and expertise with one another'.

The statistical analysis of the survey data supported all the hypotheses examined, thus the empirical data did find that not only was empowering leadership positively related to intra-team knowledge sharing, but also that team performance was also positively related to intra-team knowledge sharing.

This study therefore provides some evidence of a link between leadership and knowledge sharing processes in teams and suggests that empowering forms of leadership are likely to facilitate intra-team knowledge sharing through encouraging team members to voice their opinions, and through making them feel that their knowledge is valued and their opinions respected. Thus, in practical, managerial terms, to facilitate intra-team knowledge sharing, organizations should encourage and develop empowering leadership behaviours among its team leaders and senior managers.

1. The empowering style of leadership examined by Srivastava *et al.* appears closer to what has been called (micro) management, rather than transformational leadership (see Table 15.2). Does this suggest that *both* effective (micro) management and transformational styles of leadership have a role to play in facilitating organizational knowledge management processes?

Source: Srivastava, A., Bartol, K., & Locke, E. (2006). 'Empowering Leadership in Management Teams: Effects on Knowledge Sharing, Efficacy, and Performance', *Academy of Management Journal*, 49/6: 1239–1251.

 For further information about this journal article visit our Online Resource Centre at www.oxfordtextbooks.co.uk/orc/hislop2e/

Review and discussion questions

1   One critique of much of the leadership literature, including the concept of transformational leadership that is widely used in the knowledge management literature, is that it makes universalistic assumptions that such forms of leadership are appropriate in all contexts and situations. Thus, much of the knowledge management literature on leadership implies that transformational leadership is appropriate to all knowledge intensive firms and the management of all knowledge workers. Do you agree with this argument, or do you think that context matters and that, while transformational leadership may be useful in some contexts, different types of situation require different styles of leadership?

2   Do you agree with Alvesson & Sveningsson's (2003) argument that the unavoidable ambiguity which exists in knowledge intensive firms (for example with regard to knowing what factors enhance processes of knowledge creation) makes it difficult in such contexts to empirically verify a linkage between the leadership behaviours of specific leaders and character of knowledge processes?

Suggestions for further reading

1   S. Pan & H. Scarbrough (1999), 'Knowledge Management in Practice: An Exploratory Case Study', *Technology Analysis and Strategic Management*, 11/3: 359–374.

An interesting qualitative case study of an organization where leadership was key to the development of a knowledge sharing culture.

2   G. Yukl (2008). *Leadership in Organizations*. Pearson Education.

A good introduction to and critical review of the diverse literature on leadership.

3   D. Vera & M. Crossan (2004). 'Strategic Leadership and Organizational Learning', *Academy of Management Review*, 29/2: 222–240.

A conceptual paper only, which develops hypotheses regarding how transformational and transactional leadership relate to processes of learning in organizations.

4   M. Alvesson & S. Sveningsson (2003). 'Good Visions, Bad Micro-Management and Ugly Ambiguity: Contradictions of (Non-) Leadership in a Knowledge-Intensive Organization', *Organization Studies*, 24/6: 961–988.

A qualitative study of leadership in a knowledge intensive firm which provides a critique of the 'new leadership' perspective/discourse.

5   J. Politis (2002). 'Transformational and Transactional Leadership Enabling (Disabling) Knowledge Acquisition of Self-Managed Teams: The Consequences for Performance', *Leadership and Organization Development Journal*, 23/4: 186–197.

One of the few quantitative empirical studies which examine the relationship between leadership and knowledge processes.

Take your learning further: Online Resource Centre

Visit the supporting Online Resource Centre for resources which will extend your understanding of knowledge management in organizations. As well as web links to sites of interest, the author has provided case studies looking at knowledge management in virtual and knowledge intensive firms, and in global multinationals. These will help you with your research, essays and assignments; or you may find these additional resources helpful when revising for exams.

 www.oxfordtextbooks.co.uk/orc/hislop2e/

16

Reflections on the Topic of Knowledge Management

Introduction

The broad focus of this final chapter is on dealing with some general questions that relate to the body of writing and analysis on knowledge management in general. These issues can be embodied into three questions, each of which are dealt with separately. Firstly, what is the general quality, intellectual coherence and rigour of writing on knowledge management? Secondly, does knowledge management constitute a management fashion whose time has come (and gone)? Finally, how is knowledge on knowledge management produced and consumed, and who are involved in these processes?

Section one discusses the question of the quality of the writing on knowledge management. The second section examines the question, raised by a number of writers, of whether knowledge management represents the latest in a long line of management fashions. In evaluating this question Abrahamson's (1996) work on management fashions is utilized. The third and final section of the chapter goes beyond these debates, and the general content of the book, by considering the context in which knowledge on knowledge management is produced and consumed. This is useful as it gives an insight into the specific agents and processes through which the ideas and practices of knowledge management examined in the book have emerged.

Reflections on the knowledge management literature

As has been seen throughout the book, a diversity of perspectives exist on virtually every aspect of knowledge management. From definitions of what knowledge is, through the role of IT systems in knowledge management initiatives, to the way communities of practice should be managed and supported, debates and disagreements exist. Thus, it is hard to make general statements regarding the quality of writing on the topic, as the knowledge management literature is not coherent in character. In fact, one of the defining characteristics of the literature on knowledge management is the plurality and diversity of perspectives that exist, and continue to thrive. Never the less, this difficult task is attempted here, through discussing and commenting on two papers which have made generalizing statements about the character and quality of the literature on knowledge management (Scarbrough & Swan 2001; Alvesson & Kärreman 2001).

Scarbrough & Swan (2001), in the editorial introduction to a special issue of the *Journal of Management Studies* on knowledge management, lament what they characterize as the uncritical and unreflexive nature of the mainstream literature on knowledge management. Such literature is argued to be typically based on an objectivist perspective on knowledge (see Chapter 2), which unproblematically characterizes knowledge as an economic commodity, and fails to discuss the socially constructed, political, subjective, context dependent and dynamic characteristics of knowledge. Further, such literature is argued to be strongly managerialist in tone, being typically quite prescriptive, concerning itself with questions of how knowledge can be managed, rather than questions of can or should it be managed.

Alvesson & Kärreman (2001) are even more scathing regarding what they call the 'popular' knowledge management literature. They suggest that there are five specific problems with the way knowledge is conceptualized (see Table 16.1). Fundamentally, they argue that conceptualizations of knowledge in this literature are generally weak, sloppy, contradictory and do not stand up to rigorous criticism. This general line of argument is agreed with by Edwards *et al.* (2003). However, one weakness with Alvesson & Kärreman's analysis is that they are not very explicit about the types of work they are criticizing, giving only a few examples.

While such criticisms represent an accurate and important critique of and challenge to some of the most basic and simplistic early knowledge management literature, they do not represent an accurate comment on the full body of writing on knowledge management. Further, the heterogeneous diversity of perspectives on knowledge management that exist, and the range in quality of the work that has been produced on the

Problem	Problem description
Ontological incoherence	Blending together of incompatible constructivist and objectivist views of knowledge—for example Nonaka (1994)
Vagueness	Lack of distinctness regarding the content and character of knowledge in organizations
All embracing and empty view of knowledge	All encompassing definitions of knowledge have little clarity and make possibilities for conceptual insights difficult—for example Davenport & Prusak (1998)
Objectivity	Typically utilize objectivist definitions of knowledge unproblematically
Functionalism	Unproblematically assumes that having knowledge and managing knowledge is a good thing and neglects to deal with potential negative aspects of both having or managing knowledge

Table 16.1 Problems with conceptions of knowledge in the 'popular' knowledge management literature

Source: from Alvesson & Kärreman (2001)

TIME TO REFLECT WEAK CONCEPTUALIZATIONS OF KNOWLEDGE?

Pick an example of a popular, mainstream piece of writing on the topic of knowledge management. To what extent are the five problems of conceptualizing knowledge identified by Alvesson & Kärreman (2001) relevant to it?

topic means that the sort of generalized claims made by Scarbrough & Swan (2001) and Alvesson & Kärreman (2001) cannot be made against all the literature in this area, en mass. Thus, while there has been much writing of dubious quality on knowledge management, there has also been a significant body of writing and research of good quality which takes a sophisticated perspective on such questions as the nature of knowledge. One of the fundamental aims of this book is to demonstrate that a strong and vibrant body of critical work on knowledge management exists and has usefully questioned and challenged the assumptions of mainstream, managerialist perspectives.

However, this is not to say that the literature on knowledge management in its totality, encompassing both mainstream and critical perspectives, is not without its problems. Firstly, the comments made by Schultze & Stabell (2004) that the neo-functionalist perspective on knowledge management predominates, is still in broad terms true. While, as illustrated primarily in Chapter 3, practice-based perspectives on knowledge have been utilized by an increasing number of researchers and writers, there is still a dearth of scholarship on knowledge management which adopts what Schultze & Stabell (2004) label the critical and dialogical perspective on knowledge management. One indication of this is that the topics of power, politics and conflict are still relatively neglected and rarely written about. Thus, the lead taken by those writers examined in Chapter 12 to account for such issues is a path that has not been followed by a significant number of writers.

Another critique that can be made against some literature which talks about knowledge management is that what is actually being examined could more accurately be referred to as data or information management, rather than knowledge management (see also Spender 2008. For an example, see Dawson & Nolan 2006). This is most true of the literature on knowledge management produced by those from the academic disciplines of IS/IT and computing. This literature has deliberately not been engaged with in this book as it has been centrally focussed on knowledge management literature produced in the academic discipline of business and management.

Knowledge management as a fashion?

This section begins by considering another general critique of knowledge management: that it represents the latest in an apparently endless succession of management fads and fashions and that interest in the topic is thus likely to wane rapidly. As outlined in Chapter 1, this is a perspective adopted by a number of writers. Before this can be done it is useful to elaborate a little on Abrahamson's (1996) perspective on management fashion, whose focus is on the uptake of fashions in the business world.

Abrahamson starts from the assumption that management behaviour is shaped by norms of rationality and progress. The norm of rationality suggests that management will always use the techniques and ways of organizing which they regard as the most efficient. The norm of progress on the other hand suggests that as knowledge improves and develops over time, managers will adopt new techniques and practices as they become available. Thus, the process of fashion setting involves fashion setters attempting to utilize both the norms of progress and rationality to shape the 'collective beliefs' of managers in the business world that the particular technique they are currently advocating both represents an advance on existing knowledge, and also that it represents the most effective current technique available.

Abrahamson defines a management fashion as, '*a relatively transitory collective belief, disseminated by fashion setters, that a management technique leads to rational management progress*' (1996, 257). The transitoriness of fashions represents one of their defining characteristics, where interest in a particular topic grows quickly, but then also wanes equally rapidly. Thus, for Abrahamson, management fashions are identifiable by '*rapid bells-shaped swings*' and '*waves of interest in management techniques*' (p. 256). Thus, if interest in a topic over time is plotted on a graph a wave shaped pattern will be produced which resembles a normal distribution curve. The question addressed here is that, now that it is more than 10 years since interest in the topic of knowledge management began to take off, has there been the tell-tale rapid decline of interest in the topic which would allow knowledge management to be labelled a transitory management fashion?

As outlined in Chapter 1, Scarbrough and Swan (2001) undertook one of the most thorough analyses to determine whether the explosive growth of interest that has occurred in knowledge management could be understood as a fashion. They argued that the growth of interest in knowledge management that occurred in the late 1990s did resemble the start of a fashion, with there being a sudden ramping up of interest in the topic which resembled the first half of a normal distribution curve. While Scarbrough and Swan (2001) challenge and question various aspect of Abrahamson's (1996) fashion setting model, they concluded that it was likely that interest in knowledge management would follow the bell-shaped curve that Abrahamson suggests is evidence of a fashion, concluding that the existing evidence 'hints strongly' (p. 6) of an impending decline of interest in the topic.

However, Scarbrough and Swan's analysis ultimately represented speculation regarding how future interest in knowledge management would evolve. The data presented in Table 1.1, which extends Scarbrough & Swan's analysis by eight years to record the number of articles published on the topic of knowledge management per year up to 2006, makes it possible to more accurately judge whether interest in knowledge management has followed the normal distribution patterns symptomatic of a management fashion. The evidence presented in Table 1.1 challenges the idea that knowledge management is a management fashion, as rather than interest in the topic showing a rapid decline after 1998, there has been a plateauing of interest in the topic. Combining Scarbrough and Swan's figures with those presented in Table 1.1 it can be seen that 1998 did represent a high point of interest in knowledge management, with about 150 publications being produced in that year on the topic. However, between 2000 and 2006, rather than there being a rapid decline of interest, the number of publications on knowledge management plateaued at approximately 110–120 per year. Thus, according to this evidence, knowledge management does not represent a transitory management fashion, as since 1998 there has been a sustained level of interest in the topic. Further support for this argument is provided in the following section, which shows that the original gurus of knowledge management have continued to write and talk about the topic.

The data used in the above analysis arguably provides evidence on only academic interest in knowledge management. This data thus doesn't give a good understanding of the extent to which the business community has retained an interest in the topic of knowledge management. Gaining accurate data on this topic is difficult. One indicator of the extent to which the business community are interested in knowledge management can be gained through surveys which record the number of firms implementing knowledge management initiatives. In the late 1990s and early years of the twenty-first century a number of such surveys were conducted (such as KPMG 2000, 2003; Ruggles 1998) which suggested that there was a significant level of interest in the topic of knowledge management in the business world. However, since this time no comprehensive surveys have been conducted. The only survey that has been conducted on knowledge management use (in 2006), was a survey of global law firms (http://www.llrx.com/features/kmsurvey2006.htm). The 2002/2003 survey produced by KPMG (2003) was never updated, with the division of KPMG being responsible for conducting it and providing knowledge management services being closed (personal communication with KPMG—January 2007).

The fact that a comprehensive, up-to-date survey on the uptake of knowledge management initiatives in business has not been undertaken since 2003 could itself be understood as indicating a decline of interest in the topic in the business community. However, there is another way of interpreting this finding. It could be argued that it provides evidence of a decline in interest in certain, particular ways of managing organizational knowledge. This fits with a perspective developed by Schultze (2008), whose conclusions are based on limited anecdotal evidence: conversations with a number of friends in the business world. In explaining the apparent difference between the sustained academic interest and declining business interest in knowledge management Schultze distinguishes between what she refers to as 'knowledge management as a solution', and 'knowledge management as a problem'. The concept of 'knowledge management as a solution' (or Knowledge Management—with capital letters) represents the idea that a 'big bang' way to address and solve knowledge management issues/problems is to implement and utilize particular types of ICT. The concept of 'knowledge management as a problem' (or knowledge management—with lower case letters), by contrast refers to the day-to-day challenges and problems that workers face in using, sharing and developing knowledge in carrying out their work.

Schultze concludes that the declining interest in the business community is with the 'big bang' concept of Knowledge Management, the idea that Knowledge Management problems can be addressed through a single large-scale Knowledge Management initiative. In contrast, the need to deal with knowledge management issues in making effective use of knowledge in the conduct of day-to-day work tasks is likely to remain an ongoing challenge for firms (see also McKinlay 2005). This conclusion is also rein-forced by Nicolini *et al.*'s (2008) review of the knowledge management in the health-care sector which found that, despite the lack of initiatives which were explicitly labelled 'knowledge management', the '*healthcare sector reflects all the time on the nature and ways of managing what is known*' (p. 258). Thus, a decline in the number of large-scale knowledge management initiatives does not mean that business organizations do not require to make ongoing efforts to manage the knowledge of their workforce effectively.

Finally, a quite distinctive approach on the question of whether knowledge manage-ment represents a fashion is adopted by Spender (2008), who not only rejects this idea, but turns it on its head. Spender argues that knowledge management represents a poten-tially very important subject area which not only opens up new ways of theorizing about the nature of organizations, but also has the potential to be highly relevant to the interests of the business world in improving business performance. However, to do this he sug-gests that more 'robust' models of knowledge than those that currently predominate need to be developed.

Understanding the processes and agents in the diffusion and consumption of knowledge on knowledge management

In this section a broader focus is taken to look at how management knowledge in general, and knowledge on knowledge management more specifically, is commodified, produced, diffused and consumed. This will allow consideration of the type of people and organ-izations that are key in such processes, with a particular focus on the role of academics, business schools and universities in such processes. Such a focus is warranted not only because the role of the university sector has been relatively neglected in such processes, but also because its role has been changing dramatically in recent years.

While fashion-based analyses are useful for describing and understanding the expo-nential growth of interest in knowledge management, they are relatively broad brush and general in character. They thus have limited utility in shedding light on the particu-lar character of the processes through which knowledge on knowledge management is produced and consumed, or the actors involved in such processes. This section fills in some of these details, through making use of the cycle of knowledge production and consumption developed by Suddaby & Greenwood (2001). This cycle is relevant to the production of *all* management knowledge, and was not developed specifically in relation to knowledge management. However, this framework can be utilized to better describe and understand the context within which knowledge on knowledge management is both produced and consumed. Further, as a reader of this textbook, you are a consumer of knowledge on knowledge management, and can use the cycle to more fully under-stand the processes through which such knowledge is produced, as well as the diversity of processes through which you have acquired such knowledge (see the activity at the end of this chapter).

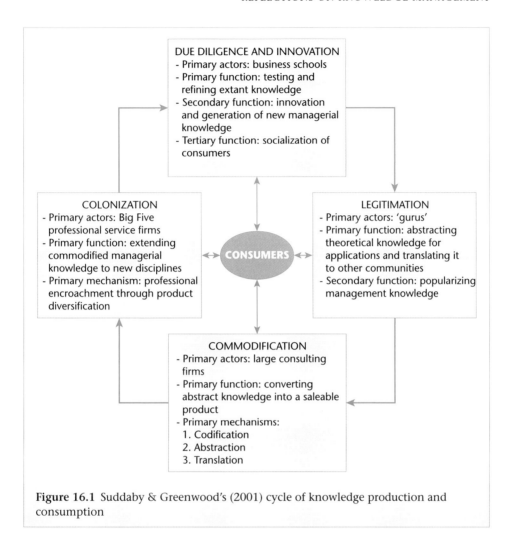

Figure 16.1 Suddaby & Greenwood's (2001) cycle of knowledge production and consumption

For Suddaby & Greenwood (2001, 933) the cycle they develop and describe represents a *'field level analysis of the process by which management knowledge is produced'*. As can be seen in Figure 16.1, the production and consumption of management knowledge involves the complex interaction via a number of discrete, but inter-related processes of a diverse range of actors including consumers, business schools and individual academics, gurus, consulting companies and large professional service firms. The cycle does not represent a simple stage model, with the production and consumption of knowledge occurring in neat, independent, sequential stages. Instead all the processes typically occur simultaneously. However, Suddaby & Greenwood suggest the process of legitimation undertaken by gurus typically represents a starting point in the production of a new body of management knowledge. Arguably, this process of legitimation is similar to the fashion setting process involving gurus which represents the starting point of management fashions in Abrahamson's (1996) model outlined earlier. The description of Suddaby & Greenwood's

TIME TO REFLECT WHAT STIMULATED *YOUR* INTEREST IN KNOWLEDGE MANAGEMENT?

Before looking at the cycle in detail, reflect upon your interest in knowledge management. When did it occur? What stimulated it? Further, through what mechanisms did/do you consume knowledge on knowledge management: newspapers, professional journals, 'airport books', management education?

cycle thus starts by examining the legitimation process. However, before doing this, the character and role of consumers—the centre of the cycle—is examined.

While consumers are at the centre of the cycle they are relatively under-conceptualized, as Suddaby and Greenwood spend little time examining the character of consumers or their role in the production and consumption of management knowledge in any detail. Further, they typically portray consumers in a way that Scarbrough and Swan (2001) criticize as being somewhat naïve (but sceptical) consumers of management knowledge. However, perhaps a more useful way of conceptualizing consumers is that portrayed by Scarbrough & Swan, where consumers, while being influenced by fashions in academic knowledge, are seen as actively seeking solutions to genuine organizational problems.

Gurus and the process of legitimation

The role of gurus in the production and consumption of knowledge can be conceptualized as the first stage in the cycle, as they play a role in popularizing and making legitimate a new body of knowledge and subject of study. For example, Peters and Waterman played such a role with the topic of culture in the 1980s through their book *In Search of Excellence* (Peters & Waterman 2004), and lecture tours which did much to popularize and legitimate the topic of organizational culture management. Gurus thus help transfer knowledge between different communities through transforming abstract theorization, or specific organizational practices, and making them generic. Gurus can be located both in the academic world and in the world of private enterprise, with many often straddling both domains. This can be illustrated via a survey of academics and practitioners conducted by Edwards *et al.* (2003), where the following writers were identified as being most influential in the area of knowledge management:

1. Nonaka
2. Nonaka & Takeuchi
3. Davenport & Prusak
4. Snowden
5. Brown & Duguid

The first observation regarding this list is that it is somewhat confusing to list Nonaka separately from Nonaka & Takeuchi. However, this appears to have been done to distinguish between the specific influence of Nonaka & Takeuchi's (1995) book *The Knowledge Creating Company*, which as was suggested in Chapter 7 represents the single most influential and widely referenced book on knowledge management, and the influence of Nonaka's other published work (of which there has been a large amount).

As outlined earlier, one of the fundamental features of Abrahamson's (1996) conceptualization of the cyclical evolution of management fashions is that particular fashions tend to be relatively transient, with interest in them declining rapidly after it has built to a rapid peak. This implicitly suggests that fashion setters, or gurus, the people who initiate interest in particular fashions, will themselves have a relatively transient interest in the topics they advocate as being important. For this reason it is worth looking at the extent to which the original gurus of knowledge management have continued to talk about the topic.

Identifying who constitute the original gurus of knowledge management is a difficult and subjective topic, with different people likely to identify different individuals. For the purposes of this book Edwards *et al.*'s (2003) survey is used. Thus, the original gurus of knowledge management are considered to be Ikujiro Nonaka (and Hirotaka Takeuchi), Thomas Davenport and Laurence Prusak, David Snowden, and John Seely Brown and Paul Duguid. Table 16.2 highlights the extent to which they have written and talked about knowledge management in the period between 2001 and 2008. This data suggests that the extent to which they have continued to regard knowledge management as a topic of importance has varied, but that in the period between 2001 and 2008 they have all continued to write about the topic of knowledge management, to some extent. This therefore arguably provides further support for the conclusion reached in the previous section that knowledge management does not represent a transient management fashion, because, as Table 16.2 suggests, the original gurus have continued to write and talk about it over a sustained period of time.

Consultants and the commodification of management knowledge

The commodification of management knowledge involves decontextualizing knowledge, and transforming it into a generic form, so that it can be sold on as a product or service to other clients. Key agents in such processes are typically consultants, with the primary goal of economic gain acting as a significant incentive for these firms to attempt such processes of codification (Morris 2001). In relation to knowledge management, consultancies have played a key role in such processes (Scarbrough & Swan 2001), which perhaps helps to explain why a significant proportion of the knowledge management solutions being sold are generic tools and technologies, and why IT based perspectives on knowledge management have been so popular.

TIME TO REFLECT KNOWLEDGE MANAGEMENT GURUS

Did you first come into contact with knowledge management as a subject through the work of a knowledge management guru? Are they one of the writers in the top five of the Edwards *et al.* survey? Who do *you* regard to be the gurus of knowledge management? Are they academics or do they work in the business sector, or both?

Guru	Evidence of interest in knowledge management 2001–2008 (in terms of written published output)
Ikujiro Nonaka	*KM related institutional affiliations* Professor in Graduate School of International Corporate Strategy at Hitotsubashi University. He is also a Xerox Distinguished Fellow in the IMIO at the University of California at Berkeley *Published output related to knowledge management* Have produced a significant amount of published work, developing their dynamic model of the knowledge creation (see Chapter 7, and bibliography)
Thomas Davenport	*KM related institutional affiliations* For most of career has worked as an academic, consultant (with McKinseys, Andersen Consulting and Ernst & Young) and public speaker. He continues with these roles and also holds the President's Chair in Information Technology and Management at Babson College (MA). Manages the Working Knowledge Research Center (along with Laurence Prusak) *Personal web resources* • http://www.tomdavenport.com/ • http://www3.babson.edu/Academics/faculty/tdavenport.cfm *Published output related to knowledge management* • 'Organizational Governance of Knowledge and Learning', *Knowledge and Process Management*, 15/2: 150–157 (2008, with Strong and Prusak) • *Thinking for a Living: How to Get Better Performance and Results from Knowledge Workers* (2005) • *Knowledge Management Case Book: Siemens Best Practises* (2002, with Probst) • 'Five Steps to Creating a Global Knowledge-Sharing System: Siemens' ShareNet', *Academy of Management Executive*, 19/2: 9–23 (2005, with Voelpel & Dous) • 'The Rise of Knowledge Towards Attention Management', *Journal of Knowledge Management*, 5/3 (2001, with Vöelpel)
Laurence Prusak	*KM related institutional affiliations* Is a researcher and consultant and was the founder and Executive Director of IBM Institute for Knowledge Management (IKM). Between 2004 and 2007 he taught in the Knowledge Management Education Program at Harvard Business School. Manages the Working Knowledge Research Center (along with Thomas Davenport) *Personal web resources* • http://www.laurenceprusak.com/ *Published output related to knowledge management* • 'Organizational Governance of Knowledge and Learning', *Knowledge and Process Management*, 15/2: 150–157 (2008, with Strong and Davenport) • *Knowledge Management and Organizational Learning: A Reader* (2006, with Eric Matson) • *Creating Value with Knowledge: Insights from the IBM Institute for Knowledge-Based Organization* (2004, with Eric Lesser) • 'Knowing What We Know: Supporting Knowledge Creation and Sharing in Social Networks', *Organizational Dynamics*, 30/2: 100–120 (2001, with Cross, Parker and Borgatti)

Guru	Evidence of interest in knowledge management 2001–2008 (in terms of written published output)
John Seely Brown	*KM related institutional affiliations*
	Was chief scientist at Xerox's Palo Alto Research Centre until 2002. Works as an independent speaker and consultant. He also has corporate roles on the advisory board and board of directors of numerous private sector companies
	Personal web resources
	• http://www.johnseelybrown.com/
	Published output related to knowledge management.
	• *Storytelling in Organizations: Why Storytelling Is Transforming 21st Century Organizations and Management* (2004, with Stephen Denning, Katalina Groh, Laurence Prusak)
	• 'Local Knowledge: Innovation in the Networked Age', *Management Learning,* 33/4: 427–437 (2002, with Paul Duguid)
	• 'Knowledge and Organization: A Social-practice Perspective', *Organization Science,* 12/2: 198–213 (2001, with Paul Duguid)
Paul Duguid	*KM related institutional affiliations*
	Worked for an extended period at Xerox's Palo Alto Research Centre. Currently is an adjunct professor at the School of Information at the University of California, Berkeley; a professorial research fellow at Queen Mary, University of London; and an honorary fellow of the Institute for Entrepreneurship and Enterprise Development at Lancaster University School of Management
	Personal web resources
	• http://people.ischool.berkeley.edu/~duguid/
	• http://www.ischool.berkeley.edu/people/faculty/paulduguid
	• http://www2.parc.com/ops/members/brown/pduguid.html
	Published output related to knowledge management
	• 'What Talking About Machines Tells Us', *Organization Studies,* 27/12: 1794–1804 (2006)
	• '"The Art of Knowing": Social and Tacit Dimensions of Knowledge and the Limits of the Community of Practice', *Information Society,* 21/2: 109–118 (2005)
	• 'Local Knowledge: Innovation in the Networked Age', *Management Learning,* 33/4: 427–437 (2002, with John Seely Brown)
	• 'Knowledge and Organization: A Social-practice Perspective', *Organization Science,* 12/2: 198–213 (2001, with John Seely Brown)
David Snowden	*KM related institutional affiliations*
	Former Director of IBM Institute for Knowledge Management. Left to form Cynefin, which evolved into Cognitive Edge, a consultancy aimed at helping facilitate corporate change and decision making in conditions of complexity
	Web resources
	• http://www.cognitive-edge.com/index.php
	Published output related to knowledge management
	• 'From Atomism to Networks in Social Systems', *The Learning Organization,* 12, 6, 152–162 (2005)

Table 16.2 Evidence on the extent to which the original gurus of knowledge management have sustained an interest in the topic in the period between 2001 and 2008

The colonizing practices of large professional service firms

Colonization represents the attempts by organizations to expand the scope of their managerial knowledge products, with the key actors in such processes being large, global professional service companies such as PricewaterhouseCoopers, Cap Gemini Ernst & Young, and Deloitte & Touche. Processes of colonization are closely related to processes of legitimation, as colonization ultimately involves specific actors struggling to be seen as more legitimate sources of management knowledge than other actors. One of the main themes in Suddaby and Greenwood's (2001) analysis relates to the importance of the not insignificant colonizing attempts by large professional service firms in transforming the cycle of knowledge production/consumption.

A specific example of their colonizing efforts are their attempts to develop a role in the creation as well as commodification and dissemination of knowledge and thus become involved in what has been a traditional university function (Huff 2000). For example, consultants are emerging as key competitors with universities in the production of research (Rynes *et al.* 2001). Specific examples of what could be interpreted as their involvement in processes of knowledge production are KPMG's efforts at publishing a series of knowledge management surveys (for example KPMG 2000), the publication of the book *Knowledge Unplugged* by consultants from McKinsey's (Kluge *et al.* 2001), and the publications of the gurus of knowledge management outlined in Table 16.2 above.

Business schools: due diligence, innovation and education

Suddaby & Greenwood characterize business schools as having three roles in the production and consumption of management knowledge. The role of business schools in the production and consumption of knowledge on knowledge management is examined in detail, not only because of the character of their role, but also the extent to which their role in these processes has been changing, arguably significantly, and also because they play a key role in the diffusion of knowledge on knowledge management, through both their research and writing and through the management education they provide.

The primary role of business schools is as quality controllers. Thus academic research typically follows, rather than leads, management practice, and plays a role in evaluating and refining management knowledge/practice (due diligence). However, this process of refinement can lead to production of new knowledge, through research led innovation, which represents the second role of business schools.

The third role of business schools is the diffusion and dissemination of management knowledge via management education. The importance of this role should not be underestimated, due to the expansion in management education that has occurred in recent years. For example, there are so many MBA programmes in existence globally, that there are web-sites which can help students identify the most appropriate programme to their needs, with one site (http://www.mbainfo.com/[1]) having information on over 2800 different MBA programmes taught at over 1400 separate institutions. This links to the

1. Site accessed 24/09/2008.

production and consumption of knowledge on knowledge management, as specific modules on learning and knowledge management are increasingly becoming a key part of a significant number of MSc. and MBA programmes. Thus, this represents an important though often under-emphasized mechanism through which people consume knowledge on knowledge management.

As outlined earlier part of the reason why it is worth looking in a little detail at the role of business schools in the cycle of knowledge production is that a number of different, external factors are impinging on them, which have implications for the cycle of knowledge production, and the role of business schools in it. Two of the most significant external factors having this influence are examined here. These are firstly, the shift from mode 1 to mode 2 knowledge production and secondly, the effects of neo-liberal/monetarist policies on the funding of universities. These pressures have had a common effect on business schools, increasing the demands on them to commercialize their work, and develop closer links with business organizations (Fuller 2002, 5; Rynes *et al.* 2001; Stevens & Bagby 2001). The extent of these pressures is visible in the development of terms such as 'academic capitalism' (Slaughter & Leslie 1997), and that the presidential address to the Academy of Management by Michael Hitt (1997) talked about the demands on business schools to become more entrepreneurial.

Gibbons *et al.* (1994) in a highly influential book, argue that fundamental changes in the nature of knowledge production processes occurred in the second half of the twentieth century. Fundamentally, they suggest that there has been a shift from what they label, inelegantly, a mode 1 based system, where knowledge production is discipline based, university centred, individualistic, largely cognitive and based on a process of peer review, to a mode 2 based system, where knowledge production is, by contrast, transdisciplinary, team rather than individual based, and where knowledge is produced and validated through use, rather than through abstract reflection. Thus, a mode 2 based system of knowledge production is highly problem oriented, and requires close collaboration with industrial/business partners. A number of writers suggest that there are pressures on business schools to undertake such a transition, and develop management knowledge through linking with relevant business partners (Gustavs & Clegg 2005; Hakala & Ylijoki 2001; Huff 2000). Thus this represents a significant external pressure, pushing business schools and private industry together.

The second factor acting to push business schools and private industry together into a closer relationship has been a change in the way that governments fund universities. In general terms governments globally have moved towards the adoption of neo-liberal, monetarist policies. Such moves involve government attempts to tightly control, if not minimize/reduce, state expenditure. In relation to universities generally, and business schools specifically, central government funding has been capped, and increasingly tied to performance based measures, with encouragement provided to business schools and universities to seek higher levels of private sector funding (Callinicos 2006; Fuller 2002; Hakala & Ylijoko 2001; Rynes *et al.* 2001).

These contextual factors thus have potentially profound implications for how business schools operate, and have contributed to an enormous debate on the ways in which business schools should adapt and change. The debates relate to a number of issues such as the nature of the relationship between business schools and universities, such as whether they should be integrated within universities, or operate as stand alone enterprises (Durand & Dameron 2007; Tieman 2008), the general value/relevance of both the research output and management education provided by business schools (Knights 2008; Pfeffer & Fong 2004; Starkey & Tempest 2005; Starkey *et al.* 2004), and the specific value/relevance of MBA courses (Legge *et al.* 2007; Volkmann & De Cock 2007; Welsh & Dehler 2007). However, it is beyond the scope of this chapter to examine, describe, compare and contrast the diversity of perspectives which exist on these questions.

Conclusion

This chapter has therefore examined three key questions related to the whole body of work on knowledge management. The general conclusions reached were as follows. Firstly, while the analytical and theoretical rigour of some of the knowledge management literature is weak, there is a growing body of work in the area that is theoretically robust. Thus it is inaccurate to say that all writing in this area is poorly theorized.

The second question examined was whether knowledge management is a contemporary example of a transient management fashion. The contradictory and partial nature of the evidence that exists on this topic means that it is impossible to give a simple unequivocal answer to this question. On the one hand, in relation to academic interest in the topic, knowledge management was not found to be a transient management fashion. This is because rather than interest in the topic rising and falling quickly, there has been a relatively high level of sustained interest in the topic in the decade between 1998 and 2008. However, in relation to the interest of the business world in knowledge management, the evidence is more uncertain and equivocal. In general there is a lack of detailed evidence to determine with any degree of accuracy the extent to which the business world remains interested in the topic of knowledge management. However, the evidence that does exist suggests that there has been a decline of interest in large scale, 'big bang' type knowledge management initiatives.

The chapter concluded by using Suddaby & Greenwood's (2001) cycle of knowledge production exploring the actors and processes involved in the production and consumption of knowledge on knowledge management. This concluded that one of the key changes involved in this cycle, which affects the production of management knowledge in general, and is not related narrowly to the production of knowledge on knowledge management, is the closer collaboration between universities and the business world in the joint production of management knowledge.

End of book activity

Name the players in the knowledge management
production/consumption cycle

Rather than provide a list of discrete questions, the book closes with an invitation to play the 'game' of naming the players and their roles in the production and consumption of knowledge on knowledge management? To do this, look in detail at Suddaby & Greenwood's cycle, and fill in the blanks.

Questions which may help you do this include:

- Where (if anywhere) is the start of the cycle?
- Who (if anyone) are the gurus of knowledge management?
  - Are they consultants? Academics? Both?
  - Through what mechanisms have their arguments been diffused (books, lectures, teaching, consultancy, . . .)
- Can you fill in more details for the unexplored category consumers?
  - Are consumers passive victims of passing fads?
  - Can you develop sub-categories of different types of consumer?
  - Are there organizations which represent collections of consumers which have been important in the knowledge management cycle? (trade associations, professional bodies?)
- What about the role of academia, business schools and individual academics?
  - Is their role primarily the testing/refinement and legitimation of existing knowledge?
  - Are there particular universities, academics or departments (business schools, IS/IT departments) that have played a particularly key role?
  - What role do university departments play in the diffusion of knowledge on knowledge management? Is this through providing education, the publication of books (such as this one)?
  - Is there evidence that academia is under pressure to commercialize its activities and outputs?
  - Is there evidence of (growing) linkages between academia and business organizations?
- What role have large professional service firms played in the production and consumption of knowledge on knowledge management?
  - Do particular organizations have a more important role than others?
  - Is there evidence of colonizing activity?
- Are there any missing actors from the cycle?
  - What about the role of the mass media? National newspapers, television? Has it had any role in the diffusion of knowledge on knowledge management?
- Is this cycle useful in understanding the processes and agents involved in the production and consumption of knowledge on knowledge management?

Suggestions for further reading

1 **J.-C. Spender (2008). 'Organizational Learning and Knowledge Management: Whence and Whither?', *Management Learning*, 39/2: 158–176.**

A beautifully written and highly insightful analysis of the relationship between the literatures on knowledge and learning which makes suggestions for how the knowledge management literature should develop.

2   M. Welsh & G. Dehler (2007). 'Whither the MBA? Or the Withering of MBAs?', *Management Learning*, 38/4: 405–424.

    Examination of the debate on how MBA courses require to change and adapt.

3   K. Starkey & S. Tempest (2005). 'The Future of the Business School: Knowledge Challenges and Opportunities', *Human Relations*, 58/1: 61–82.

    Gives a useful overview of the debate on the criticisms that have been made about business school research and education.

4   R. Suddaby & R. Greenwood (2001). 'Colonizing Knowledge: Commodification as a Dynamic of Jurisdictional Expansion in Professional Service Firms', *Human Relations*, 54/7: 933–953.

    Develops a generic model for understanding the dynamics of the production and consumption of management knowledge.

Take your learning further: Online Resource Centre

Visit the supporting Online Resource Centre for resources which will extend your understanding of knowledge management in organizations. As well as web links to sites of interest, the author has provided case studies looking at knowledge management in virtual and knowledge intensive firms, and in global multinationals. These will help you with your research, essays and assignments; or you may find these additional resources helpful when revising for exams.

 www.oxfordtextbooks.co.uk/orc/hislop2e/

REFERENCES

Abrahamson, E. (1996). 'Management Fashion', *Academy of Management Review*, 21/1: 254–285.

Abrams, L., Cross, R., Lesser, E., & Levin, D. (2003). 'Nurturing Interpersonal Trust in Knowledge-Sharing Networks', *Academy of Management Executive*, 17/4: 64–77.

Akgün, A., Lynn, G., & Byrne, J. (2006). 'Antecedents and Consequences of Unlearning in New Product Development Teams', *Journal of Product Innovation Management*, 23/1: 73–88.

Akgün, A., Byrne, J., Lynn, G., & Keskin, H. (2007). 'Organizational Unlearning as Changes in Beliefs and Routines in Organizations', *Journal of Organizational Change Management*, 20/6: 794–812.

Alavi, M., Kayworth, T., & Leidner, D. (2005–06). 'An Empirical Examination of the Influence of Organizational Culture on Knowledge Management Practices', *Journal of Management Information Systems*, 22/3: 191–224.

Allee, V. (1997). *The Knowledge Evolution: Expanding Organizational Intelligence*. Oxford: Butterworth-Heinemann.

Alter, C., & Hage, J. (1993). *Organisations Working Together*. Newbury Park: Sage.

Alvesson, M. (1995). *Management of Knowledge Intensive Firms*. London: de Gruyter.

Alvesson, M. (2000). 'Social Identity and the Problem of Loyalty in Knowledge-Intensive Companies', *Journal of Management Studies*, 37/8: 1101–1123.

Alvesson, M. (2001). 'Knowledge Work: Ambiguity, Image and Identity', *Human Relations*, 54/7: 863–886.

Alvesson, M., & Kärreman, D. (2001). 'Odd Couple: Making Sense of the Curious Concept of Knowledge Management', *Journal of Management Studies*, 38/7: 995–1018.

Alvesson, M., & Sveningsson, S. (2003). 'Good Visions, Bad Micro-Management and Ugly Ambiguity: Contradictions of (Non-) Leadership in a Knowledge-Intensive Organization', *Organization Studies*, 24/6: 961–988.

Alvesson, M., & Willmott, H. (2001). 'Identity Regulation as Organizational Control: Producing the Appropriate Individual', *Journal of Management Studies*, 39/5: 691–644.

Amin, A., & Roberts, J. (2008). 'Knowing in Action: Communities of Practice', *Research Policy*, 37/2: 353–369.

Andrews, K., & Delahaye, B. (2000). 'Influences on Knowledge Processes in Organizational Learning: The Psychosocial Filter', *Journal of Management Studies*, 37/6: 797–810.

Antonocopoulou, E. (2006). 'The Relationship Between Individual and Organizational Learning: New Evidence from Managerial Learning Practices', *Management Learning*, 37/4: 455–473.

Ardichvili, A., Page, V., & Wentling, T. (2003). 'Motivation and Barriers to Participation in Virtual Knowledge-Sharing Communities of Practice', *Journal of Knowledge Management*, 7/1: 64–77.

Argyris, C. (1990). *Overcoming Organizational Defences*. Needham Heights, Mass.: Allyn & Bacon.

Armenakis, A., & Bedeian, A. (1999). 'Organizational Change: A Review of Theory and Research in the 1990s', *Journal of Management*, 25/3: 293–315.

Armstrong, H. (2000). 'The Learning Organization: Changed Means to an Unchanged End', *Organization*, 7/2: 355–361.

Atkinson, C. (2002). 'Career Management and the Changing Psychological Contract', *Career Development International*, 7/1: 14–23.

Badham, R., Couchman, P., & McLoughlin, I. (1997). 'Implementing Vulnerable Socio-Technical Change Projects', in I. McLoughlin & M. Harris (eds.), *Innovation, Organizational Change and Technology*. London: International Thomson Business Press, 146–169.

Bacharach, P., & Baratz, M. (1963). 'Decisions and Nondecisions: An Analytical Framework', *American Political Science Review*, 57: 632–642.

Bain, P., & Taylor, P. (2000). 'Entrapped by the "Electronic Panopticon"? Worker Resistance in the Call Centre', *New Technology, Work and Employment*, 15/1: 2–18.

Ball, K., & Wilson, D. (2000). 'Power, Control and Computer-Based Performance monitoring: Repertoires, Resistance and Subjectivities', *Organization Studies*, 21/3: 539–566.

Barker, R. (2001). 'The Nature of Leadership', *Human Relations*, 54/4: 469–494.

Barnes, B. (1977). *Interests and the Growth of Knowledge*. London: Routledge and Kegan Paul (Routledge Direct Editions).

Barratt, E. (2002). 'Foucault, Foucauldianism and Human Resource Management', *Personnel Review*, 31/2: 189–204.

Bate, S., & Roberts, G. (2002). 'Knowledge Management and Communities of Practice in the Private Sector: Lessons for Modernizing the National Health Service in England and Wales', *Public Administration*, 80/4: 643–663.

Bauman, Z. (2007). *Liquid Modernity*. Cambridge: Polity Press.

Baumard, P. (1999). *Tacit Knowledge in Organizations*. London: Sage.

Baumard, P., & Starbuck, W. (2005). 'Learning from Failures: Why it May Not Happen', *Long Range Planning*, 38/3: 281–298.

Beaumont, P., & Hunter, L. (2002). *Managing Knowledge Workers*. London: CIPD.

Becerra, M., Lunnan, R., & Huemer, L. (2008). 'Trustworthiness, Risk, and the Transfer of Tacit and Explicit Knowledge Between Alliance Partners', *Journal of Management Studies*, 45/4: 691–713.

Bechky, B. (2003). 'Sharing Meaning Across Occupational Communities: The Transformation of Understanding on a Production Floor', *Organization Science*, 14/3: 312–330.

Becker, M. (2001). 'Managing Dispersed Knowledge: Organizational Problems, Managerial Strategies and their Effectiveness', *Journal of Management Studies*, 38/7: 1037–1051.

Bell, D. (1973). *The Coming of Post-Industrial Society*. Harmondsworth: Penguin.

Berman, S.L., Down, J., & Hill, C.W.L. (2002). 'Tacit Knowledge as a Source of Competitive Advantage in the National Basketball Association', *Academy of Management Journal*, 45/1: 13–31.

Berthoin Antal, A., Dierkes, M., Child, J., & Nonaka, I. (2001). 'Organizational Learning and Knowledge: Reflections on the Dynamics of the Field and Challenges for the Future', in M. Dierkes, A. Bertoin Antal, J. Child, & I. Nonaka (eds.), *Handbook of Organizational Learning and Knowledge*. Oxford: Oxford University Press, 921–940.

Bettis, R., & Prahalad, C. (1995). 'The Dominant Logic: Retrospective and Extension', *Strategic Management Journal*, 16/1: 5–14.

Blackler, F. (1995). 'Knowledge, Knowledge Work and Organizations: An Overview and Interpretation', *Organization Studies*, 16/6: 1021–1046.

Blackler, F., Crump, N., & McDonald, S. (2000). 'Organizing Processes in Complex Activity Systems', *Organization*, 7/2: 277–300.

Bock, G., Kankanhalli, G., & Sharma, S. (2006). 'Are Norms Enough? The Role of Collaborative Norms in Promoting Organizational Knowledge Seeking', *European Journal of Information Systems*, 15/4: 357–367.

Boeker, W. (1992). 'Power and Managerial Dismissal: Scapegoating at the Top', *Administrative Science Quarterly*, 37/3: 400–421.

Bogner, W., & Bansal, P. (2007). 'Knowledge Management as the Basis of Sustained High Performance', *Journal of Management Studies*, 44/1: 165–188.

Boland, R., & Tenkasi, R. (1995). 'Perspective Making and Perspective Taking in Communities of Knowing', *Organization Science*, 6/4: 350–372.

Boland, R., Tenkasi, R., & Te'eni, D. (1994). 'Designing Information Technology to Support Distributed Cognition', *Organization Science*, 5/3: 456–475.

Bolisani, E., & Scarso, E. (2000). 'Electronic Communication and Knowledge Transfer', *International Journal of Technology Management*, 20/1–2: 116–133.

Breu, K., & Hemingway, C. (2002). '*The Power Of Communities Of Practice For Subverting Organisational Change*'. Paper presented at 3rd European Conference on Organizational Knowledge, Learning and Capabilities, Athens, Greece, April 5–6.

Brown, R. (2000). 'Contemplating the Emotional component of Learning: The Emotions and Feelings Involved when Undertaking an MBA', *Management Learning*, 31/3: 275–293.

Brown, J., Denning, S., Groh, K., & Prusak, L. (2004). *Storytelling in Organizations: Why Storytelling Is Transforming 21st Century Organizations and Management*. Burlington, Mass.: Elsevier Butterworth-Heinemann.

Brown, J., & Duguid, P. (1991). 'Organization Learning and Communities of Practice: Towards a Unified View of Working, Learning and Innovation', *Organization Science*, 2/1: 40–57.

Brown, J., & Duguid, P. (1998). 'Organizing Knowledge', *California Management Review*, 40/3: 90–111.

Brown, J., & Duguid, P. (2001). 'Knowledge and Organization: A Social Practice Perspective', *Organization Science*, 12/2: 198–213.

Brown, J., & Duguid, P. (2002). 'Local Knowledge: Innovation in the Networked Age', *Management Learning*, 33/4: 427–437.

Bryant, S. (2003). 'The Role of Transformational and Transactional Leadership in Creating,

Sharing and Exploiting Organizational Knowledge', *Journal of Leadership and Organization Studies*, 9/4: 32–44.

Buchanan, D. (2008). 'You Stab My Back, I'll Stab Yours: Management Experience and Perceptions of Organization Political Behaviour', *British Journal of Management*, 19/1: 49–64.

Buchanan, D., & Badham, R. (1999). *Power, Politics and Organizational Change: Winning the Turf War*. London: Sage.

Buck, J., & Watson, J. (2002). 'Retaining Staff Employees: The Relationship Between Human Resource Management Strategies and Organizational Commitment', *Innovative Higher Education*, 26/3: 175–193.

Burchell, B., Ladipo, D., & Wilkinson, F. (2002). *Job Insecurity & Work Intensification*. London: Routledge.

Burnes, B. (1996). 'No Such Thing as . . . a "One Best Way" to Manage Organizational Change', *Management Decision*, 34/10: 11–18.

Burnes, B. (2004). 'Kurt Lewin and the Planned Approach to Change: A Re-Appraisal', *Journal of Management Studies*, 41/6: 977–102.

Burns, J. (1978). *Leadership*. New York: Harper & Row.

Burrell, G., & Morgan, G. (1979). *Sociological Paradigms and Organisational Analysis: Elements of the Sociology of Corporate Life*. London: Heinemann Educational.

Burton-Jones, A. (1999). *Knowledge Capitalism*. Oxford: Oxford University Press.

Button, G., Mason, D., & Sharrock, W. (2003). 'Disempowerment and Resistance in the Print Industry? Reactions to Surveillance-Capable Technology', *New Technology, Work and Employment*, 18/1: 50–61.

Byrne, R. (2001). 'Employees: Capital or Commodity?' *Career Development International*, 6/6: 324–330.

Cabrera, A., & Cabrera, E. (2002). 'Knowledge Sharing Dilemmas', *Organization Studies*, 23/5: 687–710.

Cabrera, E., & Cabrera, A. (2005) 'Fostering Knowledge Sharing Through People Management Practices', *International Journal of Human Resource Management*, 16/5: 720–735.

Cagerra-Navarro, J., & Sanchez-Polo, M. (2007). 'Linking Unlearning and Relational Capital Through Organisational Relearning', *International Journal of Human Resource Development and Management*, 7/1: 37–52.

Caldwell, R. (2004). 'Rhetoric, Facts and Self-Fulfilling Prophesies: Exploring Practitioners' Perceptions of Progress in Implementing HRM', *Industrial Relations Journal*, 25/3: 196–215.

Callinicos, A. (2006). *Universities in a Neoliberal World*. London: Bookmarks Publications.

Cannon, M., & Edmondson, A. (2005). 'Failing to Learn and Learning to Fail (Intelligently): How Great Organizations Put Failure to Work to Innovate and Improve', *Long Range Planning*, 38/3: 299–319.

Carlile, P. (2002). 'A Pragmatic View of Knowledge and Boundaries: Boundary Objects in New Product Development', *Organization Science*, 14/4: 442–455.

Carlile, P. (2004). 'Transferring, Translating and Transforming: An Integrative Framework for Managing Knowledge Across Boundaries', *Organization Science*, 15/5: 555–568.

Carroll, J., Hatakenaka, S., & Rudolph, J. (2006). 'Naturalistic Decision Making and Organizational Learning in Nuclear Power Plants: Negotiating Meaning Between Managers and Problem Investigation Teams', *Organization Studies*, 27/7: 1037–1057.

Castells, M. (1998). *The Rise of Network Society*. Oxford: Basil Blackwell.

Chaundy, C. (2005). 'Creating a Good Practice Centre at the BBC', *KM Review*, 8/2: 24–27.

Chen, Y-H. (2007). *Knowledge Conversion Processes and Leadership: An Exploratory Study of Taiwanese Managers*. Loughborough University: PhD Thesis.

Child, J. (2001). 'Learning Through Strategic Alliances', in M. Dierkes, A. Bertoin Antal, J. Child, & I. Nonaka (eds.), *Handbook of Organizational Learning and Knowledge*. Oxford: Oxford University Press, 657–680.

Chiva, R., & Allegre, J. (2005). 'Organizational Learning and Organizational Knowledge: Towards the Integration of Two Approaches', *Management Learning*, 36/1: 49–68.

Chua, A. (2006). 'The Rise and Fall of a Community of Practice: A Descriptive Case Study', *Knowledge and Process Management*, 13/2: 120–128.

Ciborra, C., & Patriotta, G. (1998). 'Groupware and Teamwork in R&D: Limits to Learning and Innovation', *R&D Management*, 28/1: 1–10.

Clark, P. (2000). *Organizations in Action: Competition Between Contexts*. Routledge: London.

Clegg, S. (1998). 'Foucault, Power and Organizations', in A. McKinlay & K. Starkey (eds.), *Foucault, Management and Organization Theory*. London: Sage, 29–48.

Cohen, W., & Levinthal, D. (1990). 'Absorptive Capacity: A New Perspective on Innovation and Learning', *Administrative Science Quarterly*, 35: 128–152.

Cohendet, P., & Simon, L. (2007). 'Playing Across the Playground: Paradoxes of Knowledge Creation in the Videogame Firm', *Journal of Organizational Behaviour*, 28: 587–606.

Collins, H. (2007). 'Bicycling on the Moon: Collective Tacit Knowledge and Somatic-limit Tacit Knowledge', *Organization Studies*, 28/2: 257–262.

Contu, A., Grey, C., & Örtenblad, A. (2003). 'Against Learning', *Human Relations*, 56/8: 931–952.

Contu, A., & Willmott, H. (2003). 'Re-Embedding Situatedness: The Importance of Power Relations in Learning Theory', *Organization Science*, 14/3: 283–296.

Cook, S., & Brown, J. (1999). 'Bridging Epistemologies: The Generative Dance Between Organizational Knowledge and Organizational Knowing', *Organization Science*, 10/4: 381–400.

Cook, S., & Yanow, D. (1993). 'Culture and Organizational Learning', *Journal of Management Enquiry*, 2/4: 373–390.

Coopey, J. (1995). 'The Learning Organization, Power, Politics and Ideology', *Management Learning*, 26/2: 193–213.

Coopey, J. (1998). 'Learning the Trust and Trusting to Learn: A Role for Radical Theatre', *Management Learning*, 29/3: 365–382.

Coopey, J., & Burgoyne, J. (2000). 'Politics and Organizational Learning', *Journal of Management Studies*, 37/6: 869–885.

Coyle-Shapiro, J., & Kessler, I. (2000), 'Consequences of the Psychological Contract for the Employment Relationship: A Large Scale Survey', *Journal of Management Studies*, 37/7: 903–930.

Cravens, D., Piercey, N., & Shipp, S. (1996). 'New Organizational Forms for Competing in Highly Dynamic Environments: The Network Paradigm', *British Journal of Management*, 7/2: 203–218.

Crawford, C. (2005). 'Effects of Transformational Leadership and Organizational Position on Knowledge Management', *Journal of Knowledge Management*, 9/6: 6–16.

Cross, R., Laseter, T., Parker, A., & Valasquez, G. (2006). 'Using Social Network Analysis to Improve Communities of Practice', *California Management Review*, 49/1: 32–60.

Cross, R., Parker, A., Prusak, L., & Borgatti, S. (2001). 'Knowing What We Know: Supporting Knowledge Creation and Sharing in Social Networks', *Organizational Dynamics*, 30/2: 100–120.

Crossan, M., Lane, H., & White, R. (1999). 'An Organizational Learning Framework: From Intuition to Institution', *Academy of Management Review*, 24/3: 522–537.

Currie, G., & Kerrin, M. (2003). 'Human Resource Management and Knowledge Management: Enhancing Knowledge Sharing in a Pharmaceutical Company', *International Journal of Human Resource Management*, 14/6: 1027–1045.

Currie, G., & Kerrin, M. (2004). 'The Limits of a Technological Fix to Knowledge Management', *Management Learning*, 35/1; 9–29.

Cutcher-Gershenfeld, J., Nitta, M., & Barrett, B. (1998). *Knowledge-Driven Work*. Oxford: Oxford University Press.

Cyert, R., & March, J. (1963). *A Behavioural Theory of the Firm*. Englewood Cliffs, NJ: Prentice Hall.

Daft, R., & Lengel, R. (1986). 'Organizational Information Requirements, Media Richness and Structural Design', *Management Science*, 32/5: 544–571.

Dahl, R. (1957). 'The Concept of Power', *Behavioural Scientist*, 2: 201–215.

Davenport, T. (2005). *Thinking for a Living: How to Get Better Performance and Results from Knowledge Workers*. Cambridge, Mass.: Harvard Business School Press.

Davenport, T., De Long, D., & Beers, M. (1998). 'Successful Knowledge Management Projects', *MIT Sloan Management Review*, Winter: 43–57.

Davenport, T., & Probst, G. (2002). *Knowledge Management Case Book: Siemens Best Practises*. Berlin: Wiley.

Davenport, T., & Prusak, L. (1998). *Working Knowledge: How Organizations Manage What they Know*. Harvard Business School Press: Boston, Mass.

Davenport, T., Strong, B., & Prusak, L. (2008) 'Organizational Governance of Knowledge and Learning', *Knowledge & Process Management*, 15/2: 150–157.

Davenport, T., & Vöelpel, S (2001). 'The Rise of Knowledge Towards Attention Management', *Journal of Knowledge Management*, 5/3: 212–222.

Davenport, T., Voelpel, P., & Dous, M. (2005) 'Five Steps to Creating a Global Knowledge-sharing System: Siemens' Sharenet', *Academy of Management Executive*, 19/2: 9–23.

Dawson, R., & Nolan, A. (2006). 'Metrics Collection For Process Knowledge—A Practitioners' Guide', *Knowledge and Process Management*, 13/2: 93–99.

Deetz, S. (1998). 'Discursive Formations, Strategized Subordination and Self-Surveillance', in A. McKinlay & K. Starkey (eds.), *Foucault, Management and Organization Theory*. London: Sage, 151–172.

DeFillippi, R., & Arthur, M. (1998). 'Paradox in Project Based Enterprise: The Case of Filmmaking', *California Management Review*, 40/2: 125–139.

DeFillippi, R., Arthur, M., & Lindsay, V. (2006). *Knowledge at Work: Creative Collaboration in the Global Economy*. London: Blackwell.

De Holan, P., & Phillips, N. (2004). 'Remembrance of Things Past? The Dynamics of Organizational Forgetting', *Management Science*, 50/11: 1603–1613.

De Holan, P., Phillips, N., & Lawrence, T. (2004). 'Managing Organizational Forgetting', *MIT Sloan Management Review*, 45/2 (Winter): 45–51.

De Long, D., & Fahey, L. (2000). 'Diagnosing Cultural Barriers to Knowledge Management', *Academy of Management Executive*, 14/4: 113–127.

Densten, I. (2008). 'Leadership: Current Assessment and Future Needs', in S. Cartwright & C. Cooper (eds.), *The Oxford Handbook of Personnel Psychology*. Oxford: Oxford University Press.

DeSanctis, G., & Monge, P. (1999). 'Introduction to the Special Issue: Communication Processes for Virtual Organizations', *Organization Science*, 10/6: 693–703.

Dovey, K. (1997). 'The Learning Organization and the Organization of Learning: Learning, Power, Transformation and the Search for Form in Learning Organizations', *Management Learning*, 28/3: 331–349.

Driver, M. (2002). 'The Learning Organization: Foucauldian Gloom or Utopian Sunshine?' *Human Relations*, 55/1: 33–53.

Duguid, P. (2005). '"The Art of Knowing": Social and Tacit Dimensions of Knowledge and the Limits of the Community of Practice', *Information Society*, 21/2: 109–118.

Duguid, P. (2006). 'What Talking About Machines Tells Us', *Organization Studies*, 27/12: 1794–1804.

du Plessis, M. (2008). 'What Bars Organisations from Managing Knowledge Successfully?' *International Journal of Information Management*, 28: 285–292.

Durand, T., & Dameron, S. (2007). *The Future of Business Schools: Scenarios and Future Strategies*. London: Palgrave Macmillan.

Dyck, B., Starke, F., Mischke, G., & Mauws, M. (2005). 'Learning to Build a Car: An Empirical Investigation of Organizational Learning', *Journal of Management Studies*, 42/2: 387–416.

Dyer, J., & Nobeoka, K. (2000). 'Creating and Managing a High-Performance Knowledge-Sharing Network: The Toyota Case', *Strategic Management Journal*, 21/3: 345–367.

Earl, M. (2001). 'Knowledge Management Strategies: Towards a Taxonomy', *Journal of Management Information Systems*, 18/1: 215–233.

Easterby-Smith, M. (1997). 'Disciplines of Organizational learning: Contributions and Critique', *Human Relations*, 50/9: 1085–1113.

Easterby-Smith, M., Burgoyne, J., & Araujo, L. (1999). *Organisational Learning and the Learning Organisation*. London: Sage.

Easterby-Smith, M., Crossan, M., & Nicolini, D. (2000). 'Organizational Learning: Debates Past, Present and Future', *Journal of Management Studies*, 37/6: 783–796.

Easterby-Smith, M., Lyles, A., & Tsang, E. (2008). 'Inter-Organizational Knowledge Transfer: Current Themes and Future Prospects', *Journal of Management Studies*, 45/4: 677–690.

Edwards, J., Handzic, M., Carlsson, S., & Nissen, M. (2003). 'Knowledge Management Research and Practice: Visions and Directions', *Knowledge Management Research and Practice*, 1/1: 49–60.

Elias, P., & Gregory, M. (1994). *The Changing Structure of Occupations and Earnings in Great Britain 1975–1990: An Analysis Based on the New Earnings Survey Panel Dataset*. Warwick: Institute for Employment Research.

Empson, L. (2001a). 'Introduction: Knowledge Management in Professional Service Firms', *Human Relations*, 54/7: 811–817.

Empson, L. (2001b). 'Fear of Exploitation and Fear of Contamination: Impediments to Knowledge Transfer in Mergers between Professional Service Firms', *Human Relations*, 54/7: 839–862.

Fahey, R., Vasconcelos, A., Ellis, D. (2007). 'The Impact of Rewards Within Communities of Practice: A Study of the SAP Online Global Community', *Knowledge Management Research and Practice*, 5/3: 186–198.

Felstead, A., Ashton, D., Green, F. (2000). 'Are Britain's Workplace Skills Becoming More Unequal?' *Cambridge Journal of Economics*, 24/6: 709–727.

Fenton, E. (2007). 'Visualizing Strategic Change: The Role and Impact of Process Maps as Boundary Objects in Reorganization', *European Management Journal*, 25/2: 104–117.

Fleming, P., Harley, B., & Sewell, G. (2004). 'A Little Knowledge is a Dangerous Thing: Getting Below the Surface of the Growth of "Knowledge Work" in Australia', *Work Employment and Society*, 18/4: 725–747.

Flood, P., Turner, T., & Hannaway, C. (2000). *Attracting and Retaining Knowledge Employees: Irish Knowledge Employees and the Psychological Contract*. Dublin: Blackhall.

Flood, P., Turner, T., Ramamoorthy, N., & Pearson, J. (2001). 'Causes and Consequences of Psychological Contracts Among Knowledge Workers in the High Technology and Financial Services Industry', *International Journal of Human Resource Management*, 12/7: 1152–1165.

Fosstenløkken, S., Løwendahl, B., & Revang, O. (2003). 'Knowledge Development Through Client Interaction: A Comparative Study', *Organization Studies*, 24/6: 859–880.

Foucault, M. (1979). *Discipline and Punishment*. Harmondsworth: Penguin.

Foucault, M. (1980). *Power/Knowledge: Selected Interviews and Other Writings 1972–1977*. London: Harvester Wheatsheaf.

Fox, A. (1985). *Beyond Contract: Work, Power and Trust Relations*. London: Faber.

Fox, S. (2000). Practice, Foucault and Actor-Network Theory. *Journal of Management Studies*, 37/6: 853–868.

French, J., & Raven, B. (1959). 'The Bases of Social Power', in D. Cartwright (ed.), *Studies in Social Power*. Ann Arbor: University of Michigan, 150–167.

Frenkel, S., Korczynski, M., Donohue, L., & Shire, K. (1995). 'Re-constituting Work: Trends Towards Knowledge Work and Info-normative Control', *Work, Employment and Society*, 9/4: 773–796.

Friedman, V., Lipshitz, R., & Overmeer, W. (2001). 'Creating Conditions for Organizational Learning', in M. Dierkes, A. Bertoin Antal, J. Child, & I. Nonaka (eds.), *Handbook of Organizational Learning and Knowledge*. Oxford: Oxford University Press, 757–774.

Fulk, J. (2001). 'Global Network Organizations: Emergence and Future Prospects', *Human Relations*, 51/1: 91–99.

Fuller, S. (2002). *Knowledge Management Foundations*. Oxford: Butterworth-Heinemann.

Gallie, D., White, M., Cheng, Y., & Tomlinson, M. (1998). *Restructuring the Employment Relationship*. Oxford: Clarendon Press.

Garvey, B., & Williamson, B. (2002). *Beyond Knowledge Management: Dialogue, Creativity and the Corporate Curriculum*. Harlow, UK: Financial Times/Prentice Hall.

Gherardi, S. (2000) 'Practice Based Theorizing on Learning and Knowing in Organizations', *Organization*, 7/2: 211–233.

Gherardi, S., & Nicolini, D. (2002). 'Learning in a Constellation of Interconnected Practices: Canon or Dissonance?' *Journal of Management Studies*, 39/4: 419–436.

Gherardi, S., Nicolini, D., & Odella, F. (1998). 'Towards a Social Understanding of How People Learn in Organizations: The Notion of Situated Curriculum', *Management Learning*, 29/3: 273–297.

Gibbons, M., Limoges, C., Nowotny, H., Schwartzman, S., Scott, P., & Trow, M. (1994). *The New Production of Knowledge: The Dynamics of Science and Research in Contemporary Societies*. London: Sage.

Gibson, C., & Birkinshaw, J. (2004). 'The Antecedents, Consequences, and Mediating Role of Organizational Ambidexterity', *Academy of Management Journal*, 47/2: 209–226.

Giddens, A. (1979). *Central Problems in Social Theory*. London: Macmillan.

Giddens, A. (1991). *Modernity and Self Identity: Self and Society in the Late Modern Age*. Cambridge: Polity Press.

Gittelman, M., & Kogut, B. (2003). 'Does Good Science Lead to Valuable Knowledge? Biotechnology Firms and the Evolutionary Logic of Citation Patterns', *Management Science*, 49/4: 366–382.

Glazer, R. (1998). 'Measuring the Knower: Towards a Theory of Knowledge Equity', *California Management Review*, 40/3: 175–194.

Glisby, M., & Holden, N. (2003). 'Contextual Constraints in Knowledge Management Theory: The Cultural Embeddedness of Nonaka's Knowledge Creating Company', *Knowledge and Process Management*, 10/1: 29–36.

Goles, T., & Hirschheim, R. (2000). 'The Paradigm is Dead, the Paradigm is Dead . . . Long Live the Paradigm: The Legacy of Burrell and Morgan', *Omega*, 28/3: 249–268.

Goodall, K., & Roberts, J. (2003). 'Repairing Managerial Knowledge-ability over Distance', *Organization Studies*, 24/7: 1153–1176.

Gourlay, S. (2006). 'Conceptualizing Knowledge Creation: A Critique of Nonaka's Theory', *Journal of Management Studies*, 43/7: 1415–1436.

Grabher, G. (2004). 'Temporary Architecture of Learning Knowledge Governance in Project Ecologies', *Organization Studies*, 25/9: 1491–1514.

Grant, R. (1996). 'Towards a Knowledge Based Theory of the Firm', *Strategic Management Journal*, 17, Winter Special Issue, 109–122.

Grant, R. (2000). 'Shifts in the World Economy: The Drivers of Knowledge Management', in C. Despres & D. Chauvel (eds.), *Knowledge Horizons: The Present and the Promise of Knowledge Management*. Oxford: Butterworth-Heinemann, 27–54.

Gray, P., & Durcikova, A. (2005–06). 'The Role of Knowledge Repositories in Technical Support Environments: Speed versus Learning in User Performance', *Journal of Management Information Systems*, 22/3: 159–190.

Guest, D., & Patch, A. (2000). '*The Employment Relationship, The Psychological Contract and Knowledge Management: Securing Employees Trust and Contribution*'. Paper presented at Knowledge Management: Concepts and Controversies, University of Warwick, April.

Güldeberg, S., & Helting, H. (2007). 'Bridging "The Great Divide": Nonaka's Synthesis of "Western" and "Eastern" Knowledge Concepts Reassessed', *Organization*, 14/1: 101–122.

Güldenberg, S., & Konrath, H. (2006). 'Bridging Leadership and Learning in Knowledge-based Organizations', in B. Renzl, K. Matzler, & H. Hinterhuber (eds.), *The Future of Knowledge Management*. Basingstoke: Palgrave Macmillan, 219–236.

Gustavs, J., & Clegg, S. (2005). 'Working the Knowledge Game? Universities and Corporate Organizations in Partnership', *Management Learning*, 36/1: 9–30.

Haas, M., & Hansen, M. (2007). 'Different Knowledge, Different Benefits: Towards a Productivity Perspective on Knowledge Sharing in Organizations', *Strategic Management Journal*, 28: 1133–1153.

Haesli, A., & Boxall, P. (2005). 'When Knowledge Management Meets HR Strategy: An Exploration of Personalization-Retention and Codification-Recruitment Configurations', *International Journal of Human Resource Management*, 16/11: 1955–1975.

Hakala, J., & Ylijoki, O-H. (2001). 'Research for Whom? Research Orientations in Three Academic Cultures', *Organization*, 8/2: 373–380.

Hales, C. (1993). *Managing Through Organization: The Management Process, Forms of Organisation and the Work of Managers*. London: Routledge.

Handley, K., Sturdy, A., Fincham, R., & Clark, T. (2006). 'Within and Beyond Communities of Practice: Making Sense of Learning through Participation, Identity and Practice', *Journal of Management Studies*, 43/3: 641–653.

Hansen, M. (1999). 'The Search-Transfer Problem: The Role of Weak Ties in Sharing Knowledge Across Organization Subunits', *Administrative Science Quarterly*, March: 82–111.

Hansen, M. (2002). 'Knowledge Networks: Explaining Effective Knowledge Sharing in Multiunit Companies', *Organization Science*, 13/3: 232–248.

Hansen, M., Nohria, N., & Tierney, T. (1999), 'What's Your Strategy for Managing Knowledge?' *Harvard Business Review*, 77/2: 106.

Harrison, R., & Kessels, J. (2004). *Human Resource Development in a Knowledge Economy*. Basingstoke: Palgrave Macmillan.

Harrison, R., & Leitch, C. (2000). 'Learning and Organization in the Knowledge-Based Information Economy: Initial Findings from a Participatory Action Research Case Study', *British Journal of Management*, 11/2: 103–119.

Harryson, S., Dudkowski, R., & Stern, A. (2008). 'Transformation Networks in Innovation Alliances—The Development of Volvo C70', *Journal of Management Studies*, 45/4: 745–773.

Hassell, L. (2007). 'A Continental Philosophy Perspective on Knowledge Management', *Information Systems Journal*, 17/2: 185–195.

Hayes, N., & Walsham, G. (2000). 'Safe Enclaves, Political Enclaves and Knowledge Working', in C. Prichard, R. Hull, M. Chumer, & H. Willmott (eds.), *Managing Knowledge: Critical Investigations of Work and Learning*. London: Macmillan.

He, Z., & Wong, P. (2004). 'Exploration vs. Exploitation: An Empirical Test of the Ambidexterity Hypothesis', *Organization Science*, 15/4: 481–494.

Hedberg, B. (1981). 'How Organizations Learn and Unlearn', in P. Nystrom & W. Starbuck (eds.), *Handbook of Organizational Design*. New York: Oxford University Press, 3–27.

Hemetsberger, A., & Reinhardt, C. (2006) 'Learning and Knowledge-building in Open-source Communities: A Social-Experiential Approach', *Management Learning*, 37/2: 187–214.

Hendriks, P. (2001). 'Many Rivers to Cross: From ICT to Knowledge Management Systems', *Journal of Information Technology*, 16/2: 57–72.

Hildreth, P., Kimble, C., & Wright, P. (2000). 'Communities of Practice in the Distributed International Environment', *Journal of Knowledge Management*, 4/1: 27–38.

Hindmarsh, J., & Pilnick, A. (2007). 'Knowing Bodies at Work: Embodiment and Ephemeral Teamwork in Anaesthesia', *Organization Studies*, 28/9: 1395–1416.

Hinterhuber, H., & Stadler, C. (2006). 'Leadership and Strategy as Intangible Assets', in B. Renzl, K. Matzler, & H. Hinterhuber (eds.), *The Future of Knowledge Management*. Basingstoke: Palgrave Macmillan, 237–253.

Hislop, D., Newell, S., Scarbrough, H., & Swan, J. (2000). 'Networks, Knowledge and Power: Decision making, Politics and the Process of Innovation', *Technology Analysis and Strategic Management*, 12/3: 399–411.

Hislop, D. (2002a). 'Linking Human Resource Management and Knowledge Management: A Review and Research Agenda', *Employee Relations*, 25/2: 182–202.

Hislop, D. (2002b). 'Mission Impossible? Communicating and Sharing Knowledge via Information Technology', *Journal of Information Technology*, 17/3: 165–177.

Hislop, D. (2003). 'The Complex Relationship Between Communities of Practice and the Implementation of Technological Innovations', *International Journal of Innovation Management*, 7/2: 163–188.

Hislop, D. (2008). 'Conceptualizing Knowledge Work Utilizing Skill and Knowledge-Based Concepts: The Case of Some Consultants and

Mansell, R., & SteinMueller, W. (2000). *Mobilizing the Information Society: Strategies for Growth and Opportunity*. Oxford: Oxford University Press, 2000.

Manwaring, T., & Wood, S (1985). 'The Ghost in the Machine', in D. Knights, H. Willmott, & D. Collinson (eds.), *Job Redesign: Critical Perspectives on the Labour Process*. London: Gower.

March, J., & Simon, H. (1993). *Organizations*, Second Edition. Oxford: Blackwell.

Marshall, N., & Brady, T. (2001). 'Knowledge Management and the Politics of Knowledge: Illustrations from Complex Product Systems', *European Journal of Information Systems*, 10/2: 99–112.

Marshall, N., & Rollinson, J. (2004). 'Maybe Bacon had a Point: The Politics of Collective Sensemaking', *British Journal of Management*, 15, Special Issue: s71–86.

Martin, J. (2006). 'Multiple Intelligence Theory, Knowledge Identification and Trust', *Knowledge Management Research and Practice*, 4/3: 207–215.

Martkus, L. (1994). 'Electronic Mail as the Medium of Managerial Choice', *Organization Science*, 5/4: 502–527.

Mason, K., & Leek, S. (2008). 'Learning to Build a Supply Network: An Exploration of Dynamic Business Models', *Journal of Management Studies*, 45/4: 774–799.

Massey, A., Montoya-Weiss, M., & O'Driscoll, T. (2002). 'Knowledge Management in Pursuit of Performance: Insights from Nortel Networks', *MIS Quarterly*, 26/3: 269–289.

Massingham, P. (2004). 'Linking Business Level Strategy with Activities and Knowledge Resources', *Journal of Knowledge Management*, 8/6: 50–62.

Massingham, P. (2008). 'Measuring the Impact of Knowledge Loss: More than Ripples on a Pond?', *Management Learning*, 39/5: 541–560.

Maznevski, M., & Chudoba, K. (1999). 'Bridging Space over Time: Global Virtual Team Dynamics and Effectiveness', *Organization Science*, 11/5: 473–492.

McAdam, R., & McCreedy, S. (2000). 'A Critique of Knowledge Management: Using a Social Constructivist Model', *New Technology, Work and Employment*, 15/2: 155–168.

McClure Wasko, M., & Faraj, S. (2000). '"It is What One Does": Why People Participate and Help Others in Electronic Communities of Practice', *Journal of Strategic Information Systems*, 9/1: 155–173.

McDermott, R. (1999). 'Why Information Technology Inspired but Cannot Deliver Knowledge Management', *California Management Review*, 41/1: 103–117.

McDermott, R., & O'Dell, C. (2001). 'Overcoming Cultural Barriers to Knowledge Sharing', *Journal of Knowledge Management*, 5/1: 76–85.

McDonald, D., & Makin, P. (2000). 'The Psychological Contract, Organizational Commitment and Job Satisfaction of Temporary Staff', *Leadership and Organizational Development Journal*, 21/2: 84–91.

McKinlay, A. (2000). 'The Bearable Lightness of Control: Organisational Reflexivity and the Politics of Knowledge Management', in C. Prichard, R. Hull, M. Chumer, & H. Willmott (eds.), *Managing Knowledge: Critical Investigations of Work and Learning*. London: Macmillan, 107–121.

McKinlay, A. (2002). 'The Limits of Knowledge Management', *New Technology, Work and Employment*, 17/2: 76–88.

McKinlay, A. (2005). 'Knowledge Management', in S. Ackroyd, R. Batt, & P. Thompson (eds.), *The Oxford Handbook of Work and Organization*. Oxford: Oxford University Press, 242–262.

McKinlay, A., & Starkey, K. (1998). *Foucault, Management and Organization Theory*. London: Sage.

McLoughlin, I., & Jackson, P. (1999). 'Organisational Learning and the Virtual Organisation', in P. Jackson (ed.), *Virtual Working: Social and Organisational Dynamics*. London: Routledge, 178–192.

Meeus, M., Oerlemans, L., & Hage, J. (2001). 'Patterns of Interactive Learning in a High-Tech Region', *Organization Studies*, 22/1: 145–172.

Meroño-Cerdan, A., Lopez-Nicolas, C., & Sabater-Sànchez, R. (2007). 'Knowledge Management Strategy Diagnosis from KM Instruments Use', *Journal of Knowledge Management*, 11/2: 60–72.

Meyer, J., Allen, N., & Smith, C. (1993). 'Commitment to Organizations and Occupations: Extension and Test of a Three Component Conceptualization', *Journal of Applied Psychology*, 78/4: 538–551.

Meyer, J., & Allen, N. (1997) *Commitment in the Workplace: Theory Research and Application*. London: Sage.

Meyerson, D., Weick, K., & Kramer, R. (1996). 'Swift Trust and Temporary Groups', in R. Kramer & T. Tyler (eds.), *Trust in Organizations: Frontiers of Theory and Research*. London: Sage, 166–95.

Michailova, S., & Hutchins, K. (2006). 'National Cultural Influences on Knowledge Sharing: A Comparison of China and Russia,' *Journal of Management Studies*, 43/3: 383–405.

Milne, P. (2007). 'Motivation, Incentives and Organisational Culture', *Journal of Knowledge Management*, 11/6: 28–38.

Mintzberg, H., Ahlstrand, B., & Lampel, J. (1998) *Strategy Safari: The Complete Guide Through the Wilds of Strategic Management*. Harlow: Financial Times/Prentice Hall.

Mitchell, A., Sikka, P., & Willmott, H. (2001). 'Policing Knowledge by Invoking the Law: Critical Accounting and the Politics of Dissemination', *Critical Perspectives on Accounting*, 12: 527–555.

Mooradian, T., Renzl, B., & Matzler, K. (2006). 'Who Trusts? Personality Trust and Knowledge Sharing', *Management Learning*, 37/4: 523–540.

Moorman, C., & Miner, A. (1998). 'Organizational Improvisation and Organizational Memory', *Academy of Management Review*, 23/4: 698–723.

Morris, T. (2001). 'Asserting Property Rights: Knowledge Codification in the Professional Service Firm', *Human Relations*, 54/7: 819–838.

Morris, T., & Empson, L. (1998). 'Organization and Expertise: An Exploration of Knowledge Bases and the Management of Accounting and Consulting Firms', *Accounting, Organizations and Society*, 23/5–6: 609–624.

Nadler, D., & Tushman, M. (1990). 'Beyond the Charismatic Leader: Leadership and Organizational Change', *California Management Review*, Winter: 77–97.

Nahapiet, J., & Ghoshal, S. (1998). 'Social Capital, Intellectual Capital and the Organizational Advantage', *Academy of Management Review*, 23/2: 242–266.

Nandhakumar, J. (1999). 'Virtual Teams and Lost Proximity: Consequences on Trust in Relationships', in P. Jackson (ed.), *Virtual Working: Social and Organisational Dynamics*. London: Routledge, 46–56.

Nayir, D., & Uzunçarsili, Ü. (2008). 'A Cultural Perspective on Knowledge Management: The Success Story of Sarkuysan Company', *Journal of Knowledge Management*, 12/2: 141–155.

Neef, D. (1999). 'Making the Case for Knowledge Management: The Bigger Picture', *Management Decision*, 37/1: 72–78.

Newell, S., Bresnen, M., Edelman L., Scarbrough H., & Swan, J. (2006) 'Sharing Knowledge Across Projects: Limits to ICT-led Projects Review Practices', *Management Learning*, 37/2: 167–185.

Newell, S., David, G., & Chand, D. (2007). 'An Analysis of Trust Among Globally Distributed Work Teams in an Organizational Setting', *Knowledge and Process Management*, 14/3: 158–168.

Newell, S., Scarbrough, H., Swan, J., & Hislop, D. (2000). 'Intranets and Knowledge Management: De-centred Technologies and the Limits of Technological Discourse', in C. Prichard, R. Hull, M. Chumer, & H. Willmott (eds.), *Managing Knowledge: Critical Investigations of Work and Learning*. London: Macmillan, 88–106.

Newell, S., & Swan, J. (2000). 'Trust and Inter-Organizational Networking', *Human Relations*, 53/10: 1287–1328.

Ngwenyama, O., & Lee, A. (1997). 'Communication Richness in Electronic Mail: Critical Social Theory and the Contextuality of Meaning', *MIS Quarterly*, 21/2: 145–167.

Nicolini, D., Powell, J., Conville, P., & Martinez-Solano, L. (2008). 'Managing Knowledge in the Healthcare Sector. A Review', *International Journal of Management Reviews*, 10/3: 245–263.

Nonaka, I. (1991). 'The Knowledge-Creating Company', *Harvard Business Review*, November–December: 96–104.

Nonaka, I. (1994). 'A Dynamic Theory of Organizational Knowledge Creation', *Organization Science*, 5/1: 14–37.

Nonaka, I., & Konno, N. (1998). 'The Concept of "Ba": Building a Foundation for Knowledge Creation', *California Management Review*, 40/3: 40–55.

Nonaka, I., & Peltokorpi, V. (2006). 'Objectivity and Subjectivity in Knowledge Management: A Review of 20 Top Articles', *Knowledge and Process Management*, 13/2: 73–82.

Nonaka, I., & Takeuchi, H. (1995). *The Knowledge Creating Company*. Oxford: Oxford University Press.

Nonaka, I., Toyama, R., & Byosiere, P. (2001). 'A Theory of Organizational Knowledge Creation: Understanding the Dynamic Process of Creating Knowledge', in M. Dierkes, A. Bertoin Antal, J. Child, & I. Nonaka (eds.), *Handbook of Organizational Learning and Knowledge*. Oxford: Oxford University Press, 491–517.

Nonaka, I., Toyama, R., & Konno, N. (2000). 'SECI, "Ba" and Leadership: A Unified Model of Dynamic Knowledge Creation', *Long Range Planning*, 33/1: 5–34.

Nonaka, I., von Krogh, G., & Voelpel, S. (2006). 'Organizational Knowledge Creation Theory: Evolutionary Paths and Future Advances', *Organization Studies*, 27/8: 1179–1208.

Northouse, P. (2007). *Leadership: Theory and Practice* (4th edn.). London: Sage

National Skills Task Force (2000). *Skills for All: Research Report from the National Skills Task Force*. London: Department for Education and Employment.

Nystrom, P., & Starbuck, W. (2003). 'To Avoid Organizational Crises, Unlearn', in K. Starkey, S. Tempest, & A. McKinlay (eds.), *How Organizations Learn: Managing the Search for Knowledge*. Thomson: London, 100–111.

Ogbonna, E., & Harris, L. (1998). 'Managing Organizational Culture: Compliance of Genuine Change', *British Journal of Management*, 9: 273–288.

Ogbonna, E., & Harris, L. (2002). 'Managing Organisational Culture: Insights from the Hospitality Industry', *Human Resource Management Journal*, 12/1: 33–53.

Oltra, V. (2005) 'Knowledge Management Effectiveness Factors: The Role of HRM', *Journal of Knowledge Management*, 9/4: 70–86.

O'Neill, B., & Adya, M. (2007). 'Knowledge Sharing and the Psychological Contract: Managing Knowledge Workers Across Different Stages of Employment', *Journal of Managerial Psychology*, 22/4: 411–436.

Organ, D., & Ryan, K. (1995). 'A Meta Analytical Review of Attitudinal and Dispositional Predictors of Organizational Citizenship Behaviour', *Personnel Psychology*, 48/4: 775–802.

Orlikowski, W. (2002) 'Knowing in Practice: Enacting a Collective Capability in Distributed Organizing', *Organization Science*, 13/3: 249–273.

Orr, J. (1990). 'Sharing Knowledge, Celebrating Identity: War Stories and Community Memory in a Service Culture', in D. Middleton & D. Edwards (eds.), *Collective Remembering: Memory in a Society*. London: Sage.

Orr, J. (1996). *Talking about Machines: An Ethnography of a Modern Job*. Ithaca, NY: ILR Press.

Osterloh, M., & Frey, B. (2000). 'Motivation, Knowledge Transfer, and Organizational Forms', *Organization Science*, 11/5: 538–550.

Pan, S., & Scarbrough, H. (1999). 'Knowledge Management in Practice: An Exploratory Case Study', *Technology Analysis and Strategic Management*, 11/3: 359–374.

Patriotta, G. (2003). 'Sensemaking on the Shop Floor: Narratives of Knowledge in Organizations', *Journal of Management Studies*, 40/2: 349–375.

Pauleen, D., & Yoong, P. (2001). 'Relationship Building and the Use of ICT in Boundary-Crossing Virtual Teams: A Facilitators Perspective', *Journal of Information Technology*, 16/4: 205–220.

Pavitt, K. (1984). 'Sectoral Patterns of Technical Change: Towards a Taxonomy and a Theory', *Research Policy*, 13/6: 343–373.

Pawlovsky, P. (2001). 'The Treatment of Organizational learning in Management Science', in M. Dierkes, A. Bertoin Antal, J. Child, & I. Nonaka (eds.), *Handbook of Organizational Learning and Knowledge*. Oxford: Oxford University Press, 61–88.

Pedler, M., Burgoyne, J., & Boydell, T. (1997). *The Learning Company: A Strategy for Sustainable Development* (2nd edn.). London: McGraw-Hill UK.

Peltokorpi, V. (2006). 'Knowledge Sharing in a Cross Cultural Context: Nordic Expatriates in Japan', *Knowledge Management Research and Practice*, 4: 138–148.

Perkmann, M., & Walsh, K. (2007). 'University–Industry Relationships and Open Innovation: Towards a Research Agenda', *International Journal of Management Reviews*, 9/4: 259–280.

Peters, T.J., & Waterman R.H. (2004). *In Search of Excellence* (2nd edn.). London: Harper & Row Profile Business.

Pettigrew, A., & Fenton, E. (2000). *Innovating New Forms of Organizing*. London: Sage.

Pfeffer, J., & Fong, C. (2004). 'The Business School "Business": Some Lessons from the US Experience', *Journal of Management Studies*, 41/8: 1501–1520.

Pittaway, L., Robertson, M., Munir, K., Denyer, D., & Neeley, A. (2004) 'Networking and Innovation: A Systematic Review of the Evidence', *International Journal of Management Reviews*, 5/6, 3–4: 137–168.

Polanyi, M. (1958). *Personal Knowledge*. Chicago: University of Chicago Press.

Polanyi, M. (1969) *Knowing and Being*. London: Routledge & Kegan Paul.

Polani, M. (1983). *The Tacit Dimension*. Gloucester, Mass.: Peter Smith.

Politis, J. (2002). 'Transformational and Transactional Leadership Enabling (Disabling) Knowledge Acquisition of Self-Managed Teams: The Consequences for Performance', *Leadership and Organization Development Journal*, 23/4: 186–197.

Powell, W. (1990). 'Neither Market Nor Hierarchy: Network Forms of Organization', in B. Staw & L. Cummings (eds.), *Research in Organizational Behaviour*, 12: 295–336.

Powell, W. (1998). 'Learning From Collaboration: Knowledge and Networks in Biotechnology and Pharmaceuticals Industries', *California Management Review*, 40/3: 228–240.

Powell, W., Koput, K., & Smith-Doerr L. (1996). 'Interorganizational Collaboration and the Locus of Innovation: Networks of Learning in Biotechnology', *Administrative Science Quarterly*, 41/1: 116–145.

Prencipe, A., & Tell, F. (2001). 'Inter-Project Learning: Processes and Outcomes of Knowledge Codification in Project-Based Firms', *Research Policy*, 30/9: 1373–1394.

Prichard, C. (2000) 'Know, Learn and Share! The Knowledge Phenomenon and the Construction of a Consumptive-Communicative Body', in C. Prichard, R. Hull, M. Chumer, & H. Willmott (eds.), *Managing Knowledge: Critical Investigations of Work and Learning*. London: Macmillan, 176–198.

Prusak, L., & Matson, E. (2006). *Knowledge Management and Organizational Learning: A Reader*. Oxford: Oxford University Press.

Quinn, B., Anderson, P., & Finkelstein, S. (1996). 'Managing Professional Intellect: Making the Most of the Best', *Harvard Business Review*, April–May: 71–80.

Rabinow, P. (1991). *The Foucault Reader*. London: Penguin Books.

Ravishankar, M., & Pan, S. (2008). 'The Influence of Organizational Identification on Organizational Knowledge Management (KM)', *Omega*, 36: 221–234.

Raz, A., & Fadlon, J. (2006). 'Managerial Culture, Workplace Culture and Situated Curricula in Organizational Learning', *Organization Studies*, 27/2: 165–182.

Reed, M. (2000). 'In Praise of Duality and Dualism: Rethinking Agency and Structure in Organisation Theory', in S. Ackroyd & S. Fleetwood (eds.), *Realist Perspectives on Management and Organisations*. London: Routledge, 45–65.

Reich, R. (1991). *The Work of Nations: Preparing Ourselves for 21st-Century Capitalism*. London: Simon & Schuster.

Renzl, B. (2008). 'Trust in Management and Knowledge Sharing: The Mediating Effects of Fear and Knowledge Documentation', *Omega*, 36: 206–220.

Ribeiro, R., & Collins, H. (2007). 'The Bread-Making Machine: Tacit Knowledge and Two Types of Action', *Organization Studies*, 28/9: 1417–1433.

Ribiere, V., & Sitar, A. (2003). 'Critical Role of Leadership in Nurturing a Knowledge-Supporting Culture', *Knowledge Management Research & Practice*, 1/1: 39–48.

Rifkin, J. (2000). *The End of Work: The Decline of the Global Workforce and the Dawn of the Post-Market Era*. Penguin: London.

Roan, A., & Rooney, D. (2006). 'Shadowing Experiences and the Extension of Communities of Practice: A Case Study of Women Education Managers', *Management Learning*, 37/4: 433–454.

Roberts, J. (2000). 'From Know-How to Show-How? Questioning the Role of Information and Communication Technologies in Knowledge Transfer', *Technology Analysis and Strategic Management*, 12/4: 429–443.

Roberts, J. (2006). 'Limits to Communities of Practice', *Journal of Management Studies*, 43/3: 623–639.

Robertson, S. (2002). 'A Tale of Two Knowledge-Sharing Systems', *Journal of Knowledge Management*, 6/3: 295–308.

Robertson, M., & O'Malley Hammersley, G. (2000), 'Knowledge Management Practices within a Knowledge-Intensive Firm: The Significance of the People Management Dimension', *Journal of European Industrial Training*, 24/2–4: 241–253.

Robertson, M., Sorensen, C., & Swan, J. (2001). 'Survival of the Leanest: Intensive Knowledge Work and Groupware Adaptation', *Information Technology & People*, 14/4: 334–352.

Robertson, M., & Swan, J. (2003). '"Control—What Control?" Culture and Ambiguity Within a Knowledge Intensive Firm', *Journal of Management Studies*, 40/4: 831–858.

Ron, N., Lipshitz, R., & Popper, M. (2006). 'How Organizations Learn: Post-flight Reviews in an F-16 Fighter Squadron', *Organization Studies*, 27/8: 1069–1089.

Ruggles, R. (1998). 'The State of the Notion: Knowledge Management in Practice', *California Management Review*, 40/3: 80–89.

Rynes, S., Bartunek, J., & Daft, R. (2001). 'Across the Great Divide: Knowledge Creation and Transfer Between Practitioners and Academics', *Academy of Management Journal*, 44/2: 340–355.

Sadler, P. (2001). 'Leadership and Organizational Learning', in M. Dierkes, A. Bertoin Antal, J. Child, & I. Nonaka (eds.), *Handbook of Organizational Learning and Knowledge*. Oxford: Oxford University Press, 415–427.

Sakakibara, M., & Dodgson, M. (2003). 'Strategic Research Partnerships: Empirical Evidence from Asia', *Technology Analysis and Strategic Management*, 15/2: 227–245.

Salaman, G. (2001). 'A Response to Snell: The Learning Organization: Fact or Fiction?' *Human Relations*, 54/3: 343–360.

Sapsed, J., & Salter, A. (2004). 'Postcards from the Edge: Local Communities, Global Programs and Boundary Objects', *Organization Studies*, 25/9: 1515–1534.

Sayer, A. (1992). *Method in Social Science*. London: Routledge.

Scarbrough, H. (1999). 'Knowledge as Work: Conflicts in the Management of Knowledge Workers', *Technology Analysis and Strategic Management*, 11/1: 5–16.

Scarbrough, H., & Carter, C. (2000). *Investigating Knowledge Management* London: CIPD.

Scarbrough, H., & Swan, J. (2001). 'Explaining the Diffusion of Knowledge Management', *British Journal of Management*, 12/1: 3–12.

Scarbrough, H., Bresnan, M., Edelman, L., Laurent, S., Newell, S., & Swan, J. (2004a). 'The Process of Project-Based Learning: An Exploratory Study', *Management Learning*, 35/4: 491–506.

Scarbrough, H., Swan, J., Laurent, S., Bresnen, M., Edelman, L., & Newell, S. (2004b). 'Project-Based Learning and the Role of Learning Boundaries', *Organization Studies*, 25/9: 1579–1600.

Scherer, K., & Tran, V. (2001). 'Effects of Emotion on the Process of Organizational Learning', in M. Dierkes, A. Bertoin Antal, J. Child, & I. Nonaka (eds.), *Handbook of Organizational Learning and Knowledge*. Oxford: Oxford University Press, 369–394.

Schultze, U. (2000). 'A Confessional Account of an Ethnography about Knowledge Work', *MIS Quarterly*, 24/1: 3–41.

Schultze, U. (2008). 'W(h)ither Knowledge Management?', in D. Barry & H. Hansen (eds.), *The Sage Handbook of New Approaches in Management and Organization*. London: Sage, 526–7.

Schutze, U., & Boland, R. (2000). 'Knowledge Technology and the Reproduction of Knowledge Work Practices', *Journal of Strategic Information Systems*, 9: 193–212.

Schultze, U., & Stabell, C. (2004). 'Knowing What You Don't Know: Discourse and Contradictions in Knowledge Management Research', *Journal of Management Studies*, 41/4: 549–573.

Senge, P. (1990). *The Fifth Discipline*. New York: Doubleday.

Senker, J., & Faulkner, W. (1996). 'Networks, Tacit Knowledge and Innovation', in R. Coombs, A. Richards, P.P. Saviotti, & V. Walsh (eds.), *Technological Collaboration: The Dynamics of Co-operation in Industrial Innovation*. Cheltenham: Edward Elgar, 76–97.

Sewell, G. (2005). 'Nice Work? Rethinking Managerial Control in an Era of Knowledge Work', *Organization*, 12/5: 685–704.

Sheehan, N. (2005). 'Why Old Tools Won't Work in the "New" Knowledge Economy', *Journal of Business Strategy*, 26/4: 53–60.

Shipton H. (2006). 'Confusion or Cohesion? Towards a Typology for Organizational Learning Research', *International Journal of Management Reviews*, 8/4: 233–252.

Shrivastava, P. (1983). 'A Typology of Organizational Learning Systems', *Journal of Management Studies*, 20/1: 7–28.

Singh, S. (2008). 'Role of Leadership in Knowledge Management: A Study', *Journal of Knowledge Management*, 12/4: 3–15.

Snell, R. (2001). 'Moral Foundations of the Learning Organization', *Human Relations*, 54/3: 319–342.

Skyrme, D., & Amidon, D. (1997). 'The Knowledge Agenda', *Journal of Knowledge Management*, 1/1: 27–37.

Slappendel, C. (1996). 'Perspectives on Innovation in Organizations', *Organization Studies*, 17/1: 107–129.

Slaughter, S., & Leslie, L. (1997) *Academic Capitalism*. Baltimore: John Hopkins University.

Snowden, D. (2005). 'From Atomism to Networks in Social Systems', *The Learning Organization*, 12/6: 152–162.

Somers, M. (1995). 'Organizational Commitment, Turnover and Absenteeism: An Examination of Direct and Interaction Effects', *Journal of Organizational Behaviour*, 16: 49–58.

Spender, J.-C. (1996). 'Organizational Knowledge, Learning and Memory: Three Concepts in Search of a Theory', *Journal of Organizational Change Management*, 9/1: 63–78.

Spender, J.-C. (2003). 'Exploring Uncertainty and Emotion in the Knowledge-based Firm', *Information Technology and People*, 16/3: 266–288.

Spender, J.-C. (2008). 'Organizational Learning and Knowledge Management: Whence and Whither?' *Management Learning*, 39/2: 158–176.

Spender, J.-C., & Scherer, A. (2007). 'The Philosophical Foundations of Knowledge Management: Editors' Introduction', *Organization*, 14/1: 5–28.

Srivastava, A., Bartol, K., & Locke, E. (2006). 'Empowering Leadership in Management Teams: Effects on Knowledge Sharing, Efficacy, and Performance', *Academy of Management Journal*, 49/6: 1239–1251.

Stamps, D. (2000). 'Communities of Practice: Learning is Social, Training is Irrelevant?', in E. Lesser, M. Fontaine, & J. Slusher (eds.), *Knowledge and Communities*. Oxford: Butterworth-Heinemann, 53–64.

Star, S. (1989). The Structure of Ill-Structured Solutions: Boundary Objects and Heterogeneous Distributed Problem Solving', in M. Huhns, & L. Gasser (eds.), *Readings in Distributed Artificial Intelligence*. Menlo Park, Calif.: Morgan Kaufman.

Starbuck, W. (1993). 'Keeping a Butterfly and an Elephant in a House of Cards: The Elements of Exceptional Success', *Journal of Management Studies*, 30/6: 885–921.

Starbuck, W., & Milliken, F. (1988). 'Challenger: Fine Tuning the Odds until Something Breaks', *Journal of Management Studies*, 25/4: 319–340.

Starkey, K., Hatchuel, A., & Tempest, S. (2004). 'Rethinking the Business School', *Journal of Management Studies*, 41/8: 1521–1531.

Starkey, K., & Tempest, S. (2005). 'The Future of the Business School: Knowledge Challenges and Opportunities', *Human Relations*, 58/1: 61–82.

Starkey, K., Tempest, S., & McKinlay, A. (2003). *How Organizations Learn: Managing the Search for Knowledge*. London: Thomson Learning.

Steinmueller, W. (2000). 'Will New Information and Communication Technologies Improve the Codification of Knowledge?' *Industrial and Corporate Change*, 9/2: 361–376.

Stevens, J., & Bagby, J. (2001). 'Knowledge Transfer from Universities to Business: Returns for All Stakeholders?' *Organization*, 8/2: 259–268.

Storey, J., & Barnett, E. (2000), 'Knowledge Management Initiatives: Learning from Failure', *Journal of Knowledge Management*, 4/2: 145–156.

Storey, J, & Quintas, P (2001), 'Knowledge Management and HRM', in J. Storey (ed.), *Human Resource Management: A Critical Text*. London: Thomson Learning, 339–363.

Strati, A. (2007) 'Sensible Knowledge and Practice-based Learning', *Management Learning*, 38/1: 61–77.

Strong, B., Davenport, T., & Prusak, L. (2008). 'Organizational Governance of Knowledge and Learning', *Knowledge and Process Management*, 15/2: 150–157.

Styhre, A. (2003). *Understanding Knowledge Management: Critical and Postmodern Perspectives*. Copenhagen: Liber, Copenhagen Business School.

Styhre, A., Josephson, P.-E., & Knauseder, I. (2006). 'Organization Learning in Non-Writing Communities: The Case of Construction Workers', *Management Learning*, 37/1: 83–100.

Subramaniam, M., Rosenthal, S., & Hatten, K. (1998). 'Global New Product Development: Preliminary findings and Research Propositions', *Journal of Management Studies*, 35/6: 773–796.

Subramaniam, M., & Venkatraman, N. (2001). 'Determinants of Transnational New Product Development Capability: Testing the Influence of Transferring and Deploying Tacit Overseas Knowledge', *Strategic Management Journal*, 22/4: 359–378.

Suchman, L. (2003). 'Organizing Alignment: The Case of Bridge-Building', in D. Nicolini, S. Gherardi, & D. Yanow (eds.), *Knowing in Organizations: A Practice-Based Approach*. London: M. E. Sharpe.

Suddaby, R., & Greenwood, R. (2001). 'Colonizing Knowledge: Commodification as a Dynamic of Jurisdictional Expansion in Professional Service Firms', *Human Relations*, 54/7: 933–953.

Swan, J., Bresnen, M., Newell, S., & Robertson, M. (2007). The object of knowledge: The role of objects in biomedical innovation', *Human Relations* 60/12: 1809–1837.

Swan, J., Newell, S., Scarbrough, H., & Hislop, D. (1999). 'Knowledge Management and Innovations: Networks and Networking', *Journal of Knowledge Management*, 3/4: 262–275.

Swart, J., & Kinnie, N. (2003). 'Sharing Knowledge in Knowledge-Intensive Firms', *Human Resource Management Journal*, 13/2: 60–75.

Swart, J., Kinnie, N., & Purcell, J. (2003). *People and Performance in Knowledge-Intensive Firms: A Comparison of Six Research and Technology Organizations*. London: CIPD.

Symon, G. (2000). 'Information and Communication Technologies and the Network Organization: A Critical analysis', *Journal of Occupational and Organizational Psychology*, 73/4: 389–414.

Szulanski, G. (1996). 'Exploring Internal Stickiness: Impediments to the Transfer of Best Practice Within the Firm', *Strategic Management Journal*, 17, Winter Special Issue: 27–43.

Tallman, S., & Phene, A. (2007). 'Leveraging Knowledge Across Geographic Boundaries', *Organization Science*, 18/2: 252–260.

Taylor, S. (1998). 'Emotional Labour and the New Workplace', in P. Thompson & C. Warhurst (eds.), *Workplaces of the Future*. London: Macmillan.

Taylor, P., & Bain, P. (1999). '"An Assembly Line in the Head": Work and Employee Relations in a Call Centre', *Industrial Relations Journal*, 30/2: 101–117.

Thomas, J., Sussman, S., & Henderson, J. (2003). 'Understanding "Strategic Learning": Linking Organizational Learning, Knowledge Management and Sensemaking', *Organization Science*, 1/3: 331–345.

Thompson, M. (2005). 'Structural and Epistemic Parameters in Communities of Practice', *Organization Science*, 16/2: 151–164.

Thompson, P., & Ackroyd, S. (1995). 'All Quiet on the Workplace Front? A Critique of Recent Trends in British Industrial Sociology', *Sociology*, 29/4: 615–633.

Thompson, P., Warhurst, C., & Callaghan, G. (2001). 'Ignorant Theory and Knowledgeable Workers: Interrogating the Connections Between Knowledge, Skills and Services', *Journal of Management Studies*, 38/7: 923–942.

Tidd, J., Bessant, J., & Pavitt, K. (2001). *Managing Innovation: Integrating Technological, Market and Organizational Change*. Chichester: John Wiley (2nd edn.).

Tieman, R. (2008). 'Integration of Ideas or Nimble Independence?' *Financial Times*, Business Education Supplement on European Business School: 4.

Townley, B. (1994). *Reframing Human Resource Management: Power, Ethics and the Subject at Work*. London: Sage.

Tranfield, D., Duberley, J., Smith, S., Musson, G., & Stokes, P. (2000). 'Organisational Learning— It's Just Routine!' *Management Decision*, 38/4: 253–260.

Trowler, P., & Turner, G. (2002). 'Exploring the Hermeneutic Foundation of University Life: Deaf Academics in a Hybrid "Community of Practice"', *Higher Education*, 43: 227–256.

Tsang, E. (1997). 'Organizational Learning and the Learning Organization: A Dichotomy Between Prescriptive and Descriptive Research', *Human Relations*, 50/1: 73–89.

Tsang, E. (2008). 'Transferring Knowledge to Acquisition Joint Ventures: An organizational Unlearning Perspective', *Management Learning*, 39/1: 5–20.

Tsoukas, H. (1996). 'The Firm as a Distributed Knowledge System: A Constructionist Approach', *Strategic Management Journal*, 17, Winter Special Issue: 11–25.

Tsoukas, H. (2000). 'What is Management? An Outline of a Metatheory', in S. Ackroyd & S. Fleetwood (eds.), *Realist Perspectives on Management and Organisations*. London: Routledge, 26–44.

Tsoukas, H. (2003). 'Do We Really Understand Tacit Knowledge?', in M. Easterby-Smith & M. Lyles (eds.), *The Blackwell Handbook of Learning and Knowledge Management*. Malden: Blackwell, 410–427.

Usoro, A., Sharratt, M., Tsui, E., & Shekar, S. (2007). 'Trust as an Antecedent to Knowledge Sharing in Virtual Communities of Practice', *Knowledge Management Research and Practice*, 5: 199–212.

Van der Velden, M. (2002). 'Knowledge Facts, Knowledge Fiction: The Role of ICTs in Knowledge Management for Development', *Journal of International Development*, 14: 25–37.

van Wijk, R., Jansen, J., & Lyles, M. (2008). 'Inter and Intra-Organizational Knowledge Transfer: A Meta-Analytic Review and Assessment of its Antecedents and Consequences', *Journal of Management Studies*, 45/4: 830–853.

Vera, D., & Crossan, M. (2004). 'Strategic Leadership and Organizational Learning', *Academy of Management Review*, 29/2: 222–240.

Vince, R (2001). 'Power and Emotion in Organizational Learning', *Human Relations*, 54/10: 1325–1351.

Vince, R., Sutcliffe, K., & Olivera, F. (2002). 'Organizational Learning: New Direction', *British Journal of Management*, 13: S1–6.

Voelpel, S., Dous, M., & Davenport, T. (2005). 'Five Steps to Creating a Global Knowledge-Sharing System: Siemens' ShareNet', *Academy of Management Executive*, 19/2: 9–23.

Volkmann, C., & De Cock, C. (2007). 'The Bauhaus and the Business School: Exploring Analogies, Resisting Imitation', *Management Learning*, 38/4: 389–404.

Von Hayek, F. (1945). 'The Use of Knowledge in Society', *American Economic Review*, 25/4: 519–530.

Von Hippel, E. (1976). 'The Dominant Role of Users in the Scientific Instrument Innovation Process', *Research Policy*, 5: 212–239.

Von Hippel, E. (1988). *The Sources of Innovation*. Oxford: Oxford University Press.

Von Krogh, G., Ichijo, K., & Nonaka, I. (2000). *Enabling Knowledge Creation: How to Unlock the Mystery of Tacit Knowledge and Release the Power of Innovation*. Oxford: Oxford University Press.

von Zedtwitz, M. (2002). 'Organizational Learning Through Post-Project Reviews in R&D', *R&D Management*, 32/3: 255–268.

Walsham, G. (2001). 'Knowledge Management: The Benefits and Limitations of Computer Systems', *European Management Journal*, 19/6: 599–608.

Wang, J.-K., Asleigh, M., & Meyer, E. (2006). 'Knowledge Sharing and Team Trustworthiness', *Knowledge Management Research and Practice*, 4: 75–186.

Ward, A. (2000). 'Getting Strategic Value From Constellations of Communities', *Strategy and Leadership*, 28/2: 4–9.

Warhurst, C., & Thompson, P. (2006). 'Mapping Knowledge in Work: Proxies or Practices', *Work, Employment and Society*, 20/4: 787–800.

Watson, T. (1994). *In Search of Management: Culture, Chaos and Control in Managerial Work*. London: Routledge.

Webster, F. (1996). *Theories of the Information Society*. London: Routledge.

Weick, K., & Westley, F. (1996). 'Organizational Learning: Affirming an Oxymoron', in

S. Clegg, C. Nor
Organization St
Weir, D., & Hut
beddedness ar
edge Sharing
Knowledge a
89–98.
Welsh, M., &
MBA? Or th
Learning, 38
Wenger, E.
Learning,
Cambridge
Wenger, E.,
Cultivatin
Harvard J
Werr, A.,
Manage
Systems
Wilkinson
zationa
Long R
Willem,
Capit:
Shari
Relat
Willma
& Sc
and
Hu
Wilso
Be
E
Wil
N

Wolfe, R. (1994). 'Organizational Innovation:
and Suggested Research
Studies,

nology,
versity

owledge
ournal of

I. (2001).
tion, and
chnology-
ournal, 22:

zations (6th

Knowledge
Review, 41/3:

, & Vertinsky,
ds: Facilitators
ional Learning
anagement, 13:

e Smart Machine:
Power. Oxford:

of Trust: Insti-
omic Structure,
Cummings (eds.),
aviour. Greenwich,

INDEX

(Page numbers in bold type refer to tables and figures.)